EXPLORING VANCOUVER

The Architectural Guide

EXPLORING
VANCOUVER

The Architectural Guide

Harold Kalman *&* Robin Ward

Photographs by John Roaf

Foreword by Mike Harcourt

Endorsed by the
ROYAL ARCHITECTURAL
INSTITUTE OF CANADA

DOUGLAS & MCINTYRE
D&M PUBLISHERS INC.
Vancouver/Toronto/Berkeley

12 13 14 15 16   5 4 3 2

Douglas & McIntyre
An imprint of D&M Publishers Inc.
2323 Quebec Street, Suite 201
Vancouver BC Canada V5T 4S7
www.douglas-mcintyre.com

Cataloguing data available from Library and Archives Canada
ISBN 978-1-55365-866-5 (pbk.)
ISBN 978-1-55365-867-2 (ebook)

Editing by Iva Cheung
Cover and interior design by Naomi MacDougall
Cover photographs by John Roaf
Maps by Eric Leinberger
Printed and bound in China by C&C Offset Printing Co., Ltd.
Distributed in the U.S. by Publishers Group West

The publisher gratefully acknowledges the financial support of the Canada
Council for the Arts, the British Columbia Arts Council, the Province of British
Columbia through the Book Publishing Tax Credit and the Government of
Canada through the Canada Book Fund for its publishing activities.

The authors acknowledge the financial support of BC 150 and the Vancouver
Heritage Foundation. A list of donors appears on page 327. Additional donors
are listed at www.vancouverheritagefoundation.org.

All photographs are by John Roaf except the following: A5, A33, D14, E6, F3,
F5, F11, F26, G10, G18, H9, H15, H16, H24, H37, I6, I33, I34, I37, I42, J11,
J20, K12, K16, K22, K35, K38, M23, M26 and N15 are by Harold Kalman; A17,
G25, H39, L19, M7, M11 and M15 are by Robin Ward; B4 is by Judy Oberlander;
C16 is by John Atkin; K21 is by Simon Scott; K42 and N35 are courtesy Perkins +
Will Canada; M20 is courtesy Grouse Mountain; M37 is by Steven Zhen Wang;
and N41 is by Heather Skydt.

CONTENTS

Foreword

VANCOUVERITES have always known that they live in a unique and stunning setting, surrounded by the sea, mountains and Fraser River, along with lush forests, parks and foreshores brimming with varied flora and fauna. Creating a built environment that complements and responds to this richness has been a challenge for architects and city planners—a process that's seen growing pains and close calls along the way. In *Exploring Vancouver*, Harold Kalman, Robin Ward and John Roaf show how this fascinating history has been encapsulated in the young city's diverse architecture and how bold, visionary decisions have prevailed, allowing Vancouver to take its place at the forefront of livability and urban sustainability. Vancouver may not be the first city to come to mind when one considers the world's iconic structures, but to study its architecture is to look into both its past and its future. As this book deftly shows, the mix of neighbourhoods, from historic Gastown and Chinatown to revitalized False Creek and ever-changing West End, and the mix of buildings within those neighbourhoods, are a consequence of policy decisions. These include triumphs—like the creation of Stanley Park, requested of the federal government by Vancouver's very first city council—as well as missteps—such as the short-sighted building codes that led to the "leaky condo crisis" of the 1990s.

One such disaster was narrowly avoided: in the 1960s, when I was a long-haired (sigh!) storefront lawyer, I worked with Chinatown merchants, Strathcona residents and other citizens to fight a proposed freeway that would have destroyed some of Vancouver's most characteristic neighbourhoods—from Gastown and Chinatown to Strathcona, the Grandview Woodlands and Hastings-Sunrise—and wiped out the waterfront as we know it. Our campaign to stop the freeway came to define what Vancouverites value. Today Vancouver is the only major city in North America without a major freeway going through it; our central city area has 140,000 residents, three-quarters of whom take transit, cycle, walk or telecommute instead of driving a car.

When I became mayor, my tenure was dominated by planning for Expo 86, and we successfully turned a potential $600 million deficit (the same size per capita as the Montreal 1976 Olympic deficit) into a boom in tourism and trade and a big success for Vancouver's citizens. In the lead-up to the event, we built important permanent infrastructure, such as Canada Place, Science World, a redeveloped north shore of False Creek and the Expo SkyTrain line. More recently, Vancouver built upon that experience of hosting the world, and the 2010 Olympic Winter Games gained us the expanded Trade and Convention Centre, the Canada Line, as well as new and rennovated sports facilities that will serve generations to come.

In my years of public service, I've witnessed the city evolve to embrace a planning philosophy that has come to be known as "Vancouverism"—multi-use, high-density core areas; a transit-focused transportation system; and thoughtful urban design that serves our spectacular natural setting and our vibrant, multicultural population—now a model for urban centres the world over. Over the coming decades, Vancouver has the opportunity to become a mecca for urban sustainability as we grapple with population growth, global warming and peak oil. *Exploring Vancouver* points to these challenges, while celebrating the city's history and its achievements, and I look forward to seeing the rich architectural and urban legacy that this progress will bring.

MIKE HARCOURT

Introduction

*"The magic city which grew out of a forest whose trees
were taller than our monumental buildings."*
MAJOR J.S. MATTHEWS (1878–1970), Vancouver's first city archivist

VANCOUVER was incorporated on April 6, 1886. Two months later, the Great Fire destroyed the original logging settlement, established after European maritime exploration in the late eighteenth century revealed abundant natural resources to a wider world. The city arose from that calamitous foundation, evolving as a multicultural metropolis, envied as one of the world's most livable and for its glorious natural setting. It is not generally known for its architecture.

Exploring Vancouver reveals the architecture and urbanism of the city, its history and the people and the society that made it. The story of the city's development is one of creation and reinvention— by British, Eastern Canadian and American opportunists in the late nineteenth and early twentieth centuries, through the post-WWII modernists, to the present crusade for livability and sustainability. The book also looks at a selection of old and new architecture of the municipalities that surround Vancouver.

Early settlers erected sawmills, stores, saloons and churches on First Nations territory. The opening of the transcontinental railway terminus in 1887 diversified the economy and boosted development. During Vancouver's first three-quarters of a century, architecture was mainly institutional or commercial and traditional in approach. Ambitious cultural buildings and innovative design are products of the modern era, when postwar prosperity and confidence shook off the last threads of pioneering and Depression-era austerity and colonial conformity.

When the previous (third) edition of *Exploring Vancouver* was published in 1993, the high-spirited, Art Deco Marine Building was still prominent on the waterfront. Today, it is hemmed in by new towers, part of a building boom that was the result of a unique conflation of events, including the sale by the provincial government of the Expo 86 site on False Creek to Hong Kong industrialist Li Ka-shing and the Canadian Pacific Railway's redevelopment of Coal Harbour. Consequent planning and construction have seen forests of residential high-rises shoot up on and around the downtown peninsula. New neighbourhoods, particularly False Creek and Coal Harbour, have been built out in a manner admired internationally as "Vancouverism," an ideology of dense but civilized urbanism, exported as a template for utopias worldwide. That radical transformation to the cityscape motivated this new edition.

Vancouver is at a turning point, as its citizens face challenges of sustainability in an era of global turmoil and climate change. Architecture—from basic shelter to iconic public buildings—is fundamental to how we deal with them. Global investment and the increasing population of the city raise issues of suburban sprawl and density, provision of public amenities, transit and the desire to respect the natural setting. Another concern is the loss of industrial land, rezoned for residential use. While the Port of Metro Vancouver is an exception, many industries have relocated to the suburbs near highways. This trend may be reversed because of the rising cost of fuel, and to attract a skilled young workforce that is drawn to city life. Downtown Vancouver is now largely residential—dubbed a "resort" by some commentators—as new towers are built and old ones adapted to housing. Green technologies and urban farming present architects with opportunities for mixed-use typologies, and communities and planners the question of unconventional zoning to accommodate them.

Achieving "a compact metropolitan region" was the central vision in Metro Vancouver's Livable Region Strategic Plan of 1996, which puts the burden on the City of Vancouver and the inner suburbs to increase allowable heights and floor areas. The City canonized this densification with a sustainability overlay in its EcoDensity Charter of 2008. Vancouver, often thought of as superficial, is now seriously eco-friendly. Many contemporary buildings (and rehabilitations of old ones) adapt the latest architectural trends to the regional context in pursuit of LEED (Leadership in Energy and Environmental Design) certification, an international rating of green building technology.

The drive towards densification creates enormous pressure for redevelopment. There is some recognition that the sustainable building is also the one that is not torn down, an idea that assists heritage conservation. Heritage awareness was fought for at a grassroots level when a downtown freeway was opposed in the 1960s. Since then, municipal planners have introduced innovative heritage incentive programs, with zoning relaxations, infill and the transfer of density linked to an interventionist stance regarding new development.

A pressing heritage challenge is recognition and retention of the regional modernism of the postwar era—the West Coast style—an architectural culture that is particular, if not unique, to Vancouver. Its humanity, sensitivity to architectural space and to landscape have a strong lineage that, despite globalization, remains vital. It is mainly residential, but its ethos—taken to extremes of concrete monumentality in Arthur Erickson's visionary urbanism—has been robust enough to resist a trend seen elsewhere: to jet in "starchitects" to solve urban dilemmas.

Some architects have added "planning and urban design" to their portfolios, an attempt to claim or reclaim aesthetic territory invaded by city planners, whose showpiece is Vancouverism. The latter has delivered the urbanism intended, but it may not be a suitable model to face future complexities of sustainability, patterns of settlement and affordability. Complexity will force more physical change in Vancouver. What form will that take? Organic infill, laneway housing, retrofits to the thousands of Vancouver Specials and hundreds of postwar commercial high-rises, Euro-style courtyard blocks, or the hyper-density of Hong Kong? The buildings selected for this book, each with its own social, sustainability or historical message, suggest many options.

THIS BOOK's fourteen chapters are organized as tours of the city's neighbourhoods and nearby suburbs, for walking, cycling or driving. Each entry features a photograph, along with building names, street addresses, architects and the date of completion (engineers and landscape architects are cited where their contribution is especially evident). Significant modifications are noted. Many entries also refer to buildings of interest nearby, which are highlighted in the text. The primary entries are keyed to maps, and the area covered by each chapter is shown on a map of Metro Vancouver (page 5). Readers are advised that, while private buildings can be viewed and photographed from the public roadway, and public ones entered, they should not trespass on private property. Notable buildings obscured by landscapes have been omitted; interiors are rarely mentioned unless they are open to the public.

The buildings—old and new, many changed over time—were chosen for their architectural or historical excellence, or because they represent trends in design, development and society. They reveal much about the people who built them and the communities where they are found—this is a book about neighbourhoods as much as it is of a metropolis. The selection reveals the authors' awareness of the larger environment, the spaces implied between the entries, the landscape, the views, the streets, the people.

The text often cites styles, both "high" styles used by architects, past and present (e.g., Tudor Revival, modernism) and "vernacular" types built in quantity by contractors (e.g., Craftsman, Vancouver Special). The difference between the two is often blurred. A glossary of potentially unfamiliar architectural terms, including styles, appears at the back of the book.

We wish to thank friends and colleagues who helped the preparation of this book: John Atkin, Trevor Boddy, Janet Collins, Don Harrison, David O'Laney, Anne Lee, Donald Luxton, Susan Medville, Ron Phillips, Peter and Elise Roaf, Tanya Southcott, Kate Swatek, Diane Switzer, Margaret Twohig and Cheryl Wu. Special thanks to our publisher, Scott McIntyre, editor Iva Cheung, and art director Peter Cocking. Also the many architects, city and heritage planners, building owners and managers, and authorities who provided information about or images for buildings in *Exploring Vancouver*.

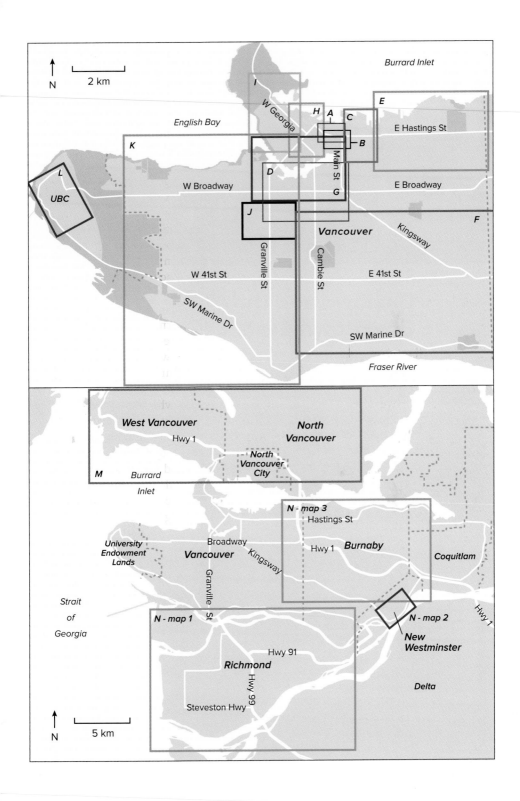

Gastown and the Downtown Eastside

A BRONZE statue at Water and Carrall Streets—"Maple Tree Square"—depicts "Gassy Jack" Deighton, a loquacious English-born mariner and riverboat skipper on the Fraser River who moved to Burrard Inlet in 1867 and opened a saloon here. The small logging community came to be known as "Gastown," after him. The saloon served workers at nearby Hastings Mill, established in 1865 to process timber from the vast forest that once covered present-day Vancouver. It became the focus of a budding settlement, which the colonial government surveyed in 1870 and officially called "Granville" for the British colonial secretary, Earl Granville.

The settlement's future was secured when William Cornelius Van Horne, general manager of the Canadian Pacific Railway, decided in 1886 to extend the tracks from Port Moody to a terminus just west of here (H28). Van Horne is credited with naming the transcontinental terminus "Vancouver," to honour the Royal Navy's Captain George Vancouver, who charted the inlet in 1792.

The rudimentary community (population around a thousand) was incorporated as the City of Vancouver on April 6, 1886, and promptly destroyed two months later by the "Great Fire," caused by forest-clearing burn-off blowing out of control. The settlement was rebuilt with brick- and stone-faced, timber-framed hotels,

Above: Woodward's Redevelopment (A25)

stores and warehouses that reflected the growth of the young shipping and commercial centre that would soon eclipse Victoria. The Klondike Gold Rush at the end of the century added distinguished architecture, much of which survived changing patterns of trade, transport and industry that caused Gastown's gradual decline.

In 1885, a new street grid was laid out west of Cambie Street by CPR surveyor Lauchlan Hamilton. His deviation from the survey of 1870, best seen at Victory Square, still marks the urban frontier between the new and old downtowns, much of the latter now dismissed as the Downtown Eastside (DTES). Centred along Hastings Street from Cambie to Main, the DTES had been the city's early commercial centre. Its architecture exhibits past prosperity. Decades of economic decline and neglect left Gastown and the DTES a shambles assaulted by chronic social problems.

Gastown's revitalization began in the late 1960s, when citizen protest cancelled a planned freeway that threatened the area, and community action led to some old buildings being rehabilitated. The provincial government responded by declaring it and adjacent Chinatown as protected historic districts in 1971. Public realm "beautification" encouraged building improvements and tourism. The City was also motivated to clean up the district's hippie-era reputation, when its warehouses offered cheap rents and allegedly concealed illegal activities. The 1971 "Gastown Riot" (commemorated in an artwork in the Woodward's atrium) followed arrests by police undercover drug squads.

Despite change, homelessness, drugs and despair prevail in the Downtown Eastside. A catalyst for the long-awaited solution is the momentous Woodward's redevelopment (A25), an innovative project that seeks to break social barriers. It also breaks physical ones, with two high-rise towers in a historic setting. Woodward's is a big fix for the Downtown Eastside, but smaller creative enterprise is introducing edgy retail and chic residential conversions, to the concern of many low-income residents.

Non-conformist behaviour—and the present social tensions in the Downtown Eastside—are rooted in Vancouver's origin as a logging settlement and seaport and to the individualism that founded its most popular early building: Gassy Jack's saloon. Today, the site of the saloon could not be further removed from the spirit of the past: it is now a polished Gastown heritage conversion that mixes hip retail and loft-style dwellings.

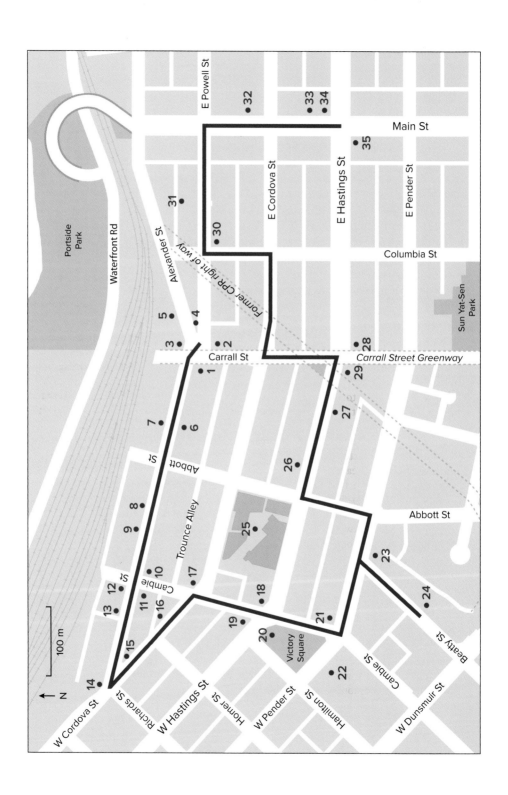

A1 Byrnes Block

2 Water Street

Elmer H. Fisher 1887; 1969; Acton Ostry
Architects, Donald Luxton & Associates 2010

"Gassy Jack" Deighton, for whom Gastown is named, built a saloon in 1867 on this site on Maple Tree Square, Vancouver's first outdoor public space. The present building was erected by realtor George Byrnes after the Great Fire of 1886. The Victorian Italianate frills—ornate window surrounds, top-floor pilasters and decorative cornice—announced it as someplace special. It was first occupied by the Alhambra Hotel, one of the few charging more than a dollar a night, justified by its claim to be "Vancouver's most modern . . . with running water and a wood stove in most rooms." The accommodation later dropped a few notches when it became the city's first courthouse and jail (the name "Gaoler's Mews" for the courtyard records this).

Architect Fisher, who claimed to have been born in Edinburgh and to have fought in the American Civil War, arrived in Victoria in 1886 by way of the American West and established a busy office. He then opened offices in Port Townsend and Seattle, exploiting the opportunity set by the latter's fire of 1889, and designed that city's finest Romanesque Revival work, the Pioneer Building (1892).

The Byrnes Block has twice played a vital role in the revitalization of Gastown. Developer Larry Killam rehabilitated it in 1969, inspiring other property owners to give their dreary, run-down buildings facelifts and the City to upgrade the public realm. Some forty years later, renewed confidence in the district was shown by developer Robert Fung, who reinvested in the Byrnes Block/Alhambra Hotel and its four western neighbours—the **Cordage Building** (c. 1890) and **Nagle Brothers Garage** (12 Water Street, the latter by McCarter & Nairne 1930, originally two storeys), the **Grand Hotel** (26 Water Street, c. 1890), and the bay-windowed **Terminus Hotel** (30 Water Street, Bunning & Kelso 1886) which had been gutted by fire in 1998.

The stylish package included conservation, seismic upgrading, geothermal heating and salvaged building materials. Underground parking, retail and forty-six residential units (including new penthouse floors) added profitable density. At the rear, the elevations are contemporary (their height difference indicates the original lots). They face **Blood Alley Square**, created as part of an earlier heritage project that linked Gaoler's Mews to Cordova Street with a passage through the Stanley Hotel (21 West Cordova Street, c. 1907; rehabilitated by Henriquez & Todd 1971).

A2 Ferguson Block
6 Powell Street
William Tuff Whiteway 1887

Victorian Italianate with a trace of the frontier, this building was constructed for Alfred Graham Ferguson, a CPR tunnel contractor-turned-developer. It was one of the first masonry buildings erected after the Great Fire, which destroyed the pioneer settlement of Granville—a.k.a. Gastown—and its wood buildings (including Ferguson's on this site) in twenty minutes. The fire started in Yaletown, where CPR crews were clearing land for the Roundhouse (G20). Hastings Mill (C19), east of Gastown, was spared, and its manpower and lumber aided swift

rebuilding. The new Ferguson Block became a focus for that effort because it housed the CPR land office, with the City Magistrate's law office upstairs (it was extended south in 1889). Like other post-fire buildings, its structural materials were timber, stone and brick. Whiteway, a Newfoundlander, had his name carved on the cornerstone.

A3 Dunn Block
1 Alexander Street
N.S. Hoffar 1900

Merchant Thomas Dunn, an alderman on the first Vancouver City Council, expanded his "Headquarters for Klondike Supplies" from the pedimented **Lonsdale Block** (8–28 West Cordova Street, N.S. Hoffar 1889) to this Romanesque Revival warehouse. The attic made it three and a half storeys, supported on interior columns. The rear portion was built at the same time; the east addition 1907. The building housed the office of the Union Steamship Company, whose dock was at the foot of Carrall Street.

Vancouver's pioneer architects were mostly a nomadic and opportunistic lot. Hoffar was typical. Born and educated in Washington, D.C., he mined in Nevada, learned the building trades in San Francisco and worked his way up the West Coast before settling in Vancouver in 1886. Here he found opportunity and a good supply of clients after the Great Fire.

A4 Europe Hotel
43 Powell Street
Parr & Fee 1909; Adolph Ingre &
Associates 1983

The hotel sails into this intersection like
a ship parting a sea of traffic. It was built
to a triangular "flatiron" plan for Italian-
born proprietor Angelo Calori, whose
name is above the entrance. The cornice caps six rather than the eight storeys intended. The contractor was the
Ferro-Concrete Construction Company
from Cincinnati, Ohio; this was the first
reinforced-concrete building in Vancouver. Glass blocks on the sidewalks
lighted "areaways," which added space.
They were filled with gravel by City Engineering in a 1990s safety campaign, lest
trucks mount and collapse the sidewalk.
Once noted for its palatial bar, the Europe was a decrepit rooming house when
the Canada Mortgage & Housing Corporation stepped in to renovate it for affordable housing. Heritage features include a
floridly tiled lobby, Ionic-columned window mullions on the curved prow and

the conspicuous cornice. Calori's adjoining, earlier **Europe Hotel** (49–51 Powell
Street, 1886; 1890; Adolph Ingre & Associates 1983), has twin, vaguely Venetian
elevations, one on Powell, the other on
Alexander Street. Enlarged westward in
1890, it was retained as the new Europe's
annex.

A5 100-block Alexander Street
c. 1900–1912; 1990–2000

Short, medium and tall warehouse façades lined the north side of this block
for almost a century. The streetscape was
so convincingly of the past that the producers of the 1994 movie *Legends of the
Fall* hardly needed to dress it as a stand-
in for Helena, Montana, c. 1910. The film
could not be shot here now. Only the **Captain French Building** (41 Alexander Street,
Parr & Fee 1909; Paul Merrick Architects
1990), named for its first owner, a tugboat skipper, retained its original height
during loft conversions on the block.

There is a contextual justification for
add-on lofts: extra floors were fitted to
many of Gastown's buildings during the
Edwardian economic boom. Additions
increase density, an aspect of the City's
heritage management that evolved after
the provincial government, at the City's

request, designated Gastown a historic district in 1971. That led to renovations and streetscape improvements. Planners have since tried to balance conservation with the commercial investment and changes of use that keep the buildings alive. Contemporary interventions are now accepted behind historic façades.

A6 Inform Interiors
50 Water Street
1906; Busby + Associates Architects 2005

In a Gastown that is trendy, Inform Interiors is a design-led symbol of continuity. Its Danish-born designer, Niels Bendtsen, opened a store in the district in 1970. His modernist furniture, crafted in a converted warehouse on Railway Street (C20) four blocks east, continues a manufacturing tradition in Gastown that goes back to the nineteenth century. This showroom for owners Niels and Nancy Bendtsen retains the cornice, concrete blocks (cast to look like stone) and storefront I-beam from the Kane Building, as the structure was first known. A green roof has been added. Designer and project architect Omer Arbel introduced concrete floors and columns (to replace wooden posts), and a skylight to illuminate the see-through showroom's contemporary furniture and twentieth-century design classics. An elegant new stair structure is poised in the centre of the showroom.

A7 Malkin Building
55 Water Street
Parr & Fee 1907; John Macfarlane McLuckie 1912; Merrick Architecture 2002

Wholesale grocery magnate and sometime mayor of Vancouver William Harold Malkin built this brick-clad, Douglas-fir-framed structure—his third warehouse on Water Street in a decade of thriving business (his previous, smaller warehouses are at 353 and 141 Water Street—see A9). The building was extended to the east in matching style, doubling the floor space. This part of Water Street was the hub of grocery distribution until the 1930s, when many of these big buildings were taken over by the garment trade. Rehabilitation as live-work studios by developer Jon Stovell's Reliance Properties included a seismic upgrade, an underground parkade and a lofty glazed retail space on an empty lot to the west.

A8 Gaslight Square
131 Water Street
Henriquez & Todd 1975

The CPR's Marathon Realty developed this infill site, a concession to a revitalized Gastown after their Project 200 (A17) urban renewal scheme in the late 1960s failed. Project 200 caused "planning blight," as building owners were unwilling to maintain properties likely to be torn down. Gaslight Square, the first new building to recognize Gastown's historic character, gave a lesson in how to stitch the district together.

Early postmodern with a façade rendered at its western edge as a faux false front, it is a reinterpretation of the Wild West–style false fronts on the wooden buildings destroyed in the Great Fire. The use of brick is contextual; bay windows echo those on the Terminus Hotel (A1). Behind the façade, a modernist glazed roof slides away to a split-level courtyard with retail and offices. Across the street, **Gastown Parkade** (150 Water Street, Paul Smith 1971; Henriquez Partners Architects 2005), originally part of Project 200, was rebuilt with contextual elevations, to fit the streetscape's historic character.

A9 First Malkin Warehouse
141 Water Street
c. 1898; c. 1903; Paul Merrick Architects 1996

Water Street is aptly named: the backs of the first warehouses on its north side were supported on wooden piles along the shoreline. Boardwalks connected to a CPR trestle above the water on the tidal strip parallel to the street, allowing freight to be off-loaded from boxcar to building. The back of this block was built on piles. Its loading bays faced tracks laid when the trestle was dismantled and the land reclaimed around 1900. Three east bays were added (the Klondike boom saw many structures in Gastown enlarged). A condo rehab included mansard-roofed lofts, set back, sensitive to the streetscape.

A10 Leckie Building
170 Water Street/220 Cambie Street
Dalton & Eveleigh 1909; 1913; Vladimir Vit, Gower Yeung & Associates engineers 1991

Around 1900, Vancouver overtook Victoria as B.C.'s main trading centre. Canneries, mineral strikes (particularly the gold in the Klondike) and logging operations were supplied from, and many products manufactured, here. The Leckie Building is a symbol of that commerce because its owner made what every logger needs: a

sturdy pair of boots. John Leckie, a Scottish immigrant, founded the company whose boots were "The Best in the West," so a rooftop sign claimed. The building, framed with cedar posts and beams behind load-bearing brick-and-masonry walls, was converted to offices by Novam Development, which pioneered warehouse makeovers in Vancouver. The work included a seismic upgrade, unique in the city at the time. Steelwork anchored in concrete 27 metres below grade braces the structure; two tension rods crossing diagonally on each elevation were exposed to allow the ingenuity to be seen.

A11 **Edward Hotel**
302 Water Street
1906

The CPR in Vancouver connected to the company's coastal and trans-Pacific shipping routes. Its train station (H28) and piers were built on the western edge of Gastown. Almost as many hotels were built in the district as there are warehouses. The Edward replaced the wood-frame Regina Hotel, one of the few buildings saved during the Great Fire. Romanesque lingers in the rusticated stone bands on the elevations here, but

the feel is Italianate, almost like a miniature palazzo (with a sheet-metal cornice). Prestige was sought with façades clad completely in stone, expensive and uncommon. The ground floor retains its cast-iron columns, I-beam headers with cast rosettes and storefront articulation and glazing. A bistro continues the tradition of hospitality.

A12 **Gastown Steam Clock**
Water and Cambie Streets
1977

Horologer Raymond Saunders and metalwork specialist Doug Smith (at the Vancouver Technical School) designed and fabricated this faux-antique, allegedly steam-powered clock, funded as a business improvement to put Gastown on the tourist map. Only the whistle, which toots the chimes of Big Ben, is activated by steam. The steam is generated at Central Heat Distribution's plant (720 Beatty Street) and delivered by underground pipes, a network that also heats many buildings downtown. The adjacent globe-clustered street lamp is of nineteenth-century design, introduced as a "heritage" feature in Gastown in the 1970s.

A13 Hudson House
321 Water Street
Charles Osborn Wickenden 1894; 1903;
Werner Forster 1977

This former Hudson's Bay Company fur and liquor warehouse—and the **Greenshields Building** across the alley (341–345 Water Street, 1902; 2004)—symbolize Canada's pioneering westward expansion. The HBC's fur traders opened the West; other merchants followed, particularly after the CPR was completed. Wholesaler Greenshields was founded in Montreal and expanded west; the Water Street warehouse is attributed to J.H. Cadham, architect of the company's building in Winnipeg.

The HBC warehouse was enlarged by two storeys, added after the Klondike boom. Their arched windows sprang from the existing piers; twin pediments were aligned vertically with the street entrances. Both buildings were inspired by the Marshall Field Wholesale Store (1887), a now-demolished Chicago landmark, which was designed by Henry Hobson Richardson, the master of the Romanesque Revival in America. The repetitive arch-and-spandrel window treatment here is characteristic of

A

the style; so too the shallow, corbelled cornices and the rusticated and carved stonework, especially at sidewalk level. The Greenshields Building's carved capitals, representing indigenous and immigrant peoples, are particularly fine.

A14 The Landing
375 Water Street
William Tuff Whiteway 1905;
Soren Rasmussen 1988

Robert Kelly and Frank Douglas formed Kelly, Douglas & Company in 1896. It supplied Klondike gold rush prospectors, became known for its Nabob-brand tea and coffee and grew to be one of the biggest grocers in the Lower Mainland. This building, enlarged to the west within a few years, was the largest produce warehouse in the country. It was timber framed. Steel-frame (A19, A23) and reinforced-concrete construction (A4) soon superseded wood for buildings of this size and larger. The McLean Group rehabilitated it as offices, shops, restaurants and a brew pub, with a picture window inserted in the north wall to open up views of the harbour and North Shore.

A15 Holland Block
364 Water Street
1891

The street grid of downtown Vancouver, laid out after a survey by the CPR's Lauchlan Hamilton in 1885, joined that of the Granville townsite at an angle. The shift between the two grids is visible in the flatiron shape of the Holland Block, built for developer James M. Holland at the western entrance to Gastown. The style is Italianate in the San Francisco manner, with a projecting roof, originally curved above corner bay windows, which flow back on both façades. The storefronts are framed in cast iron, with the B.C. Ironworks trademark on the base of the columns.

A16 Horne Block
309-311 West Cordova Street
N.S. Hoffar 1889

This Italianate caprice, flatiron in shape, was originally decorated with a classical cornice, half-moon pediment, balustrade, cast-iron filigree and a cupola that defined the one-bay corner where only a "Juliet" balcony survives. Vancouver City Foundry made the cast-iron storefronts,

whose capitals display an "H," not for the architect but for Toronto-born owner James Welton Horne, who arrived in 1885 and profited from real estate during the post-CPR boom.

The abutting **Springer–Van Bramer Block** (301 West Cordova Street, N.S. Hoffar 1888), once known as the Masonic Temple for its tenants, is also Italianate, angled to the street corner. As with the Horne Block, its weathered cornice was removed for public safety. The owners were tugboat captain James Van Bramer and Ben Springer, manager of the Moodyville sawmill on the North Shore.

A17 Canadian Pacific Telecommunications Building
175 West Cordova Street
Francis Donaldson 1969

The architecture of this building was influenced by the "New Formalist" style, a pseudo-classical offshoot of modernism, expressed here with a vertically finned curtain wall that turns the street corner gracefully. It is one of two structures by Donaldson (H29) for Project 200, proposed by Marathon Realty, department stores Woodward's and Simpsons-Sears and Grosvenor-Laing

Investments, inspired by the sweep-the-old-stuff-away mania of post-WWII urban redevelopment.

A18 Flack Block
163 West Hastings Street
William Blackmore 1900; Acton Ostry Architects, Donald Luxton & Associates 2008

Thomas Flack struck it rich in the Klondike, sold his claim and expressed his good fortune in this Richardsonian Romanesque commercial block. The tripartite, granite façade with twin-columned articulation commands the corner facing Court House (now Victory) Square. Time was not kind to its status as a preferred location for lawyers, mining, logging and

insurance brokers, gold dealers and retail tenants. When developer Robert Fung's Salient Group took it over, a marijuana grow-op and rooms of stolen goods were discovered, and misguided modernization had destroyed the ground floor and cornice.

Hastings Street was massively (for the time) redeveloped in the late 1940s, just after WWII. Many shops were rehabbed with modern glass-and-aluminum storefronts and neon signs. The lower part of the terracotta and brick-faced **Ormidale Block** (151 West Hastings Street, G.W. Grant 1900), also Richardsonian, was altered in this way. The Flack Block shows how such buildings can be revived. Salient's thorough and tasteful renewal included seismic and mechanical and electrical system upgrades, as well as a steel-and-glass rooftop addition. The elevator cage within the staircase was retained as a memory. The name was restored to its position above the cornice and to the main entrance, where the long-lost sandstone archway was accurately reconstructed.

A19 Dominion Building
207 West Hastings Street
J.S. Helyer & Son 1910; Read Jones Christoffersen engineers 1998

The Imperial Trust Company promoted this steel-frame, brick- and terracotta-clad extravaganza as "an object of pride to every citizen [of the] most prosperous go ahead commercial city on the continent." The firm promptly went bust, and its debt was taken over by Dominion Trust, which finished the colourful landmark, briefly the tallest office building in the British Empire. The roofline looks French and the elevations are flamboyantly classical, in the early skyscraper manner. Two titanic granite columns mark the main entrance, which is recessed and richly appointed. The interior retains its marble, terrazzo and wood finishes and ten-storey staircase.

A20 The Cenotaph
Victory Square
George Lister Thornton Sharp 1924;
Pechet & Robb 2002

Soldiers, sailors and aircrew killed in two world wars are commemorated by this obelisk, which follows the precedent established with the Cenotaph in London (Sir Edwin Lutyens 1920). Lutyens's cenotaph is four sided in response to the urban design of Whitehall; Sharp's three-sided version reflects the shape of Victory Square, a recruiting ground during WWI and where Remembrance Day ceremonies are held. The Cenotaph's "steel" helmets and formality inspired Pechet & Robb's Victory Square Lighting Project, a public realm enhancement encouraged by the Friends of Victory Square.

A21 The Architecture Centre
440 Cambie Street
Alfred Arthur Cox 1911; Busby + Associates
Architects, Roger Hughes Architects, Robert
G. Lemon Architecture & Preservation,
Rockingham Engineering 1988

This truncated Chicago Style building was built for Edgett Brothers, retail and wholesale grocers. It was linked, in 1924, by a bridge across the alley to the **Province Building** (198 West Hastings Street, Cox & Amos 1909), home of *The Province* newspaper, for which it became the printing plant. (The Province Building, originally the Carter-Cotton Building, for the publisher of the *News-Advertiser*, is full-blown Chicago Style.)

Glass block lights on the sidewalk and a modern entrance are a clue to changes inside the old printing plant, where floors were opened up for an atrium, offices and public exhibition space for the Architectural Institute of B.C. In the boardroom, a 2-ton steel truss replaced a concrete column taken out to create a workable space. The truss, exposed along with fragments of the column to show how it was done, is a metaphor for whole approach, which was rational and remains visible. The old elevator hoist in the skylight shows the position of the shaft that was removed; high-tech fittings are a perfect foil to the original concrete, distressed from years of pressmen's knocks.

A22 Vancouver Community College Downtown Campus
250 West Pender Street
Sharp & Thompson, Berwick, Pratt 1949

Robert Berwick and C.E. "Ned" Pratt, trained in modernism at the University of Toronto, joined the established office of Sharp & Thompson in 1945. The buildings that followed gained the firm a reputation as the most progressive in

Canada (H48). The downtown campus of VCC (opened as the Vancouver Vocational Institute) was one of the city's first International Style designs, with characteristic clean lines inspired by the seminal Bauhaus, itself a vocational school in Germany (Walter Gropius 1926). Three classroom blocks were positioned to create a sunlit courtyard. The original elevations and twin glazed stairs offset by symmetrical brick corners are intact.

A23 Sun Tower
100 West Pender Street
William Tuff Whiteway 1912; Ted Murray Architect, Donald Luxton & Associates 2011

The World Building, as this was first called, summed up Vancouver's Edwardian boom with an exclamation mark—a tower capped by a French Second Empire dome, from where the Michigan-born publisher of the *Vancouver World*, Louis Denison Taylor, could survey the city he would rule with Citizen Kane-style populism as a long-serving mayor. "There is no limit to the possibilities of this city," he once declared. His tower succeeded the Dominion Building (A19) as the tallest in the British Empire. A huge globe was mounted on the dome. The terra-

cotta caryatids supporting the podium's cornice were cast in England and later inspired the name of the Nine Maidens Restaurant, from where their Rubenesque proportions could be admired.

The *World* was absorbed by *The Vancouver Sun*, which occupied the "Sun Tower" from 1935, adding a huge neon sign, recalled by "newspaper row" ex-reporter and author Pierre Berton as "electric blue; you could see it all over town." *The Sun* (with *The Province*) relocated to 6th and Granville in 1965; both papers moved back downtown, to Granville Square (H29), in 1997 and their printing to a new plant in Surrey.

A24 Five-Fifty Beatty
550 Beatty Street
1906; Bruno Freschi 1981

A continuous row of Edwardian warehouses created this muscular streetscape, now lined with lofts behind the elevations. The trendsetter was Five-Fifty Beatty, a conversion of the Johnston Terminals warehouse by developer Robert MacIntyre, who was inspired by artists' lofts in SoHo, the old garment industry district in New York. Behind its postmodern façade, original big spaces were adapted and brick walls and timber posts and beams retained. The project was the first in the city to convert a heritage building to strata apartments, aimed at reversing the decline of this downtown edge.

Freschi's influence lingers all along the street, particularly at the timber-framed **Bowman Block** (528 Beatty Street, 1906; Gair Williamson Architects 2007), where floor plates were cut back from the front elevation to make two-storey lofts, with a modern two-storey roof addition set back to add floor space while preserving the heritage streetscape.

A25 Woodward's Redevelopment
151 West Hastings Street,
108-128 West Cordova Street
Various architects 1903–71;
Henriquez Partners Architects 2010

Retail pioneer Charles Woodward built a flagship department store (W.T. Whiteway 1903) at Hastings and Abbott, with additions over the next seventy years covering most of the block. When the store closed in 1993, owing to the failure of the corporation, it had become a sad relic of the Downtown Eastside's days as a business and transit hub (A29). The loss of the store highlighted the area's social problems. The "Woodward's Squat" in 2002, in which many of the neighbourhood's homeless people occupied the store for months, protested these and the neglect of the district and raised awareness of its need for affordable housing.

In an attempt to jump-start revitalization, the City of Vancouver bought the Woodward's site in 2003. City councillor and activist Jim Green had long promoted the idea that redevelopment should serve the existing community and sustain the memory of Woodward's. Architect Gregory Henriquez and developers Westbank/Peterson Group responded with "a real village on one super-block" comprising three new building blocks and the rehabilitated original 1903–08 building. The project and its inclusive social ideals got a popular stamp of approval when the condos in the flatiron "W" Tower, evoking memories of the Dominion Building (A19), presold in one day in 2006.

Architecture dominates this utopian vision of homes and workplaces where people of all ages and incomes might co-exist harmoniously. The built form accommodates two hundred social housing units, five hundred market condos, Simon Fraser University's School for the Contemporary Arts, offices for the City and for non-profit groups, a daycare centre, retail, a bank (the first major bank to open in the area in a half-century) and federal government offices. Heritage and amenity density bonuses enabled the huge amount of floor space—about one million square feet.

The vertical and horizontal integration of this complexity is deft: the urban design, with sidewalk access points penetrating to a large atrium, opens the block to public passages, and green credentials are made visible on the "W" Tower's steel "eco skeleton," intended as a green wall. The two extant façades and the internal structure of the timber-framed, brick-faced heritage building were retained, with its period cornice and the painted names of the retail departments restored (Commonwealth Historic Resource Management, Jonathan Yardley Architect). The iconic "W" sign and tower, too

deteriorated to reuse, were rebuilt on top of it, and the original "W" was preserved in its rusted condition on the Cordova Street plaza. An interpretive program including the sidewalk display windows and reuse of salvaged fragments from the old building—and calling the supermarket "Woodward's Food Floor"—ensures that residents and users understand the heritage of the site and the neighbourhood. The glazed atrium features a huge photomural of the 1971 Gastown Riot (Stan Douglas 2009).

Woodward's Parkade (125 West Cordova Street, 1957; Henriquez Partners Architects 2005), part of the city-owned Gastown Parkade (A8), was rebuilt to feel safer and be more user friendly and was linked by a new bridge to the redevelopment.

A26 Paris Block
53 West Hastings Street
Hooper & Watkins 1908; Gair Williamson Architects 2010

The ground floor was once occupied by boot maker and shoe retailer Pierre Paris, an immigrant from the Basque re-

gion of southwest France; the Strathcona Hotel had the upper floors. Ghost signs on the exterior walls remained, along with a much altered façade. The revitalizing—some say gentrifying—influence of the Woodward's project is evident in the conversion to condos. The building's clear-span I-beams and brickwork were retained à la mode; the *savoir faire* includes a chic annex (Gair Williamson 2012), clearly contemporary but scaled to coordinate with the old building. Another revival is at **43 West Hastings** (1899), where Save-on-Meats (1957–2009) was reopened (2011) by restaurateur Mark Brand as a deli-diner complete with the original flying pig neon sign.

A27 Portland Hotel
20 West Hastings Street
Nick Milkovich Architects, Arthur Erickson 1999

The non-profit Portland Hotel Society (PHS) drove this project forward, with various government agencies. The architects came on board after the PHS, which accommodates many of the Downtown Eastside's "hard to house," called Erickson, whose designs for the privileged are better known. The response rejected the brick-faced heritage look in favour of

metal cladding, with bay windows contextual with those on the Pennsylvania Hotel (see next entry). The bays, which divide above a cornice, animate the utilitarian elevation, which is duplicated at the rear, as is the mansard roof. There are eighty-six single room occupancy (SRO) units, with residents supported by on-site staff. Cornelia Hahn Oberlander designed the back-court garden.

A28 Pennsylvania Hotel
412 Carrall Street
William Tuff Whiteway 1906; Merrick Architecture, Donald Luxton & Associates 2008

San Francisco urbanism ripples on the façades of what was originally the Woods Hotel, a classy hostelry-turned-SRO hotel. It has been completely rehabilitated, with façades restored for the Portland Hotel Society, which provided

forty-four safe, clean bachelor suites for the needy. The Downtown Eastside was Vancouver's "Skid Road" (a loggers' term from the wood "skids" on which logs were rolled), which morphed from a haven for transient loggers to one for the transient poor. This building's revival, besides the social benefits, saw the replication of a long-removed corner turret and a 1920s neon sign with the hotel's later name. The Carrall Street entrance, previously boarded up, is first class—Romanesque Revival and original.

Around the corner is the **Only Seafoods** neon sign (1950), on the former Brunswick Pool Room (20–26 East Hastings Street, H.A. Hodgson 1911). It's a classic diner, established by two Greek brothers; the "Only" dates from 1916. It changed hands around 1992 and closed in 2009, after police alleged drugs were being dealt on the premises. The sign was removed, restored (Pattison Sign Group 2011) and returned to its original location for the Portland Hotel Society, which has leased the restaurant.

A29 B.C. Electric Railway Company Building
425 Carrall Street
Somervell & Putnam 1912; Sharp & Thompson 1945

B.C. Electric's interurban tram network, once the most extensive in Canada, was run from this head office and depot. Trams ran into the terminus through a clear span on Hastings Street; the first two arches on the Carrall Street arcade were open to the station concourse. The structure, with steelwork "fire-proofed" with concrete, was preloaded for additional storeys (one was added in 1945). The building accommodated three hundred workers. The company was the biggest employer in the area, whose decline was accelerated when the interurban ser-

vices to the terminus ceased in 1955, and to the region in 1958 (also the year North Vancouver ferries, which docked at the foot of Columbia Street, stopped sailing). In the 1990s, the BCER Building was adapted for high-tech and media tenants.

The same architects' **Merchants Bank** (1 West Hastings Street, 1913), a neoclassical pile of faded grandeur facing pocket-size Pigeon Park, was also designed for additional floors. The end of the Edwardian boom prevented any. The façade detailing is exceptionally fine. The building's steel frame was angled to avoid the CPR spur line from Burrard Inlet to rail yards at False Creek. Steam locomotives crossed Hastings Street at this point until the Dunsmuir Tunnel was opened in 1931. The City's Carrall Street Greenway, which follows the eastern boundary of the Granville townsite, revives the route as a pedestrian and cycle link between the creek and the inlet (in the 1860s, it was possible to paddle a canoe between the two at high tides).

A30 The Warehouse Studio
100 Powell Street
N.S. Hoffar 1887; Don Stuart Architect 1991;
Davidson Yuen Simpson Architects 1999

Brothers David, Charles and Isaac Oppenheimer, members of a large family that hailed from Germany, immigrated to the U.S. in 1848 and arrived in B.C. in 1858. Charles Oppenheimer & Company, provisions, was founded in Victoria around 1858, with a second store around 1860 at Yale, where riverboats dropped off prospectors headed for the Cariboo Trail. The company was renamed Oppenheimer Brothers in 1871, with David and Isaac as partners (by 1881, they controlled the business). They acquired land in Granville, and moved here about 1885 (David had joined a syndicate with contractor Andrew Onderdonk to raise money for the construction of part of the Canadian Pacific Railway, near Yale). By 1887, the assessed value of their holdings was the richest after Hastings Mill and the CPR. That year, they opened their wholesale grocery business in Vancouver. Both were acclaimed aldermen; David was elected the city's second mayor, serving from 1887 to 1891, and was a major influence in the city's development. He remained active in the civic and Jewish communities and is honoured in the name of Oppenheimer Park (C21) and at

Stanley Park (125). This warehouse, one of the city's oldest structures (originally two storeys), was one of their ventures. It has been converted considerably, as a recording studio for another prominent Vancouverite, singer Bryan Adams.

A31 Four Sisters Housing Co-operative
133–153 Powell Street,
188 Alexander Street
Davidson/Yuen Partners 1987

The architects won an AIBC award in 1988 for this innovative design, which was short-listed for the World Habitat Awards in 1991. The 153-unit, three-building complex for families, singles and seniors with low incomes was conceived by the Downtown Eastside Residents Association, founded in 1973 to improve living conditions in the area. Administered by the residents, the development includes a communal courtyard, adaptive reuse of heritage buildings and new construction.

Across the street is the **Smart Building** (168 Powell Street, Busby Perkins + Will 2009). With apartments arranged around a south-facing deck to maximize natural light, it updates the West End courtyard model (H45). A smart fit in this historic area, it achieves a similar density to Vancouverism's tower and townhouse formula, with which its developer, Concord Pacific, is normally associated (G19).

A32 Vancouver Court Services (Provincial Criminal Court)
222 Main Street
Harrison, Plavsic & Kiss 1974

The traditional courthouse façade of cut stone and classical columns, seen at the old Provincial Courthouse at Robson Square (H50), was transcribed here—with a testimony from Le Corbusier—into concrete piers and walls without any loss of dignity, although an addition at Main and Powell seems a case for prosecution. Many police and magistrates' courts spread around the area were centralized here. Nearby is the former **Coroner's Court** (240 East Cordova Street, Arthur Julius Bird 1932), a Georgian Revival gem that became the Vancouver Police Museum in 1986.

A33 Bruce Eriksen Place
380 Main Street
Henriquez Partners Architects 1998

Named for ironworker, city councillor and cofounder of the Downtown Eastside Residents Association Bruce Eriksen, this thirty-five-unit infill for the Main & Hastings Housing Society fits between the **Public Safety Building** (312 Main Street, Townley & Matheson 1953) and the Bank of Montreal (see next entry). Its structural frame rises from the sidewalk, with units recessed for balconies, a visual effect that mediates the gap between the neighbours. The façade has an

agitprop photomontage (Blake Williams 1998) screen printed on ceramic tiles. The balconies are tiled with inspiring words. City planners grumbled that the art should be subject to the sign bylaw. Jim Green, the provincial coordinator for the project, said, it was "a poetic insight."

A34 Bank of Montreal
390 Main Street
Honeyman & Curtis 1930

Neoclassicism distinguishes this miniature "temple bank" with fluted Corinthian columns and a pedimented entrance. The pilasters along the sides are rendered in shallow bas-relief, typi-

A

cal of the modern classicism of the day. The bank's coat of arms, with its fur trade imagery of Indians and a beaver above the entablature, adds a message and delight. The interior was refurbished in 1996 by Four Corners Community Savings, a short-lived initiative that gave low-income people fairer financial services than those provided by cheque-cashing marts and loan sharks.

East of the bank is a lively heritage ensemble that includes the **Ovaltine Cafe** (251 East Hastings Street, 1942) in a former apartment building (A.J. Bird 1912). Across the street is the Beaux-Arts-style **Royal Bank of Canada East End Branch** (400 Main Street, Howard Colton Stone 1910).

A35 Carnegie Community Centre †
401 Main Street
George William Grant 1903; Downs/
Archambault 1980

Scottish-American steel magnate Andrew Carnegie funded libraries around the globe. Vancouver benefitted from his largesse. The resulting building housed

the Vancouver Public Library until it left for Burrard Street (H46) in 1957 and the municipal museum from 1905 until it departed to Kitsilano Point (K1) in 1968. City Hall was located next door on Main Street.

Architect Grant had designed New Westminster Court House in the Romanesque Revival style (N19) and varied it here with a dome, faintly Byzantine, and turned the Main and Hastings corner with a two-storey entrance flanked by two Ionic columns. Rusticated stone and round-arched windows on the façades are typical of the style. Not so the copper roof, which is inspired by French Second Empire buildings. After a campaign led by the Downtown Eastside Residents Association, the Carnegie became a community centre, with a postmodern addition on Main Street. The centre opened in 1980, a beacon on Skid Road. Users are greeted by portraits of Robbie Burns, Shakespeare and other writers in stained-glass windows (Henry Bloomfield & Sons 1903) set in the wall of its marble, spiral staircase.

Chinatown

BRITISH Columbia's Chinese population had its origins in the gold fever that lured prospectors from California to British Columbia in 1858 and also in the recruitment of labour from the South China coast two decades later to build the Canadian Pacific Railway's transcontinental line through the Rocky Mountains and Coast Range. Many Chinese workers later settled in Vancouver, where they found work in hotels, sawmills and canneries. They were allowed to build their community on the low neck of land between the False Creek tidal flats and Burrard Inlet, which flooded periodically. Even with this physical limitation, Vancouver's Chinatown became an established community in the late 1880s. The first generation of buildings were wood-frame structures, many with distinctive recessed balconies, an architectural feature remembered from the homeland.

The Chinese called Vancouver "Saltwater City," a term evocative of sea air, the voyage many had made to reach the city and the bitter experience for many after arrival. Following their unsung (until recently) contribution to nation building by working on the CPR, Chinese labourers were viewed by Vancouver's European working class as low-wage competition, which provoked anti-Oriental prejudice exploited by the press and politicians. In

Above: Chinese Benevolent Association (B9)

1885 a federal "head tax" was levied on Chinese immigrants, and a full ban on immigration was in place from 1923 until 1947. Despite this persecution, the local Chinese merchant class grew and prospered. Its members kept the community together by funding schools and the benevolent society buildings that still stand on East Pender Street.

The most serious threat to Chinatown—and to neighbouring Gastown and Strathcona—was a 1967 freeway plan that would have bisected the community and destroyed its social and architectural cohesion. The plan was halted by local outrage and opposition, which gained support from outside the areas that would have been affected. In 1971, Chinatown and Gastown were designated by the provincial government as historic districts, with every building listed for protection. The Chinatown Historic Area Pender Street Improvement Project (1979) introduced streetscape improvements with "Chinese" elements.

Chinatown's traditions and lifestyles were not always appreciated by new immigrants from Hong Kong and Mainland China who arrived in the late-twentieth century, a cultural bias that was resented by some in the local community, which had survived racism and hard times. Moreover, Vancouver's Chinese-Canadian population vastly outgrew the neighbourhood. For new arrivals and many children of older Chinatown residents, the suburbs—particularly Richmond—offered a fresh start, with dream housing and glittering malls.

Chinatown's fortunes have since improved, partly the result of planning initiatives by the City, which have relaxed the need for strict adherence to heritage protection. The Vancouver-Chinese diaspora, Vancouver's non-Chinese population and tourists alike patronize Chinatown businesses and appreciate the appealing buildings, restaurants and cultural amenities. At this critical point, the area's historic urban scale and character may yet be threatened, not by the horizontal intrusion of the notorious freeway but by a vertical one—selective high-rise zoning to serve the mantra of "densification."

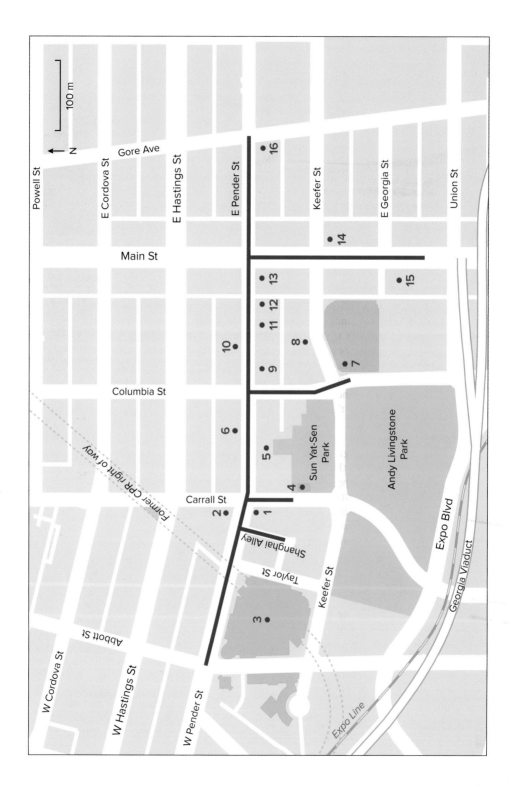

B1 Sam Kee Building
8 West Pender Street
Bryan & Gillam 1913; Birmingham & Wood 1966;
Soren Rasmussen 1986

Famed by the *Guinness World Records* as the "world's narrowest building," this is a unique structure, 4 feet 11 inches deep on the ground floor; 6 feet 2 inches deep including the bay windows. It was the response of merchant Chang Toy (a.k.a. Sam Kee) after the City expropriated most of his property—a valuable corner location for his Sam Kee Company—to widen the street. The bay windows and an areaway (A4) maximized the space that remained. In 1966, architects Birmingham & Wood bought and restored the Sam Kee building "close to original condition." It was their office when they worked on pioneering proposals to preserve Gastown's and Chinatown's architecture. Insurance agent Jack Chow bought it in 1986. Chow proved as pugnacious as Chang Toy. After he rehabilitated the building, the city increased his property assessment. Chow fought that but the city then taxed his bay windows. Finally, in 1988, council voted to waive all fees.

The road widening that provoked Chang Toy was amplified in 1967 when City Council approved an elevated freeway through Chinatown. That prospect, linked to "slum clearance" in Strathcona (C2), sparked opposition from the Chinese and other communities. The

"Strathcona freeway" was dropped: the "livable city" that is present-day Vancouver was born.

The **Chinatown Millennium Gate** (Joe Y. Wai Architect 2002) celebrates the entrance to Chinatown. Shanghai Alley, just west of the Sam Kee Building, was given a public realm makeover (Joe Y. Wai 2002). The focal point is a plaza, Allan Yap Circle, with replica Han Dynasty bell gifted by the City of Guangzhou (once known as Canton) and interpretive panels that tell of Chinatown's past.

B2 Chinese Freemasons Building
5 West Pender Street
1907; Joe Y. Wai Architect, Commonwealth Historic Resource Management 2008

Chinatown was designated as a historic district (at the same time as Gastown) by the provincial government in 1971. This building's façades show characteristics of both: Gastown's Italianate on Carrall Street, Chinatown's recessed balconies on Pender. Guangdong province was where the majority of B.C.'s Chinese immigrants came from. China was also the source of the recessed-balcony style of architecture (often with a sidewalk arcade in the home country, and in Southeast Asian cities with "overseas Chinese" populations).

Philanthropist and former chancellor of Simon Fraser University, Milton Wong, bought this building (where his father had opened a tailor shop in 1913) and hired long-time Chinatown architect Joe Wai to rehabilitate it. Housing was fitted into the upper floors, and the ground floor is commercial, where a seismic brace, patterned like a Chinese screen, is visible. The interior had been gutted and replaced with a steel structure in 1975, so only the exterior elevations' significant features could be conserved or restored. These include painted signage on the Carrall Street elevation and the window on the west elevation that reportedly illuminated the bedroom in which Dr. Sun Yat-Sen (B4) stayed in 1911.

B3 International Village and International Village Mall
88 West Pender Street (Mall)
International Village Architects (Baker McGarva Hart, Davidson Yuen Simpson Architects, Downs/Archambault), Kirkor Architects
1990s–2011

Like a fusion chef trying to match flavours, this megaproject struggled with

the blend. It mixed Vancouverism with the Hong Kong developer's (Henderson Development) and Toronto architects' (Kirkor) taste for globalizing additives. The marketing was "themed" with references from afar; the architecture could be anywhere.

Unlike the Coal Harbour and False Creek projects (I36, G19), it does not have a waterfront advantage. It abuts Beatty Street's backside, Pacific Boulevard, the Chinatown heritage district (to which planners wanted it to relate sensitively) and the Downtown Eastside. Its 21-acre site was part of the Expo Lands acquired by Concord Pacific Developments, which flipped it in 1989. The scheme includes a shopping mall, multiplex cinema, sidewalk retail, office space, a supermarket, parkades and almost 1,400 apartments (108 units subsidized, in the zigzag-canopied **Sorella**, 505 Abbott Street, Gomberoff Bell Lyon 2011) and the 10-acre Andy Livingstone Park. It was expected to revitalize the area, but few tourists or locals visited, and it had competition from Richmond's Asian malls (N4). A reviving Chinatown—and the Woodward's effect (A25)—may help it serve the eastside, to which its urban geography is connected (the developer ignored that).

Solid urbanism was the project's starting point: a pedestrian-oriented circular plaza (Paris Place) linked by Keefer Steps to Beatty Street and Stadium-Chinatown SkyTrain station; high-rises (and the Sorella) scaled to the Sun Tower and other buildings to the heritage height of Chinatown. The mall's concourse is aligned as a memory of the CPR track that linked False Creek and Burrard Inlet (a fragment of track crosses West Pender Street at the north entrance to the mall). These attributes were a local, not global, base for the recipe.

**B4 Dr. Sun Yat-Sen
Classical Chinese Garden**
578 Carrall Street
Joe Y. Wai Architect; Don Vaughan
landscape design 1986

Artisans from Suzhou employed traditional techniques and materials imported
from China to construct this tranquil
"scholar's garden" based on traditional
architectural and landscape design. Joe
Wai described it "as an ever-changing
universe which fluctuates between op-
posites, such as hard and soft, light and
dark; to achieve harmony, such contrasts
are included in the journey of life." It was
the first full-size Ming Dynasty–style
garden outside China and is named for
Dr. Sun Yat-Sen, prodemocracy leader
and founder of the Kuomintang (nationalist) party (B16), who visited Vancouver
to raise funds for the revolution of 1911
that overthrew the Qin Dynasty and created the Republic of China, of which he
was the first president.

**B5 Chinese Cultural Centre
of Greater Vancouver**
50 East Pender Street
James K.M. Cheng Architects, Romses,
Kwan & Associates, Don Vaughan landscape
design 1981; Joe Y. Wai Architect 1998

A Wong Benevolent Association ban-
quet in 1972 was the genesis of the centre, which includes a public park and the

Dr. Sun Yat-Sen Classical Chinese Garden.
The administration and education buildings were completed in 1980, followed by
storefront space in 1981. WWII military
volunteers and CPR workers are remembered on plaques at the entrance, which
is fronted by the China Gate, refashioned
with bas-reliefs (Arthur Cheng 2005); it
was first erected outside the Chinese pavilion at Expo 86. The built form echoes
traditional Chinese urbanism—walled,
with an inner courtyard—rendered without overt imitation. The Chinese Cultural
Centre's Museum and Archives Building
(555 Columbia Street, Joe Y. Wai 1998) is
more conspicuous with a roof characteristic of the Ming Dynasty.

Only one Chinese-Canadian architect (who was not accepted into
the professional association) has been
noted as working in Chinatown before WWII—W.H. Chow, whose **Ming
Wo Store** (23 East Pender Street, 1914;
store established 1917) and the similarly

recessed-balcony-style **Yue Shan Society Building** (33–39 East Pender Street, 1920) still stand. Hidden behind the latter is an old-style courtyard and housing (34 Market Alley).

B6 Rennie Collection at Wing Sang ↑
51 East Pender Street
1889; T.E. Julian 1901; Walter Francl Architecture, mcfarlane green biggar, Robert Lemon Architect, Donald Luxton & Associates 2009

Three related but dissimilar buildings were converted as cohesive and serene spaces for condo marketer and arts patron Bob Rennie to house his private museum of international contemporary art and the business that funds it. The original Wing Sang Building—the oldest in Chinatown—accommodates a main-floor gallery that preserves the volume of the original structure and leads, through minimalist exhibition spaces, to a spacious rooftop sculpture garden.

The Wing Sang Building was built for Guangdong-born Yip Sang, a gold panner and cook in California who moved to B.C. in 1881. He recruited Chinese labour for the CPR and was a passenger agent for the railway's steamships to China. A rags-to-riches entrepreneur, he established the Wing Sang Company in 1888. A new bay-windowed block absorbed the original in 1901 and was connected to a tenement (1910) across an alley—a stereotypically "secret" Chinatown alley—where Yip Sang lived with his extended family. Part of the tenement's brick wall was retained to divide gallery space, and as a memory of the alley. The curious door on the second floor of the 1888 building would have accessed a wooden verandah, either never added or undocumented. The Rennie Collection can be viewed by guided tour.

B7 Chinatown Plaza
180 Keefer Street
Joe Y. Wai Architect 1995

Business leaders lobbied City Hall for this mixed-use, seven-level, nine-hundred-plus stall parkade to compete with the suburbs. It contains shops and a thou-

sand-seat Chinese restaurant, the biggest in Canada. The elevations are postmodern, on Columbia Street evoking a Chinese city gate, with allusions on Keefer Street to recessed-balcony heritage façades. History and achievements of Chinese Canadians are noted on the Keefer Triangle, where statues of a railway worker and soldier flank the **Chinatown Memorial Monument** (Arthur Cheng 2003). The plaza's bilingual neon sign (John Atkin 2010) evokes the 1950s, when neon seemed to light up every Chinatown block and advertise every eatery and shop.

B8 The Keefer
135 Keefer Street
Sharp & Thompson 1910; Gair Williamson Architects, John Bryson & Partners engineers 2009

False Creek's tide rose and fell outside this former Vancouver Gas Company warehouse, a minor work by Sharp & Thompson, now a major style statement, with artworks by Douglas Coupland. The only liquid flowing now is in the ground

floor bar, where lush design hints at the luxe life (and more liquid) upstairs—three full-floor suites, plus a penthouse with a steel-supported, glass-bottomed pool. Heritage features were preserved for the customary loft look. After the market collapse in 2008, owner Cameron Watt opened the upper floors as a boutique apartment hotel.

B9 Chinese Benevolent Association
108 East Pender Street
1910; Joe Y. Wai Architect, Commonwealth Historic Resource Management 2010

Rusticated stone piers and decorative iron on the recessed balconies animate this façade in the Chinatown style, restored to original colours with assistance from

B

the Vancouver Heritage Foundation and the City's Heritage Incentive Program. The Benevolent Association, begun in 1895, was founded officially in 1906. Chinese clan and benevolent societies provided social services, accommodation and support for a community that was isolated from mainstream society and whose people were often valued only as a source of cheap labour. Perceived from a racist point of view as a threat to European-Canadian jobs, that labour force provoked a white protest in 1887 after contractor John "Chinese" McDougall hired Chinese workers to clear the forest in the West End; a march in 1907—incited with speeches in the Protestant Orange Hall (C23)—turned violent when crowds swept through Chinatown and on to Japantown (C18), vandalizing stores as they passed.

B10 Mon Keang School ↑
121 East Pender Street
J.A. Radford & G.L. Southall 1921

A lovely piece of stained-glass chinoiserie decorates the entrance to this atmospheric building, whose unaltered stairway ascends to rooms that resonate with the click-clack of mah-jong tiles. The mezzanine "cheater storey" was designed for extra floor space without incurring property tax. The façade is a reconstruction of a 1904 structure, with two storeys and recessed balconies added by the Wong Benevolent Association, whose name appears on a curved pediment above the cornice. The Mon Keang School (the first in Canada to offer classes at high-school level in Chinese) opened here in 1925; children attended after their regular school days.

The adjacent **Lee Building** (127–131 East Pender Street, 1907; Henriquez & Todd 1973) also patterns the streetscape with recessed balconies. The original façade was reconstructed as a free-standing screen after a fire; a modern structure was erected behind and includes a cozy courtyard. This "façadist" approach to heritage revitalization, in varied forms, has become popular (if disapproved by many in the heritage sector) and can be profitable.

B11 Chin Wing Chun Society
160 East Pender Street
Robert A. McKenzie 1925

Chinatown's recessed balcony style—also found in Victoria and San Francisco—was often embellished or stacked with Western features, here a crescendo of Tuscan columns, classical mouldings and a prominent pediment. The building is a hybrid, rather like present-day Vancouver, with its blend of Euro- and Asian-Canadian business, culture and history. Architect McKenzie could claim knowledge of both societies, having worked for more than five years in northern China.

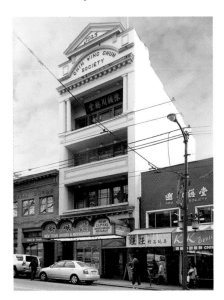

B12 Vancity Chinatown Community Branch
188 East Pender Street
Birmingham & Wood 1971

Built for the Bank of Montreal, this is a sensitive reworking of the Chinatown built form, filling a deep narrow lot, visible here because of the lane. It incorporates a tiled roof (used on temples and other buildings) between walls. Its scale and depth echo nineteenth- and early-twentieth-century shophouses, an Asian building-type often decorated with Chinese and Western features, with the family living above the store. The architects' office was in Chinatown (B1), and they acquired intimate knowledge of its architecture, as this gem of a building shows. It is neither a pastiche nor patronizing.

B13 Canadian Imperial Bank of Commerce
501 Main Street
Victor Daniel Horsburgh 1915

Four stupendous, banded columns rise to a classical pediment on this unconventional elevation. A caduceus (a winged staff with entwined snakes), once a symbol of commerce, appears on the pediment. Horsburgh was from Edinburgh, but he saw nothing in that city to spark this improbable design, which would be at home in the colonial grandeur of Shanghai's Bund. He was based in

Toronto, where he was the chief architect of Dominion Realty, a subsidiary of the bank. The supervising architect in Vancouver was W.F. Gardiner, an Englishman, a WWI hero and a future president of the Architectural Institute of B.C.

B14 HSBC Building
608 Main Street
W.T. Leung Architects 1995

This confident addition to the historic streetscape marked a revival of Chinatown's sagging fortunes, as did Chinatown Plaza (B7). Its recessed balconies acknowledge the area's heritage, while the bay windows and a cornice relate to those on **Keefer Rooms** (c. 1912) across the alley. The cylindrical corner feature, which can be compared with the Carnegie Centre (A35), strengthens the urban scale, turning the corner more forcefully than the likable three-storey Victorian building, home of On-On Tea Gardens, it replaced.

B15 Murrin Substation
721 Main Street
McCarter & Nairne 1947

The B.C. Electric Company operated Vancouver's power and transit systems until 1961, when it was nationalized and became B.C. Hydro. Its pride in its purpose is shown in the quality of the architecture here—functionally a concrete box but with delightful decor applied. Two Art Deco doorways display chevron and swash mouldings; panels flash with flames and bolts of electricity to symbolize the power generated inside. Variegated brickwork and fluted pilasters add texture to the façades, which are strongly composed, classical and dignified. The substation was named for company president W.G. Murrin.

B16 **Nationalist League (Kuomintang) Building**
525 Gore Avenue
William Edwardes Sproat 1920

The Chinese Nationalist League, a.k.a. the Kuomintang, was founded in 1905 by Dr. Sun Yat-Sen (B4); it survives as the government of Taiwan. This was the league's Western Canadian headquarters, financed by Chinese Canadians inspired by Sun Yat-Sen's vision of a democratic China. The architect introduced contextual features to the concrete, brick-faced structure, with arches that were originally open with recessed balconies and a Chinese pagoda-style turret, since removed, at the corner.

B

Strathcona

S TRATHCONA, "Vancouver's oldest neighbourhood," was named for Lord Strathcona, the Scottish-born director of the Canadian Pacific Railway and the man who drove home the last spike on the transcontinental line. The neighbourhood was established in the 1860s for its proximity to Hastings Mill. Other mills, canneries, the port and the railway also provided employment as the city developed. Early residents were from the British Isles or Canadians of British origin, reflecting the dominant demographic of nineteenth- and early-twentieth-century Vancouver.

After the completion of the CPR, the city's social elite settled on property being developed in the West End or the East End. Strathcona remained a working-class immigrant community. Through the twentieth century, like the British before them, other Europeans—many from Scandinavia, Russia, Germany, Portugal and Italy, as well as Jews, Chinese, and other religious and racial minorities—moved in and moved on when and if their circumstances improved.

In the 1960s, some planners and politicians claimed the neighbourhood was a "slum," which they wanted to remove with ambitious urban renewal and by slicing a freeway through it—the same freeway that would have gouged Chinatown and Gastown. The freeway was stopped, and only two fragments of the renewal

Above: 500-block Hawkes Avenue (c11)

plans were built (C2) before a rethink, forced by local protest and regime change at City Hall. Strathcona's residents led the protest that stopped both schemes, saving their neighbourhood and—as is now generally acknowledged—rescuing the City from planning megalomania and total auto-dependency.

In the last generation, the civilized urbanism of communities such as Strathcona has been praised by architects and planners and enjoyed by residents. The combination of walkable streets, adaptable heritage buildings and green spaces is seen as a template for social and environmental sustainability, not only in Vancouver but throughout North America, where many cities that took the freeway route are now trying to remedy its consequences.

The Strathcona neighbourhood was never a slum, nor has it since become a heritage theme park. The community is genuine and evolving—to some extent it is being gentrified, but more gently than elsewhere—and it still retains its "authenticity" in that change responds to its character without being too precious. The architectural serendipity on its leafy sidewalks and rustic lanes is a delight: Victorian fretwork gables decorate the same street as a stout Edwardian school; condos occupy a converted synagogue (C10); onion domes sprout from a Russian Orthodox church (C14); and corner groceries and three-storey walk-ups are mixed lot by lot with heritage homes, Vancouver Specials and eco-conscious rehabilitations and infill dwellings.

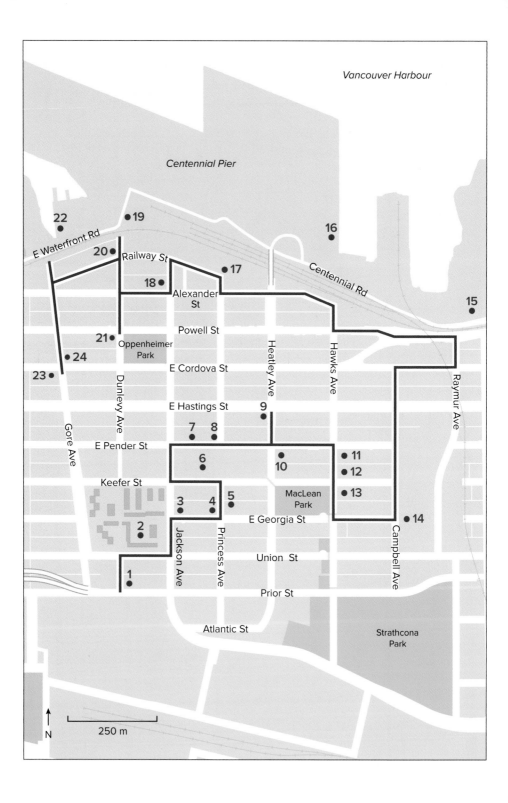

Vancouver Harbour

Centennial Pier

22
19
E Waterfront Rd
20
Railway St
16
18
17
Alexander
St
Centennial Rd
Powell St
15
21
Oppenheimer
Park
24
E Cordova St
Heatley Ave
Hawks Ave
23
Raymur Ave
Dunlevy Ave
E Hastings St
9
7   8
Gore Ave
E Pender St
6
11
10
12
Keefer St
13
MacLean
Park
3   4   5
14
Campbell Ave
2
E Georgia St
Jackson Ave
Princess Ave
Union St
1
Prior St
Atlantic St
Strathcona
Park

N
250 m

c1 Winchcombe House
844 Dunlevy Avenue
1899; 2006

Chinatown stops abruptly east of Gore Avenue, where a social and architectural mix of Victorian homes, schools, churches, corner groceries and public housing projects makes up Strathcona. This was Vancouver's earliest residential neighbourhood, first established around Hastings Mill (c19) to accommodate millworkers. Successive waves of immigrants settled. Strathcona's old homes stayed old, unmodernized—heritage paradise but residentially substandard.

This Victorian house, typical of the first generation of homes in Strathcona, would have been demolished had the 1960s urban redevelopment scheme not been halted (see next entry). Planners and politicians saw the neighbourhood's homes as not worth saving and of no historic value. In 2004, when new owners took possession, the house was almost terminally decayed, fitting that 1960s preconception. It was fixed up "shingle by shingle, board

by board," aided by the Vancouver Heritage Foundation, and has history. It was built by New Brunswick–born Frederick William Sentell, a contractor who built homes after the Great Fire and an early City Hall—a plain, wood-frame, two-storey building on Powell Street. Despite the name, Strathcona was not part of the CPR's land grant but owned by a competitor, David and Isaac Oppenheimer's (A30) Vancouver Improvement Company.

c2 MacLean Park Housing Project
Gore and Jackson Avenues,
Keefer and Jackson Streets
Central Mortgage & Housing Corporation
1963, 1970; Canada–B.C. Affordable
Housing Initiative 2011

Much of old residential Strathcona would have been swept away by a 1950s federal government urban redevelopment program, to be rolled out across the nation. To implement it, the City's planning and public health experts chose Strathcona. Fifteen blocks and the Georgia Viaduct (1915) were demolished; a new twin viaduct was built as part of the proposed "Strathcona freeway" before grassroots protest halted the grand plans.

Two projects were completed: **Raymur-Campbell Housing Project** on Campbell Avenue (Duncan McNab & Associates 1967) and **MacLean Park**—named after Vancouver's first mayor, Malcolm Alexander MacLean). Both variously exhibit the clichés of postwar planning: separation of people from amenities (to leave the streets for traffic); concrete "skywalks," point towers, slab blocks and low-rise maisonettes, all set on communal open space. The built form is the antithesis of the old (now fashionably "new") urbanism of Strathcona's heritage streetscapes. Yet Raymur Place and MacLean Park were once fashionable too, in professional circles, as utopian solutions to worn-out housing. The

C

problem was less the architecture (which derived from European modernism and ideals of social progress) and more that the professionals chose not to ask the people what they thought or wanted.

An arch-enemy of comprehensive redevelopment was planner and author Jane Jacobs, whose love of human-scale neighbourhoods has had a significant influence in Vancouver. Her style of urbanism influenced the 1971 Strathcona Rehabilitation Project, funded by the Central (now Canada) Mortgage & Housing Corporation, as an alternative to 1960s redevelopment. (The Strathcona experience led to the CMHC's national Residential Rehabilitation Assistance Program in 1974.) The City's Strathcona Community Plan in 1992 sought to deal with zoning and heritage issues and social problems overflowing from the DTES. The committee that liaised with the City through the three years of the planning process became the successful Strathcona Residents' Association. MacLean Park and Raymur-Campbell remain viable projects that have received funding for upgrades.

c3 Jackson Apartments
501 East Georgia Street
E.E. Blackmore 1910

This typical West Coast walk-up retains a convenience store at the corner, a characteristic of Strathcona. The district never developed its own commercial area (it was well served by the Main Street shops). B.C. Electric Railway streetcar lines connected it to the city. A proposal to run the trams across the Georgia Viaduct prompted apartment construction, and the Jackson is one of the results. The viaduct never took the trams, reportedly too poorly built to support them.

Residents in the building witnessed a shoot-out in 1917, when Vancouver Police Chief Malcolm MacLennan was murdered by a known offender, Bob Tait, in a nearby house, and a boy on the street was killed by crossfire. Tait was black and was branded a drug addict by the press. The incident confirmed the East End's reputation, held by many Westsiders and City Hall, as a problem area needing a big fix. That perception played out in the 1960s redevelopment plans and informed the Woodward's project (A25). MacLennan is commemorated by a mosaic on the sidewalk outside Jackson Apartments.

c4 The Schoolhouse
595 East Georgia Street
George Aspell 1940; Hotson Bakker
Boniface Haden 2009

Strathcona's virtues are sociability, serendipity and no mandated style, although neo-heritage seems preferred. Change can fit in, as this intervention shows. Take Root Properties built five residential units plus optional commercial space in the corner-store manner. An old schoolhouse (St. Francis Xavier, built for the Chinese Catholic Mission) was retained. It was jacked up to excavate a new foundation, which supports structural steelwork. Because of the tight site, the steel was rolled in by hand. Hand crafted

is how the abutting additions on Princess Avenue look, complementing the heritage. The project gained LEED Platinum certification.

c5 McNair House
630 Princess Avenue
1900

Offset porch, bay windows, gables and jigsaw trim in typical Victorian style are seen on this house, built for New Brunswick-born James Archibald McNair, the "Shingle King of the Northwest." He arrived from Quebec in 1892 and opened a mill east of Hastings Mill with one of his brothers. Their company, Hastings Shingle Manufacturing, expanded in 1902 with a shingle mill near the north foot of Commercial Drive that was the biggest in the world. Tugboats pulled North Shore timber across Burrard Inlet to feed it. McNair followed a familiar Strathcona pattern: when he could, he moved—in his case to a mansion in North Vancouver (M13).

c6 Lord Strathcona Elementary School
592 East Pender Street
Thomas Hooper 1891; William Blackmore 1897;
F.A.A. Barrs 1921; C.L. Morgan 1914; H.W. Postle
1929; Gardiner Thornton Partnership 1972

This traditionally multicultural school evolved from the Hasting Mill community school (1865), a clapboard building with fifteen pupils, to this medley of five buildings, which includes a modernist community centre. The site is the Vancouver School Board's oldest in continuous use. Bricks and granite from the original 1891 structure were recycled in the Primary Building (1921). Architect Blackmore's Junior Building on Keefer Street, with a central tower flanked by gabled bays, all on a stone base, is the most imposing in the group.

The **Queen Anne house** (602 Keefer Street, 1902), with a witch's hat turret, gables, porch, faceted entrance and gingerbread trim, was built for school principal Gregory Henry Tom. Number 636 was the **Anglican Chinese Mission** (Townley & Matheson 1935; 2002), the scissor-truss interior rehabilitated as live-work space by a new owner; **658 Keefer** was the home of Mary Chan, who inspired the creation of the Strathcona Property Owners & Tenants Association, which fought redevelopment in the 1960s.

c7 Jackson Garden
503 East Pender Street
H. Hou 1983

This mews-style development, similar in scale to preceding low-rise projects on False Creek (G8) was designed with

C

Strathcona's Chinese population in mind. The layout and use of brick recall the Hutong manner of urbanism in China, where the dwellings form a compound, laced with alleys linking one or more courtyards. The form was common in Beijing, before that city adopted the comprehensive redevelopment ideas that once threatened Vancouver. Jackson Garden is low-rise but dense, a good neighbourhood fit, although its inner focus seems defensive. The composition's curving forms are inventive.

c8 Korean Foursquare Gospel Church
431 Princess Street
J.G. Price 1910

Strathcona's changing but consistent immigrant makeup is revealed in the successive congregations that have worshipped in this Gothic Revival church. Previously, it was St. Francis Xavier Chinese Catholic Parish Church, St. Mary's Ukrainian Greek Church, St. Stephens Greek Catholic Church and First Swedish Evangeli-

cal Lutheran Church. The style is rather French, like Holy Rosary Cathedral (H12), a mode preferred by the Roman Catholic diocese.

c9 Heatley Block
696 East Hastings Street
1931

When the City bought this building in 2008 as the site for a new library, vigilant locals saw the implications and protested—not against the library but against proposed demolition of the Heatley Block, a classic of its type and the only survivor on this strip of Hastings Street. The wood-frame apartment and retail building was built by Samuel Plastino, an Italian-born hotelier who moved two Klondike-era houses to the back of the lot to make space for it. The houses are still there. Heritage Vancou-

ver called the ensemble "unique" for its combination of building-types and social history. A preservation group gathered seven thousand signatures on a petition to prevent demolition. The City took note and acquired a site for the library on the next block east, and the Heatley Block was spared.

C

c10 Schara Tzedeck Synagogue
700 East Pender Street
1921; Spaceworks Architects 1987

The Schara Tzedeck congregation built the first permanent synagogue in Vancouver here in 1911, soon replaced by this larger structure. It became a gym after the congregation moved to Oak Street in 1947 and forty years later was rehabilitated as condos. The Pender Street entrance was altered but the overall style respected, with buttress-like features, round-arched windows and a dome retained. These were originally intended to evoke the Romanesque style that was favoured by many Jewish temple builders for its Mediterranean origins and because classical and Gothic styles were associated with Christian worship.

c11 500-block Hawkes Avenue
Walter Scott builder 1900; Clare McDuff-Oliver 1987

Strathcona's streetscapes generally exhibit a looser urbanism than these identical workers' rental cottages, lined up in a row, suggest (the community's lanes, for example, are completely accidental in their variety). They typify the end-of-block solution found in the early city; instead of two houses on the two lots, there are six across the lot lines. Four cottages were extant when renovations began; the two missing ones (at either

end) were replicated. Rehabilitation here was a sign of a neighbourhood on the cusp of change; the Smart Cars and Minis parked on the streets show it is happening, though not yet on every block. The cars and cheerfully painted homes suggest "gentrification," but "evolution," as Strathcona resident and historian John Atkin has said, is a more accurate word.

c12 Koo's Corner
568–598 Hawkes Avenue
1947; Bruce Haden Architect 2002

The neighbourhood's evolution is seen at this adaptation of and addition to Koo's Garage, established in 1973 in a former haulage company depot built in 1947 on an empty lot, once the site of a Victorian home. Developer Robert Brown commissioned this eco-conscious intervention that rejected the faux-heritage look, while referring to the past with porches, slanted gables and siding in a contemporary blend of the area's industrial and residential features. Two of the project's six units are in the shell of the garage, which was reoriented; there are three row houses and an intermediate unit. The streetscape thus created is idiosyncratic— like old Strathcona. The garage appears as a "laneway house," the type of infill promoted by planners as a model for moderate density, affordability and sustainability city wide (F11).

c13 Paneficio
800 Keefer Street
1894; c. 1935

This funky corner and artists' studio was the site of the Montreal Bakery from 1935 to 1955, owned by Italian-born Lucien Zanon, who enclosed the Victorian house with an Art Deco extension to the sidewalk, with a shop at the corner. The artists renamed it as a memory of the bakery. Similarly organic is the house (1905) at **708 Hawkes Avenue**, wrapped in 1923 by the Di Tomaso family for a candy store, now residential, called the "fish bowl" because of its storefront windows. A reminder that Strathcona once had a black community is **417 East Georgia Street**, formerly the home of guitarist Jimi Hendrix's grandmother.

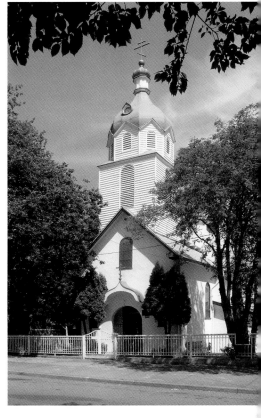

c14 Holy Trinity Russian Orthodox Church
710 Campbell Avenue
Alexander Kiziun 1940

Strathcona has always been a home for new immigrant groups; only the Chinese have remained in the area in large numbers, still the majority. This onion-domed jewel, built by priest and carpenter Kiziun, is less incongruous than it seems, because Russians and Ukrainians escaping Stalin's regime immigrated to Vancouver in numbers in the 1930s. The nearby Raymur-Campbell Housing Project (c2) stands in as a suitably Soviet-style social housing backdrop.

C

C15 Rogers Sugar Warehouse
123 Rogers Street
1903; various additions

New Orleans–born Benjamin Tingley Rogers arrived in Vancouver from Montreal to build a sugar plant, with financial backing promised from the CPR's Donald Alexander Smith (Lord Strathcona) and William Van Horne. He founded B.C. Sugar in 1890 and persuaded the City to grant him free water for ten years and a fifteen-year tax holiday. The City provided the site, but Council stipulated that Rogers not hire Chinese labour. The refined sugar warehouse is the oldest structure on the site. Behind its long brick façade, which faces the Powell Street railway tracks, is a honeycomb of industrial structures, storage bins, a moderne-style steam plant (1941) and a dock built as the plant was enlarged. Rogers invested in plantations in Fiji, made a fortune and flaunted it with two of the most luxurious mansions in Vancouver (I11, K39).

C16 Ballantyne Pier
655 Centennial Road
1923; Musson Cattell Mackey Partnership 1996

Four storage sheds were embellished with colossal façades in the Beaux-Arts manner favoured for transportation terminals in the early twentieth century, usually railway stations (H28). One façade (and an interior fragment) was saved as part of modifications and a breezy addition for a facility to berth overflow Alaska cruise ship traffic from Canada Place (H30). The contractor (Kiewit Corporation) also built a massive bulk cargo shed, primarily for wood pulp, which required a seismic upgrade to the pier (its concrete caissons had been set in landfill, potentially unstable in the event of an earthquake).

Vancouver was the site of federal relief camps during the Depression and much social tension. The "Battle of Ballantyne Pier" took place here, when port workers and police clashed during a bitter labour dispute in 1935. The same year, Mayor Gerry McGeer, backed by two hundred police, stood at the Cenotaph at Victory Square (A20) and read the Riot Act to the relief camp protesters.

c17 American Can Company
611 Alexander Street
Carl G. Preis 1925; Bruno Freschi 1988

North America's largest tin can producer brought modern industrial architecture to Vancouver with this reinforced-concrete and glass factory building. Preis was in charge of American Can's engineering and architecture and designed plants across North America, including one in Montreal, during the company's expansion after WWI. His crisp corporate style is liberated here with moderne modelling on the office block. Bruno Freschi's makeover (designers' showrooms, artists' studios, architects' offices off an internal atrium) is announced with a striking, see-through steel-and-glass elevator pylon at the entrance.

c18 Vancouver Japanese Language School & Japanese Hall
475 Alexander Street
Sharp & Thompson 1928; Shigeru Amano 2000

Japanese immigrants arrived in the 1880s and worked at Hastings Mill (see next entry). Little remains of the community that bloomed as "Japantown," before its businesses were seized by the government when Japanese Canadians were expelled from Vancouver in 1942 (E19). The school, established in 1906 in a wood-frame building at 439 Alexander Street, moved to this cultural centre, lightly detailed with a Spanish Colonial brush. Like the Japanese-Canadian people interned as "enemy aliens" in camps in B.C.'s interior, the centre became a prisoner of war, requisitioned by the army. In 1953, it was returned to the community—the only item from countless possessions confiscated in 1942 and sold. An addition

C

reinterpreted the original's tiled entrance in 2000. A larger Japanese-Canadian cultural facility, the National Nikkei Museum & Heritage Centre, opened in the same year (6688 Southoaks Crescent) in Burnaby.

c19 Mission to Seafarers "Flying Angel Club"
401 East Waterfront Road
1906

Captain Edward Stamp, who arrived in Victoria from England in 1858, founded Hastings Mill, originally the Vancouver Island Spar, Lumber & Sawmill Company, near this site in 1865 (k13). It was the nucleus of early settlement; its thirsty workers inspired Gassy Jack Deighton to build a nearby saloon (a1). Sailing ships were loaded with lumber from "Stamp's Mill," as Hastings Mill was called, near the present Port Metro Vancouver container cranes. In 1891 it became the B.C. Mills, Timber & Trading Company, which milled lumber and shipped houses, schools, banks and churches in kit form to any location in Western Canada. The surviving prefabricated building here was the mill office and sales centre. In 1930, the Vancouver Harbour Commission moved in. Since 1973, it has been occupied by the local branch of the Mission to Seafarers, which was established in England by the Anglican Church in 1855.

c20 Empire Stevedoring
395 Railway Street
Watson & Blackadder 1941

Railway Street was a neglected enclave of docklands architecture until the Gastown live-work lifestyle moved eastward in the 1990s, romanticizing the look of labour. The buildings are attractive because they have high ceilings, visible structural columns, brick façades and a feeling of the past. Empire Stevedoring outdoes this crowd with a moderne, fluted façade and a flashy frieze of Art Deco typography. The unpretentious warehouse at **365 Railway Street** (1948) was rehabilitated in 1998 for furniture manufacturing by designer Niels Bendtsen (a6).

c21 Tamura House
398 Powell Street
Townsend & Townsend 1913; Robert G. Lemon Architecture & Preservation 1991

The Lookout Emergency Aid Society runs this 110-unit block, bought by the provincial government in 2008 as part of a program to secure affordable housing. Previously the New World Hotel, it was built for Shinkichi Tamura, Canada's first commissioner of trade to Japan. The style and ornament are Western, with sheet-metal cornices and Corinthian columns

applied to enhance Tamura's Canada & Japan Trust Savings Bank. The intersection at Powell and Dunlevy was "Little Tokyo" until wwii; ghost lettering survives on the former **Maikawa Department Store** (365 Powell Street, 1908; T.L. Kerr 1936).

Across the lane from Tamura House is the **Franciscan Sisters of the Atonement** (255 Dunlevy Avenue, 1929). The Sisters, who arrived in 1926 to operate the Catholic Japanese Mission School, later bought the 1887 building at 385 East Cordova Street, now recognized as the oldest house in the city. During wwii, they set up schools in the internment camps

(c18) and still serve this north Strathcona neighbourhood. **Oppenheimer Park**, once home field of the renowned Vancouver Asahi baseball team (winner of ten city championships between 1919 and 1940), is an important open space in this disadvantaged zone, which seems ripe for revival, and also the focus the Japanese community's annual Powell Street Festival. The park had a reputation for substance abuse and violence until reclaimed by a thoughtful intervention (mcfarlane green biggar, space2place landscape design 2010).

c22 Canadian Fishing Company †
Foot of Gore Avenue
1906 and later

The company (now called Canfisco) was begun by entrepreneurs trading halibut from Vancouver in 1906. The industrial vernacular structures at its Vancouver base date from that era and included freezing, cold storage and ice-making facilities, offices and a fish dock constructed in 1910. The plant was rebuilt after fire in 1917, a remarkable survivor

C

redolent of a once buccaneering fishery now eco-conscious. The company also operated the Gulf of Georgia Cannery (N9) on the Fraser River, where it launched its famous "Gold Seal" canned salmon brand in 1940.

c23 Firehall Arts Centre ↑
280 East Cordova Street
William Tuff Whiteway 1907; Roger Hughes 1976

Five Renaissance-arched bays and an Italianate tower indicate the building's public stature, as it was the headquarters of the Vancouver Fire Department. The arches spring from terracotta capitals and once supported a cornice crowned with a pediment (since removed) above the three central bays. They were filled in after the firefighters left in 1975, and the building was converted to a 175-seat studio theatre. A new **Fire Hall (No. 2)** was built nearby (199 Main Street) in basic brutalist style.

Next door to the arts centre is the former **Coroner's Court** (A32). Around the corner is **Orange Hall** (341 Gore Street, J. Gillott 1907), erected for the Grand Orange Lodge of B.C., whose members notoriously stormed out of the building to join the Chinatown Riot in 1907 (B9). The hall later had a stint as a wrestling arena. The Richardsonian Romanesque entrance arch is the most pleasant feature. The **Salvation Army Temple** (301 East Hastings Street, Mercer & Mercer 1949), down at heels now, was a shining example of moderne style when built.

c24 St. James' Anglican Church →
303 East Cordova Street
Adrian Gilbert Scott 1937

The first St. James' Church was built on the waterfront in 1881 and burned in the Great Fire in 1886. It was resurrected as an "English country style" church (Thomas Charles Sorby 1888), which stood on this site for fifty years until this extraordinary vision appeared. Scott, a scion of the London dynasty of architects, was the lead designer of this exotic, concrete structure: an octagon rising from a Greek Cross plan. Massive walls, tipped with Art Deco-influenced neo-Gothic

fluting and stylized gargoyles, step up like a ziggurat to a pyramid belfry. The entrance is wide, almost processional, High Anglican. At the time, Scott was designing All Saints' Cathedral, Cairo (1938; demolished 1978), in an Orientalist deco style; the personality, if not the form, of the Vancouver building is not far removed from that. Concrete dominates the interior. Daylight is filtered through Gothic lancets. The space is mysterious, Byzantine. Costs imposed a flat ceiling, which prevents the octagonal height to the lantern from being expressed. Scott also wanted brick cladding, a wish fulfilled in London's East End, where he reworked St. James in the almost identical ss Mary & Joseph Roman Catholic Church (1954). Reverend Canon Wilberforce Cooper of St. James was related to the Scott family and commissioned the architect. Scott called his design a "modern version of fourteenth-century Gothic"; Sharp &

Thompson, designers of the adjacent Arts and Crafts ensemble—**Parish Hall** (1925), **Clergy House** (1927) and **St. Luke's Home** (1924)—oversaw the building program.

C

Mount Pleasant and Fairview

MOUNT Pleasant and Fairview occupy the rise south of False Creek, extending from Fraser Street in the east to just beyond Granville Street in the west. Densely forested, scored by salmon-bearing creeks and traversed by First Nations trails, the slopes were logged in the 1870s. Access across False Creek was provided by a bridge at Main Street in 1872, followed by bridges at Granville Street in 1889 and Cambie Street two years later. In 1891 the "Fairview Beltline" offered regular streetcar service from downtown along Broadway between Main and Granville Streets, opening the area for rapid development.

Mount Pleasant, straddling Main Street, was Vancouver's first streetcar suburb. Residential development began in the 1880s, and before long the area was mostly built out with single-family homes and a few apartment buildings (D6). The commercial core developed along Main Street between Kingsway and Broadway, as well as along Broadway. Attempts to expand business up the hill, encouraged by the federal government's imposing post office (D8), failed to attract investment. A number of churches sprang up southwest of Main and Broadway (D9, D10), once known as "church hill."

Above: Heather Court (D20)

The area never prospered and became run down in the second half of the twentieth century. As a result, many old houses remain intact. The rehabilitation and gentrification of Mount Pleasant began in the 1970s (D12) and continues today.

West of Cambie Street the slopes were named "Fairview" and opened for settlement by CPR surveyor Lauchlan Hamilton in 1890. Before long it filled with homes for the middle class (D24) and for workers engaged in the many industries along False Creek (D22). Institutions took root in Fairview, including Vancouver General Hospital (D17), King Edward High School and the Model and Normal Schools (D16). City Hall moved to 12th and Cambie in the 1930s, reinforcing the vitality of its neighbourhood.

Beginning in the 1920s, and again after WWII, single-family houses west of Cambie began to be replaced by two- and three-storey apartment buildings (D29). A few high-rises were built west of Granville. The Fairview slopes were rezoned in the 1970s to encourage condominium construction within tightly controlled building envelopes to ensure that every building had a share of the view (D20). Hardly any of Fairview's older houses survive; a few are visited towards the end of the chapter.

The tour indicated on the map has been optimized for driving. Cyclists and pedestrians should proceed to the closest building rather than following the map.

D

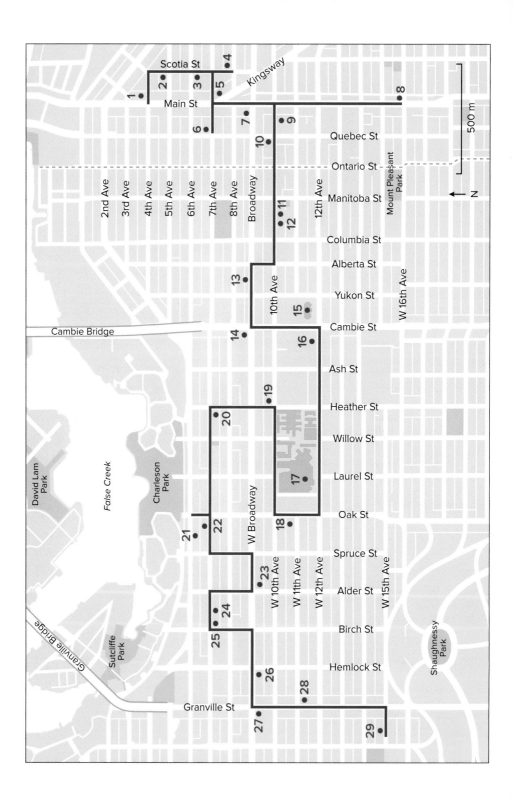

D1 Artworks
237 East 4th Avenue
Kasian Kennedy 1993

The City rezoned this area in 1993 to accommodate a community of high-density, live-work loft spaces intended to assist the arts community with affordable housing while revitalizing the neighbourhood. This and the nearby Brewery Creek Building (D3) were first off the mark; since then, more than one thousand units have been constructed. Artworks—its name makes the market explicit—set a precedent with its corrugated metal siding and exposed I-beams, providing an industrial vocabulary to respect the now rapidly disappearing historical context. Half the seventy-six strata-titled units are double-height to accommodate sleeping lofts; the remainder have 11-foot ceilings. Two others nearby are across the street at **272 East 4th Avenue** and **The Artiste** at 2050 Scotia Street. Artists began to populate the neighbourhood in 1973, at the Western Front (D4).

D2 NEC Native Education College
285 East 5th Avenue
Larry McFarland 1985

Inspired by the traditional coastal longhouse, wood posts support huge wood beams—13.2 metres long and 30 × 80 centimetres in cross-section—cut from old-growth Douglas-fir. Small classes of adult aboriginal students from around B.C. study here for one year. The totem pole at the entrance is by Nisga'a master carver Norman Tait, who participated in the 1970s revival of First Nations culture; another pole by him stands with the group in Stanley Park (131).

D3 Brewery Creek Building
280 East 6th Avenue
1904; Kasian Kennedy 1993

Charles Doering and Otto Marstrand opened this brick-and-stone building to accommodate the Vancouver Brewery,

which featured electric bottle-washing machinery and an ice-making plant. Other brewers in search of clean fresh water soon followed their lead—hence the name Brewery Creek, commemorated on a cairn across Scotia Street. The building was converted from dereliction to live-work studios—the first (with D1) of what are now many in the neighbourhood—with a floor added and set back on the roof. The Fell's Candy Factory sign from the 1920s was retained.

D4 Western Front Society Building
303 East 8th Avenue
1922; alterations 1973 and later

The Western Front, an artists' collective specializing in exploring new and interdisciplinary art, acquired this former Knights of Pythias lodge in 1973. It converted the frame building to gallery and performance space, production facilities and living quarters for artists, marking the beginning of the neighbourhood as an artists' enclave (D1). The exaggerated boomtown-style parapet was installed in 2009 by sculptor Reece Terris. A nearby old-timer is the **Ledingham House** (2425 Brunswick Street, 1895; Edward De Grey 1988), now the centrepiece of a nonprofit housing complex.

D5 One Kingsway
Busby Perkins + Will 2009

In an attempt to revitalize failing neighbourhoods such as Mount Pleasant, City-Plan, a long-range planning exercise carried out in the 1990s, envisioned "neighbourhood centres" that would bring together civic services and stimulate renewal—a goal that is achieved here. The Mount Pleasant community centre and branch library, supplemented with child care facilities, were relocated in the low-rise block, while ninety-eight rental units occupy the mid-rise block that slices into the intersection of Main Street and angled Kingsway (once the trail to New Westminster). One Kingsway responds to the scale and brickwork of the Lee Building (D7) and replaces it as the primary neighbourhood icon.

D6 Quebec Manor
101 East 7th Avenue
Townsend & Townsend 1912

Two immodest female figures energetically support the heavy pediment that forms the frontispiece of this marvellous concoction. Originally the Mt. Stephen

Apartments, it is now the thirty-two-unit Quebec Manor Housing Co-operative. Diamond-patterned brickwork, a heavy bracketed cornice, wrought-iron balconies and a tiled entrance hall with an elaborate, double-height wooden baroque screen all add interest.

D7 Lee Building
175 East Broadway
Stroud & Keith 1912

For many years, the largest commercial building outside the downtown core, the seven-storey brick-and-stone-faced building, developed by H.O. Lee, is a sym-

bol of the high aspirations once held—but never realized—for the Mount Pleasant neighbourhood. The arcade accommodated the new sidewalk required when Broadway was widened in the 1950s. The intersection has suffered a number of recent fires and is being renewed.

D8 Heritage Hall
3102 Main Street
Archibald Campbell Hope, David Ewart, Department of Public Works 1915; Downs/ Archambault, Baker McGarva Hart 1984

Local boosters hoped Mount Pleasant would become a bustling commercial centre. All they got were the Lee Building (D7) and this Postal Station C, the latter standing on the rise from Broadway. For seven decades, this delightfully eclectic Edwardian confection, with its rusticated stone base, coupled pilasters, steep roof and tall clock tower, contained federal government offices, including the RCMP from 1963 to 1976. An alliance of four community groups prompted a successful campaign to rehabilitate it in the 1980s as a social and cultural centre.

D9 Holy Trinity Ukrainian Orthodox Cathedral
154 East 10th Avenue
Serhyj Tymoshenko 1948–53

Two spires flanking the entrance and a third one atop the central cupola ensure that this Ukrainian Orthodox church—elevated to cathedral in 1983—is something special. The Eastern-Rite congregation was organized in 1937, and construction of the ambitious building began soon after the war. The area was nicknamed "church hill" for its spiritual skyline. A half-dozen blocks east, the **Protection of the Blessed Virgin Mary Ukrainian Catholic Church** (550 West 14th Avenue, Julian Jastremsky 1982), which looks to Rome for theological guidance, adopts similar architectural sources but renders them in a more modern idiom.

D10 The Cornerstone
85 East 10th Avenue
Parr & Fee 1910; Gomberoff-Policzer 1994

Originally Mount Pleasant Presbyterian Church, the stolid structure combines Romanesque Revival entrance arches and a corner turret with touches of Gothic Revival and Craftsman. The eclectic mix is brought together by brickwork trimmed with stone. After stints as an evangelist tabernacle and a performing arts venue, the building was converted to thirty-five dwelling units, including a four-storey wing added to the west. Mount Pleasant Baptist Church (Burke, Horwood & White 1910) stood kitty-corner until destroyed by fire in 2004; the site is now occupied by **Maison Quebec** (2600-block Quebec Street, Formwerks Architectural 2006), an apartment block clad in half-timber in its memory.

D11 Isis & Isis Cottage
122–26 West 10th Avenue
1907; Richard Fearn 1987

Inspired by the Davis family's initiative (see next entry), builder Richard Fearn reproduced the original "cast stone" (concrete) blocks of this Edwardian-era house to reconstruct the front porch and to build Isis Cottage, the small infill dwelling at the rear—an antecedent of the laneway house (F11). Much of the original house's detailing, such as the

rusticated quoins and arched inset balcony, are mirrored in the cottage. Other good makeovers nearby include the former **Bloomfield Home and Studio** (2532, 2544 Columbia Street, c. 1900), built for Charles and James Bloomfield, whose father, Henry, founded the renowned firm of art-glass makers (I11); the Queen Anne–style **McLean House** (356 West 11th Avenue, Campbell & Bennett 1910); **Ardencraig** (355 West 11th Avenue, 1910; Allan Diamond Architect, Bruce Haden 2000), an innovative eco-makeover; and the bulbous-towered house at **410 West 12th Avenue** (Parr & Fee 1909), across from City Hall.

D12 Davis House
166 West 10th Avenue
1891; 1973

This charming streetscape of Victorian and Edwardian houses preserves the conviviality of a turn-of-the-twentieth-century streetcar suburb, thanks to the efforts of four members of the Davis family. John Davis began in 1973 by restoring this simple frame house built in the earliest years of Mount Pleasant, with its bay window, two-storey porch and intricate wood detailing. He and his kin went on to improve virtually all the homes on the south side of the block, serving as a catalyst for the revitalization of the wider

neighbourhood. In recognition they received a City of Vancouver Heritage Award in 1990, a Heritage Canada Award the following year and the City's first annual "Most Beautiful Block" award in 2000. The street trees and historic paving blocks along West 10th and Columbia were saved, thanks again largely to the Davis efforts.

D13 Labour Temple
307 West Broadway
Dominion Construction 1949

This stretch of Broadway was a hub of activity for Vancouver's strong labour movement, many of whose political activities were centred in this, the former Labour Temple. Labour and its skilled workers are celebrated above the entrance in a bas-relief that depicts the solidarity of Canadian (the beaver) and American (the eagle) unions during WWII. The sculptor was Beatrice Lennie, whose style owed much to heroic socialist realism and the influence of Charles

Marega (D15), her mentor at the Vancouver School of Decorative & Applied Arts (now Emily Carr University, G4). The building is now used for retail and called Clydemont Centre. The neighbourhood retains a leftist orientation, as the area's federal and provincial ridings are regularly represented by the New Democratic Party.

D14 The Crossroads
522 West 8th Avenue
Busby Perkins + Will 2008

Rapid transit attracts development. Vancouver learned this in the late nineteenth century when the BCER streetcar and interurban lines stimulated the growth of new neighbourhoods—including Mount Pleasant and Fairview. The same holds true today. The cut-and-cover construction of the Canada Line (2009) beneath Cambie Street (a tunnel was bored downtown and under False Creek) severely harmed existing low-density retail shops, but the transit line and rezoning encouraged a new generation of high-density development. Located kitty-corner from the **Broadway–City Hall Canada Line Station** (Stantec Architecture 2009), The Crossroads is one of several new projects to provide ground-level big-box retail, in this case with offices and residential condo units above. Just down Cambie Street, **The Rise** (411 West 8th Avenue,

Nigel Baldwin Architects 2009) is another example of the trend, with yet a third a block further north.

D15 Vancouver City Hall →
453 West 12th Avenue
Townley & Matheson 1936; 1970

After a decade of bickering, this "remote" site for City Hall was chosen in 1935 with the prodding of Mayor G.G. McGeer, who wanted to strengthen links with newly annexed South Vancouver and Point Grey. The massing, setbacks, unadorned classical shafts and grey finish are a touch totalitarian, as was much government architecture of the day. Superb Art Deco ornament emerges at the tops of the blocks, below the windows, around the entry and in the less-intimidating lobby. An energy-saving illumination (*Ice Light*, Gunda Förster 2010) draws on the forceful composition. The four-storey somewhat modernist **East Wing** along Yukon Street was designed by the same firm (Townley, Matheson & Partners 1970). The statue of Captain George Vancouver enjoying the fine view of the city is by Italian-born and -trained Charles Marega. Construction of the nearby Canada Line station (D14) prompted landscape improvements (Durante Kreuk 2009), with a retaining wall and stepped access to City Hall's expansive grounds at the northwest corner of the site.

D16 City Square
555 West 12th Avenue
E.E. Blackmore 1905; Pearce & Hope 1909;
Paul Merrick Architects 1989

Two Edwardian schools, the **Provincial Normal School** (1909; a teachers' college) and the **Model School** (1905; an elementary school where student teachers trained), have been subsumed within this shop-and-office complex. The main entrance, squeezed between two six-storey office blocks, opens to a cruciform-plan mall, skylit and transparent at the crossing, almost Gothic in the arrangement of steel columns and struts. The schools' historic sandstone walls can be appreciated from within the atrium as well as from the landscaped grounds to the north (Phillips Farevaag Smallenberg). Paul Merrick's sensitive homage to Frank Lloyd Wright, the **UBC Medical Student & Alumni Centre** (1990), stands a block west at 2750 Heather Street.

D17 Jim Pattison Pavilion, Vancouver General Hospital
899 West 12th Avenue
Hemingway Nelson Architects 1990–2006

Vancouver General Hospital, which succeeded the downtown City Hospital in 1902, erected its first building on the Fairview Slopes, a distinguished granite structure with four towers. Fragments survive as part of the **Heather Pavilion** (Grant & Henderson 1906; additions 1910-59). In the mid-twentieth century, hospital expansion begot a hodgepodge of buildings in styles ranging from Georgian to moderne (e.g., **Health Centre for**

D

Children, 715 West 12th Avenue, Townley & Matheson 1944). All were dwarfed by the cruciform **Centennial Pavilion** (855 West 12th Avenue, Townley, Matheson & Partners 1958). The dominant facility today is the Pattison Pavilion, the massiveness of its precast concrete walls broken up by multiple recesses and setbacks. Just to the west the **Gordon & Leslie Diamond Health Care Centre** (2775 Laurel Street, IBI Group, Henriquez Partners Architects 2006) accommodates ambulatory care services and the UBC Faculty of Medicine's VGH offices. It occupies the site of the old **King Edward High School** (built as Vancouver High School, W.T. Whiteway 1903; destroyed by fire 1973), used temporarily as the first UBC campus (see Chapter L) and remembered by its stone boundary wall.

D18 B.C. Lung Association
2675 Oak Street
Gardiner & Mercer 1929

This stalwart stone building is the home of the B.C. Lung Association, whose primary focus has shifted from tuberculosis to research, education, prevention and advocacy for all respiratory diseases. It was built as Vancouver's first Jewish Community Centre, as that community migrated across False Creek from Strathcona (C10), which remained the

first neighbourhood for many immigrant groups. Two large synagogues, the Orthodox **Schara Tzedek** (3476 Oak Street, John Harvey 1947; Ross A. Lort 1955) and the Conservative **Beth Israel** (4350 Oak Street, Kaplan & Sprachman 1948; later additions) as well as the **Vancouver Talmud Torah School** (998 West 26th Avenue) stand nearby. A planned extension to the community centre with a gymnasium and six-hundred-seat theatre was never built because of the onset of the Depression. By the time the means were available, Vancouver's Jewish population had shifted south, and a new **Jewish Community Centre** was built at 950 West 41st Avenue (1950s; many later additions).

D19 B.C. Cancer Agency Research Centre
675 West 10th Avenue
IBI Group, Henriquez Partners Architects 2004

The B.C. Cancer Agency provides both research and treatment: the former focused here and the latter in the building across the street (**B.C. Cancer Agency**, 600 West 10th Avenue, 1984). Architect Richard Henriquez approached the research centre in his signature storytelling manner, in which his narratives, in his words, "give people a new way of looking at what they take for granted." The laboratory side of the building is illuminated by large

D20 Heather Court
730 West 7th Avenue
James K.M. Cheng 1980

The Fairview Slopes were rezoned in 1972 to encourage multi-family townhouse complexes with carefully calculated heights that gave every building a minimal view of the mountains. This is one of three adjacent complexes on West 7th by James Cheng that meet the guidelines. All have the same general plan, with units accessed from central courtyards and reached by a series of stairs and landings ascending from the street, and all are faced with the same brick but with differences in detail. The other two are **Willow Arbor** (744 West 7th Avenue, 1981) and **Willow Court** (766 West 7th Avenue, 1980).

D21 The Sixth Estate
1060–1090 West 6th Avenue, 2201–2251 Oak Street, 2202–2256 Spruce Street
Hughes Baldwin Architects 1982

A former warehouse complex on a busy street exemplifies adapted commercial architecture. Four of six units were reused, while the others were replaced. The elevation on 6th Avenue is all business, with offices occupying the ground floor and glass blocks muffling the street noise. The front block screens infill housing on the rise behind, the two portions

circular windows representing the petri dishes that form a basis for scientific research; the pattern of vertical windows on the office side is an abstraction of Chromosome 6, central to cancer research; and the spiral staircase joining the twelve office floors represents the DNA spiral. All these features contribute to the dynamic design and composition. The architects appreciated the links between environmental quality and health: the building is salubrious and achieved LEED Gold certification. This is one of many recent facilities that make the large Vancouver General Hospital campus a hub of cutting-edge medical research. Others include the **Blusson Spinal Cord Centre** (818 West 10th Avenue, Musson Cattell Mackey Partnership 2008), supported in part by the Rick Hansen Foundation, and the **Robert H.N. Ho Research Centre** (2635 Laurel Street, Musson Cattell Mackey Partnership 2011), specializing in prostate, hip and ovarian cancer research.

two at the 7th Avenue grade) down the steep slope in steps, covered the 18-foot-wide frame with clapboard siding and built a catwalk along the east side that drops with the hill. The property was confiscated in 1944, when B.C.'s Japanese Canadians were interned. The density squeezed into the narrow lot has a "floor space ratio" similar to a West End high-rise. The exterior wood siding was replaced in a recent rehabilitation. Just west is **Choklit Park**, a gift to the City from Purdy's Chocolates when the firm relocated from here to larger premises (F29).

separated by a quiet interior landscaped "street." Structural bracing and corrugated siding anticipate the "live-work" look (D1). Workshop-style gables on the lane elevations read as a memory, not only of the industries on False Creek but also of postmodernism's passing fancy.

D22 Takehara Tenements
1017 West 7th Avenue
Genya Yada and R. Takehara 1913; 1992

This curiosity is an isolated survivor of the bunkhouses for workers—in this case Japanese—who sweated in the sawmills on False Creek. Builders Yada and Takehara took the building's three floors (only

D23 BowMac/Toys "R" Us Sign
1154 West Broadway
Neon Products 1959; Urban Design Group 1997

The prominent two-message sign has been praised and ridiculed. The toy store chain leased the site of long-time car dealership BowMac (Bowell McLean

Motor Company), including its 29-metre-high sign, able to be seen for miles and illuminated with 3,500 flashing incandescent bulbs and lots of neon tubing. It dates back to when Vancouver was called "the neon capital of North America." When the Heritage Commission offered Toys "R" Us the options of superimposing a new semi-transparent and "reversible" (that is, removable) sign on the landmark or replacing it with a small new sign that met the City's restrictive sign bylaw, the toy company wisely chose the former for its visibility. Old neon is back in vogue, and this project helped.

D24 Hodson Manor
1254 West 7th Avenue
1894; J.J. Honeyman 1903;
Rhone & Iredale 1974

In June 1974, Fairview residents were treated to the spectacle of this fine early house being moved here from its former location at 1417 West 8th Avenue. This was the first time the City bought a property rather than allowing its demolition.

The left and central bays were built for Captain James J. Logan, and the right side was added ten years later for the eleven-child family of sometime alderman and yachtsman William Hodson. The City rents the building to non-profit societies.

D25 James England House
2300 Birch Street
1910

A number of fine homes, such as this gracious Queen Anne-style residence (so-called for its verandah and tower), were built on the Fairview Slopes. It is now used as offices, typical of many re-purposed former houses. Others were built in the neighbourhood, but the area never became particularly classy, especially after the CPR created Shaughnessy Heights, with its larger building lots and exclusive setting.

D

D26 Holy Trinity Anglican Church
1440 West 12th Avenue
S.B. Birds, E.E. Blackmore 1912; Keith Sullivan
Donald Architecture 1994

Holy Trinity Parish, which has served Fairview since 1899, relocated here in 1994 to the former Chalmers United Church (originally Presbyterian, the name celebrating a Scots churchman). The original entrance on Hemlock Street retains the Chalmers name over the entrance, expressing the continuity of use. The somewhat Georgian, somewhat Baroque Revival style, with its columned porticos and central dome, was often favoured by Presbyterians over the more Anglo-Catholic Gothic Revival. Holy Trinity removed the semicircular, galleried Presbyterian interior to suit the Anglican liturgy and added a wing to the west that is respectful, but not imitative, of the original building. Two community tenants are the South Granville Seniors Centre and Pacific Theatre, a professional company that balances artistic and spiritual content in its 126-seat facility.

D27 1508 West Broadway
Musson Cattell Mackey Partnership 2001

This mixed-use complex by Bentall Developments fills an entire city block and displays the "urbanity" that has come to

be associated with new Vancouver buildings. A low podium "streetwall" with well-patronized retail stores hugs the sidewalk, a glazed office tower rises at the busy Granville-Broadway corner, the Vancouver School Board offices are on the west half of the site, a residential tower faces 10th Avenue, and a landscaped park occupies the southwest corner. The whole is politely inoffensive, with density much higher than meets the eye, all characteristic of what is termed "Vancouverism" (G19). Two blocks north is the strikingly modernist **Amanat Architect Office** (1515 West 7th Avenue, Amanat Architect 2009) designed and occupied by Iranian-Canadian Hossein Amanat.

D28 Stanley Theatre
2750 Granville Street
H.H. Simmonds 1930; Proscenium Architecture
+ Interiors 1998

This gem of a Moorish/Art Deco picture palace was closed by Famous Players in 1991 and nearly demolished. After a campaign by Heritage Vancouver and others,

it was acquired and rehabilitated by the Arts Club Theatre Company, which also operates 200- and 400-seat stages on Granville Island. The façade features a small cupola and a neon marquee and sign, installed in 1947 and lovingly repaired. The gilded-domed and arcaded audience chamber has been reduced to become an intimate, 650-seat house with superb acoustics, and the lobby expanded and redecorated as a lively contemporary space for intermission socializing. The sensitive blend of old and new (by Proscenium, with Commonwealth Historic Resource Management) is exemplary. As architect Thom Weeks explained, "audiences shouldn't be too aware that we've been here."

D29 Madrona Apartments
1575 West 15th Avenue
1930

The Madrona's fancy dress is Spanish Colonial Revival, the adobe effect rendered in crisp brickwork, with curved gables flanking a tile overhang and arched openings. Three siblings with different styles of clothing continue the uniform streetscape to either side: the **Margaret Rose,** named after the newly born Princess Royal (1545 West 15th Avenue, 1930), the **Oxford** (1585 West 15th Avenue, 1930) and **Allandale Manor** (1565 West 15th Avenue, 1940). Across the street, the **Mont Royal** (Gardiner & Mercer 1927) sports Tudor Revival. All are delightful examples of the three-storey walk-ups that give this South Granville neighbourhood a consistent scale and character, a balance too easily upset by intrusive development.

Grandview and East Vancouver

THE neighbourhood known today as Grandview began to be settled after the opening of the interurban railway to New Westminster in 1891. The trains stopped on the rise near today's Commercial Drive and East 1st Avenue, which was quite a distance from Strathcona and Mount Pleasant, the eastern limits of development. Local lore tells that the name of the community was coined by an early resident who affixed a sign saying "Grand View" at the stop. Residential construction finally began in earnest early in the new century, with retail focused along Commercial Drive (E2).

Many "eastenders" had worked in the pioneering resource industries before the arrival of the CPR and considered themselves distinct from "westenders," primarily Eastern Canadians who came with the railway. Some early landowners hoped to see Grandview become an upper-crust neighbourhood and sowed the seeds by building their own large homes there (E5, E9). They were few in number.

Developers also built groups of middle- and working-class houses on smaller lots (E11). They accommodated expansion from Strathcona and immigrants, mainly from the British Isles. Over the years the demographics have changed markedly, as first Italians—the area focused on "The Drive" was known as "Little

Above: Commercial-Broadway SkyTrain Station (E24)

Italy"—and then other European, Asian and African immigrant groups settled into Grandview. Today's population is diverse, reflecting that of the city as a whole.

Development spread east of Nanaimo Street in the 1920s, particularly east along Hastings Street to Hastings Park and to areas then known as Hastings Manor and Rosedale, part of today's Hastings-Sunrise and Renfrew. Hastings Park has long been the site of the Pacific National Exhibition (E17, E19), Hastings Racecourse and the former Empire Stadium, facilities that attracted crowds from all Metro Vancouver. Local residents have been lobbying for years to have it returned to the status of a neighbourhood park.

Industry expanded along the Burrard Inlet waterfront in the 1920s and subsequently, including the construction of grain elevators (E7). Until recently the public could drive along Commissioner Street from Clark Drive to east of Renfrew, but post-9/11 security concerns have unfortunately closed the waterfront to general traffic.

SkyTrain, the automated light rail system constructed in conjunction with the transportation-themed Expo 86 (G14), came east to Commercial Drive; the Millennium Line (2002) serves East Vancouver along the Broadway corridor, continuing to Burnaby.

Pressures for growth have affected Grandview and East Vancouver somewhat less than other parts of the city. A number of three- and four-storey apartments were built a half-century ago, and some recent densification has occurred, but the area remains dominated by single-family housing. Gentrification is evident in the vicinity of cosmopolitan, artsy Commercial Drive.

The residential streets around The Drive have been the object of "traffic-calming," which makes it difficult to reach destinations by car. The map does its reasonable best to provide a navigable route.

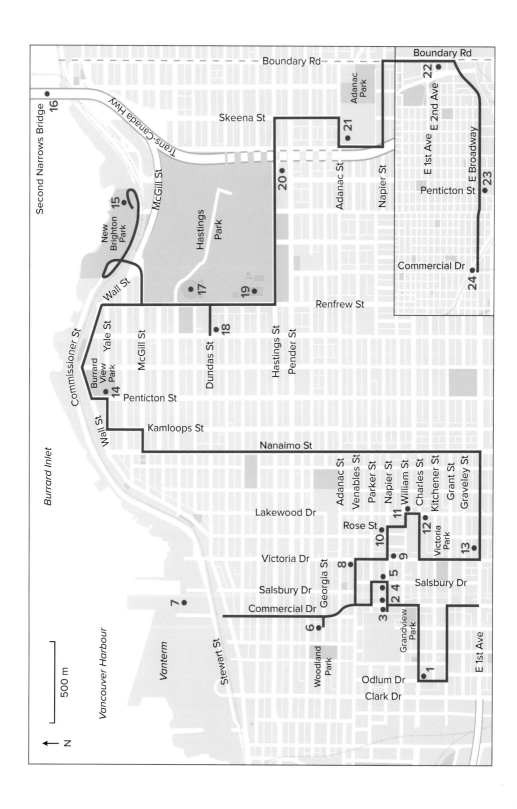

E1 Odlum Drive Live–Work Studios
1332–1334 Odlum Drive
Peter Cardew Architects 1998

In contrast to nearby Grant Street, a typical series of Grandview residential blocks with mature street trees and mostly old homes, this gritty setting is a mix of plain dwellings and light industry. The studios' tough materials strike an appropriate contextual note, responding to the unassuming structures across the street and ignoring the old houses to either side. This is the east and not the west side, with a different aesthetic and different values. The highly glazed modernist elevation is slashed by visible, diagonal seismic bracing in steel. The four-studio project has a communal inner courtyard, a defensible space evoking ambiguity and tension in contemporary urban life. The street is named after scientist, ethnographer and landowner Edward Odlum, whose nearby turreted residence (1774 Grant Street, 1905) was one of the first houses in Grandview.

E2 Beck Block
1046 Commercial Drive
1910

Commercial Drive—known simply as "The Drive"—is the high street of Grandview, whose development was sparked by waterfront industry and the arrival of the interurban railway in 1891. The neighbourhood was originally British in makeup, then became Little Italy, and is now more diverse in character. "The Drive's Big Three groups," writes author Charles Demers, "are the Italians, the Lesbians and the Leftists." Coffee houses, ethnic and vegetarian restaurants and funky retail predominate. The ensemble is artistic (with a popular annual art walk) and trendy yet not overly gentrified. The bay-windowed Beck Block, characteristic of its time, features Tony's Deli, opened in 1972 by Tony Baruci and still busy after forty years. A block south

are **Joe's Café** (1150 Commercial Drive), which has been serving cappuccino since 1974, long before the arrival of the coffee chains, and the **Portuguese Club of Vancouver** (1144 Commercial Drive), which sponsors soccer teams and has a public restaurant.

E3 Britannia Community Services Centre
1661 Napier Street
Downs/Archambault, Britannia Design 1976

This unique complex is a legal partnership between the community, City and Vancouver School Board that fully

E

integrates educational (Britannia Elementary School), social, library and recreational facilities. Citizen involvement played an important role in the design of the cluster of low, non-institutional-looking buildings that break away from the street grid in the manner of a new urban village. **Britannia Secondary School** (Norman Leech 1910; E.D. King 1955; 1973) has been located here since 1910, when its classical main block was completed. Grandview's diversity is revealed by the provision of Chinese, Vietnamese and Spanish translators for the school's parent-teacher interviews.

E4 Shiv Mandir Hindu Temple
1795 Napier Street
B.C. Mills, Timber & Trading Company 1908, 1921

Built as Robertson Presbyterian Church, the building's vertical batten strips dividing the walls into 3-foot sections of narrow clapboard reveal it to be a rare survivor of the B.C. Mills prefabrication system (C19). The original structure is around the corner on Salsbury Drive; the south wing on Napier Street, now partly stuccoed (both B.C. Mills prefabs), is a 1921 addition. Since 1977, it has served the Shree Sanatan Dharam Ramayan Mandali, a Hindu temple and cultural centre for about six hundred worshippers who trace their roots to Fiji.

E5 Kurrajong
1086-1098 Salsbury Drive, 1803-1823 Napier Street
1908; later alterations; Stuart Howard Architects 1999

This showy mansion was built for John J. Miller, the creative force behind the PNE (E17, E19). Raised on a sheep station in Australia, he came to B.C. in 1903 with experience in agriculture, business and politics. He named his turreted house Kurrajong (a bushy Australian evergreen) for the town in New South Wales where he had married and lost his fortune five years later. Later converted to Glen Hospital, a residential care home, the house briefly became a notorious squat and *X-Files* location. It has been rehabilitated with five suites and enveloped by two detached houses and eight townhouses. Kurrajong was moved closer to the corner to accommodate the infill, which remains subordinate to the main house and is sympathetic to its appearance.

E6 Georgia Green
1665–1671 East Georgia Street
Shape Architecture 2010

This fourplex, which achieved LEED Platinum (the highest rating), helps to shift the conventions of residential design into the era of sustainability. The styling is restrained and contemporary, the form and materials determined by function. The roof pitch was set for solar panels; siding is durable cement plank, western red

cedar and stucco. Interior space is organized to maximize natural light; concrete floors have radiant heating from solar power; rainwater is harvested. The building—set back from the street in a landscaped yard that absorbs rainwater into the water table—is a paradigm for eco-density and an example of how the significant carbon footprint of residential construction can be reduced. Around the corner is the **York Theatre** (637 Commercial Drive; J.Y. McCarter 1913; H.H. Simmonds 1940), rescued by developer Bruno Wall and being rehabilitated for live theatre (Henriquez Partners Architects 2012), to be operated by The Cultch (E8).

E7 Stevens' Folly ✝
North foot of Salisbury Street
1914

Predicting a boom in the international grain trade following the opening of the Panama Canal, local MP H.H. Stevens persuaded the Dominion government to build this, Vancouver's first grain elevator. WWI rendered it idle, making it the focus of public ridicule—hence the

E

nickname. Increased postwar trade produced more elevators, a concrete structure-type praised by architect Le Corbusier as a pivotal expression of modernism. Stevens' Folly is best seen from the foot of Commercial Drive, at Powell Street. The industrial waterfront has been closed to the public and set behind barbed wire as a result of post-9/11 security.

E8 Vancouver East Cultural Centre
1895 Venables Street
1909; John Keith-King 1973; Derek Neale 1977; Proscenium Architecture + Interiors 2009

"The Cultch" has been popular since opening night in 1973 as a three-hundred-seat venue. Arts writer Max Wyman likened it to a "miniature European opera house." Built as the Grandview Methodist Church, it has been much changed, most recently with a seismic, structural and sustainability overhaul as well as a new cubic wing to the east, the Vancity Culture Lab, an eighty-eight-seat rehearsal and performance hall with support spaces. The Craftsman house immediately west is **The Green House** (1885 Venables Street), built as the Church manse and now a performance studio. The former church hall and gymnasium immediately north (882 Adanac Street, 1926) is the **WISE Hall**, opened in 1958 as the Welsh-Irish-Scottish-English Club and now used for rock and folk performances.

E9 W.H. Copp House
1110 Victoria Drive
J.P. Malluson 1911

Another of the larger homes built during the initial development of Grandview was the residence of realtor W.H. Copp. A domed corner turret, columned portico and impressive stained and bevelled glass lend elegant airs. The house has been subdivided into suites and given the name Aberdeen Mansion.

E10 St. Francis of Assisi Church & Friary
2025 Napier Street
George Aspell 1938

The religious focus of Little Italy was opened by the Franciscan Order in 1938. Its Romanesque Revival façade and campanile evoke romantic images of the old

country. The unaltered interior includes relics of Saints Francis and Antonio. The adjacent Craftsman house (Beam & Brown 1910), built for the brother of John Miller (E5) and acquired by the order in 1925, was used for mass until the church was built; it is now the Friary (rehabilitated 1990s). The Church faces **Rose Street**, a charming streetscape of heritage houses.

E11 Harris House
1210 Lakewood Drive
1908

This is one of eight virtually identical builders' houses (1204-1246 Lakewood Drive) constructed between 1908 and 1910, showing that from the start Grandview's residences comprised both mansion and modest. Number 1210 was lovingly preserved inside and out by Evelyn Harris, whose father bought it in 1919. Harris, "a Vancouver treasure," received a City of Vancouver Heritage Award in 1989 in recognition of her achievements in conservation. The first owner was the Reverend David James, the minister at nearby Robertson Church (E4).

E12 Lakewood Residence
1333 Lakewood Drive
c. 1970s; Pechet & Robb 2001, 2008

A small Vancouver Special (F13) was entirely made over in this award-winning intervention, demonstrating the flexibility of these much-ridiculed, low-budget,

E

cookie-cutter houses. Architect and occupant Stephanie Robb removed the interior walls and drywall ceilings to create open-plan living on the ground floor and skylit bedrooms upstairs. A second phase added a garage-studio and garden at the rear. The result is creative, honest and sustainable. The pyramidal roof on the house to the right (**1323 Lakewood Drive**) reveals it as another makeover, this of a much earlier inexpensive Vancouver house-type, the Pioneer Cottage of c. 1900.

E13 Victoria Court
1943 East 1st Avenue
Victor Daniel Horsburgh, W.F. Gardiner 1915;
Iredale Partnership 1982

Built as a long-term storage vault for the Imperial Bank of Canada's records, this handsome brick warehouse, with cast keystones and the bank's symbol over the cornice, was sensitively converted into townhouses in 1982. New windows and iron balconies are in keeping with the original character of the building. Original contractors Baynes & Horie owned the Port Haney Brick Company, which supplied bricks for this and countless buildings in Vancouver, including many schools.

E14 Babies Cottage
2625 Yale Street
Sharp & Thompson 1923; William McCreery
Architects 1999

This Arts and Crafts gem in Burrard View Park was built as an infant orphanage by the Children's Aid Society. It later became a youth detention centre and is now the St. James' Cottage Hospice, operated by the Downtown Eastside–based St. James Community Service Society, whose mission is to support the most vulnerable in the community. Exquisitely complementary recent additions provide a peaceful lounge for residents and a community room in the basement.

E15 New Brighton Park
New Brighton Road
(accessed from Commissioner Street)

Just north of the PNE is New Brighton Park, an 11-hectare park with a swimming pool, tennis courts, sandy beach

and superb views of the industrial waterfront, It also looks out on the Second Narrows Crossing (E16) and the North Shore harbour and mountains. The park occupies the site of Brighton Beach, once a fashionable watering place for New Westminsterites, established in 1860 when Douglas Road was created by the Royal Engineers. This was the first European settlement on the south shore of Burrard Inlet, boasting the first hotel, first pier and first store. In 1869, the larger area south of here was named Hastings Townsite, and seven of its forty-seven surveyed lots were sold (to only three buyers). Hastings never became a going concern and amalgamated with Vancouver in 1911.

E16 Ironworkers Memorial Second Narrows Crossing ✝
Highway 1
Swan Wooster Engineering 1960

This high-level cantilever bridge, seen from New Brighton Park and Road, crosses Burrard Inlet at the Second Narrows. It replaced a low-level road and rail bridge (1925), which had been damaged frequently by errant ships. The present bridge was named as a memorial to eighteen men killed when part of the structure collapsed during construction. Trains use the adjacent CNR bridge (1969), whose robust lift span allows large oil tankers to pass up the inlet to the refineries at Burnaby. The First Narrows are spanned by the Lions Gate Bridge (M1). Between the bridge and the park is the impressive **Viterra Cascadia Terminal** grain elevator (3333 New Brighton Road, C.D. Howe Company 1927) and office (Wright Engineers 1991).

E17 Pacific Coliseum
Exhibition Park
W.K. Noppe 1967

The Pacific National Exhibition (PNE) and its predecessor, the Vancouver Exhibition Association, have presented a late summer fair here since 1910. Recreational facilities animate the grounds with year-round activity. The Coliseum is a 15,600-seat arena, whose ring of white panels represents the formalist architecture of the day. It attracted the NHL Vancouver Canucks in 1970. The 5 1/2-furlong **Hastings Racecourse** (1947) replaced a track that had been here since the 1880s.

E

Playland, the PNE's amusement park, features a spectacular wooden **roller coaster** (Carl Phare 1958). The 38,000-seat Empire Stadium was built for the Empire Games of 1954 (demolished 1993) and hosted the famous "Miracle Mile" in which Roger Bannister and John Landy both broke the four-minute barrier. The stadium also attracted a major league franchise in football's B.C. Lions. Both the Canucks and the Lions have relocated downtown (G18), and the Coliseum is now home to hockey's minor-league Vancouver Giants. The stadium site was occupied temporarily by the prefabricated **Empire Field** (Nussli Group 2010), used while B.C. Place (G18) was being renovated and as the first home of soccer's major league Vancouver Whitecaps.

E18 First PNE Prize Home
2812 Dundas Street
1934

A highlight of the Pacific National Exhibition (E17, E19) has been the Prize Home raffle, held annually since 1934. The very first one stands here a stone's throw from the fairgrounds, where it was built and whence it was dragged by a team of Clydesdales. The winner of the tidy 800-square-foot furnished home was Spencer's Department Store deliveryman Leonard Frewin, for whom the prize also won him the hand of his girlfriend, Emily

Leitch, since her parents now judged him sufficiently prosperous. Although the house looks much the same, every detail has been changed over the years, including the siding, the windows and door, the porch, the basement and the roof overhang. This northeast corner of Vancouver is Hastings-Sunrise, made up largely of the former Hastings Townsite (E15) and extending east from Nanaimo Street and north from Broadway. It developed between the 1920s and '40s as a working-class neighbourhood dominated by small single-family houses.

E19 Garden Auditorium
2901 East Hastings Street
Townley & Matheson 1940

The initial wood-frame PNE buildings were replaced by concrete structures between the late 1920s and early 1940s. The Garden Auditorium is the best of the bunch, a streamlined moderne concoction with round towers flanking the entrance and horizontal bands in the concrete walls. Other survivors of this group are the **Forum** (McCarter & Nairne 1933), used as a hockey rink, and **Roller-land** (H.H. Simmonds 1931), a multi-purpose auditorium and sometime roller rink. The PNE occupies 160-acre Hastings Park, founded in 1889. The Exhibition's moment of shame came in 1942, when it was used as a holding area for eight thousand Japanese Canadians expelled to the interior of the province. Hastings-Sunrise residents would like to develop the park as green space and relocate the PNE, caring little about the historical factoid that the PNE attracted the streetcar here, which in turn led to the development of their neighbourhood in the first place.

E20 E-Comm
3301 East Pender Street
Architectura 1998

Metro Vancouver's 24/7 Regional Emergency Coordination Centre is a communications hub from which 911 responses are directed and post-disaster emergency operations coordinated. Its structure is rated to survive a 7.5-Richter-scale earthquake. The architects attempted to humanize this high-stress workplace; facilities elsewhere were mostly concrete bunkers with high staff turnover. The skylit entrance atrium with post-and-strut support is airy and welcoming; the steel roof has a built-in acoustic deck to filter interior ambient noise. The visible roofscape is syncopated with curves, corrugations and cantilevers.

E21 Provincial Industrial Home for Girls
868 Cassiar Street
A.A. Cox 1913; H.R. Hatch Architect, McGinn Engineering & Preservation 1997

This institution opened in 1914 for the "education, industrial training and moral reclamation" of girls under sixteen convicted of an offence punishable by imprisonment. Superintendent Margaret Bayne directed the school with a firm but compassionate hand. The Mission Style design, with the characteristic curved gables, seems to have referred to a mission of a very different sort. The school moved to Burnaby in 1959 and the building was used for provincial offices. It was recently rehabilitated as twelve residential units, with an additional seventy-six units built in seven new, low-key buildings on the site (called **Terra Vita**)—a case of the City's permitting bonus density in

E

return for heritage conservation. A second home for indigents—this time senior citizens—was built on the other end of this large lot in this edge-of-city neighbourhood: **Taylor Manor** (951 Boundary Road, Perry & Fowler 1915). Originally called the Old People's Home, it was renamed in 1946 to honour former mayor Louis D. Taylor. It has sat empty since 2000, when a new **Adanac Park Lodge** (851 Boundary Road) was built immediately adjacent to it. Between them is the 160-unit **Adanac Housing Cooperative** (John Keith-King 1977).

E22 Trev Deeley Motorcycles/ Deeley Motorcycle Exhibition
1875 Boundary Road
Stantec Architecture 2006

Design-conscious, premium-brand automotive retailers polish their product image with slick outlets such as this. Trevor Deeley, "Canada's Mr. Motorcycle," took over Fred Deeley Motorcycles, founded by his grandfather in 1917 as an early Harley-Davidson dealership. Among his achievements was a collection of bikes, the Deeley Motorcycle Exhibition, now housed in this warehouse retrofitted as a showroom and museum. The dynamic entrance canopy functions like a traditional auto dealer's advertising sign (compare D23).

E23 Vancouver Technical Secondary School →
2600 East Broadway
Townley & Matheson 1928; F.A.A. Barrs & H.W. Postle 1941; E.D. King 1954; Colborne Architectural Group Pacific 2008

Van Tech was the first school in B.C. designed for vocational education. Initially only boys attended; girls were admitted in 1941—when the boys were away at war—with the construction of a new, segregated wing, which was the first designed for female vocational and technical (as opposed to commercial) instruction. The "modernized Tudor" main building, built of concrete and finished in stucco, features a relief panel over the main entrance by Charles Marega. It forms a contrast with the sawtooth roof of the workshop wing (1928) and the modernist east wing (1954). More than two thousand students attend Van Tech, whose buildings and grounds are spread over 10 acres between Broadway and Grandview Highway. The structures were seismically upgraded in 2008, including using bonded fabrics of fibre-reinforced polymers (FRP) to reinforce the concrete walls—the largest use of FRP in Canada—and inserting fibreglass rods and anchors to stabilize the hollow-clay and glass-block walls.

E24 Commercial-Broadway SkyTrain Station
Architektengruppe U-Bahn, Allen Parker & Associates 1986; VIA Architecture 2002, 2009

This interchange station serves the Expo and Millennium Lines of SkyTrain, the automated light-rail system built in conjunction with the transportation-themed Expo 86 (G14). The Expo Line (1986) passes over, the Millennium Line (2002) beneath, 12th Avenue. The Expo Line runs from Waterfront Station (H28), through the Dunsmuir Tunnel (cut by the

CPR in 1932 to link its False Creek yards with Burrard Inlet), then emerges onto an elevated guideway on its way to New Westminster and subsequently Surrey. The route follows closely that of the B.C. Electric Railway interurban line, begun around 1890 and abandoned in 1958 (F31). The elevated Broadway Station, as it was first called, is typical of the Expo Line's austere Euro-modernism, the work in part of Viennese design consul-

tants. It was later deemed to lack regional character. Consequently the stations on the Millennium Line, which goes east to Burnaby, sport high-tech steelwork softened by wood—the traditional B.C. material—without sacrificing durability or the appearance of modern efficiency. Commercial-Broadway has three levels. A street-level concourse (2009), linked to the Expo Line platform (renovated 2009), contains shops, services and ticketing. The Millennium Line addition, reached by a footbridge, is set in the Grandview Cut, a deep trench excavated in 1908–13 by the Great Northern Railway (G16).

South Vancouver

THE District of South Vancouver, incorporated in 1891, originally encompassed nearly all the lands south from 16th Avenue—the southern boundary of the City of Vancouver (1886)—to the Fraser River, from the Strait of Georgia to today's Burnaby border. At the time it was mostly agricultural land with a scattering of small villages.

The large area to the east was never properly surveyed. The residents were primarily working-class people, mostly British or Canadian born but also members of immigrant minorities. The western portion, in contrast, was populated by the professional and managerial classes. Conflicting attitudes and social tensions drove frustrated West Side residents to separate from South Vancouver in 1906 and incorporate the Municipality of Point Grey (see Chapter K).

The residents of South Vancouver consistently voted for low taxes and minimal services. Streets were narrow and irregularly aligned, few parks were planned, and conflicting land uses often existed side by side. As recently as the 1970s a furniture factory was in use near 20th and Ontario, hidden away on a lane and completely surrounded by houses. The land along the Fraser River largely developed with lumber and marine industries,

Above: Bloedel Conservatory (F4)

but in recent decades these have been replaced by residential development.

The district was also an important transportation corridor. Kingsway (F27, F30) follows the route of the old military trail that connected New Westminster with Burrard Inlet as a defence against the threat of American invasion. Colonel Richard Moody and the Royal Engineers built the trail in 1861. The interurban railway was built in 1891 along a parallel route; today it is the route of SkyTrain elevated light rail.

South Vancouver and Point Grey were reunited when both amalgamated with the City of Vancouver in 1929. Despite the supposed equalization of services, divisions remain. To a large extent, Cambie Street still forms a boundary between the working and middle classes—between the East Side and the West Side. The designation "East" and "West" on the city's avenues provide a constant reminder of the divisions.

This chapter visits much of South Vancouver, including many former villages that retain their identities as neighbourhoods—Hillcrest, South Hill, Killarney, Collingwood, Cedar Cottage, and others. Since the once agricultural area developed largely as a dormitory for downtown and waterfront industry and business, the focus is on residences. South Vancouver remains dominated by single-family housing, although that has changed in recent years in response to a drive towards densification. The variety of house types visited includes early-twentieth-century cottages (F14), post-WWII tract housing (F21), "Vancouver Specials" (F13), townhouses (F24) and a spanking new laneway house (F11) and prototype row house (F5).

F

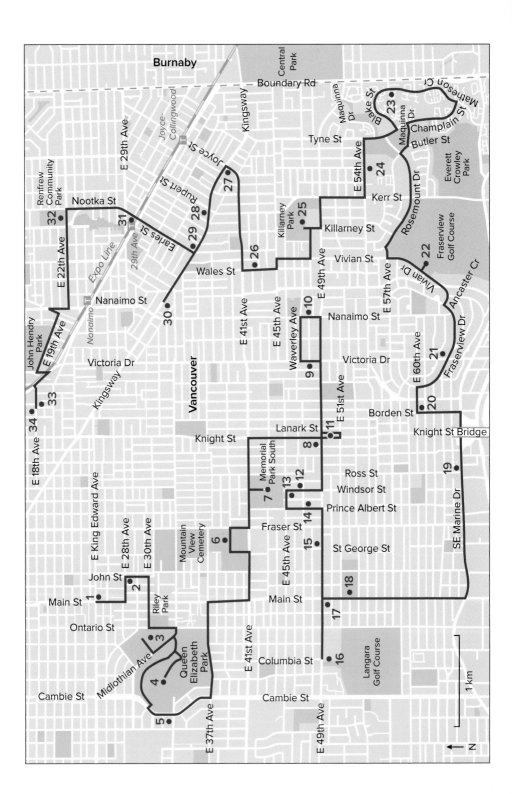

F1 Walden Building
4120 Main Street
1910

Main Street was intended to be South Vancouver's high street, but south of Mount Pleasant it never lived up to its name. One of the few older substantial structures is this three-storey commercial block, with its (now white-painted) brick façade, contrasting with the more cheaply finished stuccoed wood elsewhere. The adjacent building and one across the street are similar in scale; otherwise the area is a strip of minimarts and eateries, being mildly gentrified and sprinkled with three- and four-storey residential blocks.

F2 300-block East 28th Avenue
Various builders and dates

The development of South Vancouver was far less consistent than that of Point Grey to the west. This block contains sixteen houses (one a former corner store), which apart from three that were once identical (numbers 350–366, c. 1912) are unrelated in size or design. Number 369 is a tiny "pioneer cottage," perhaps built around 1905; the remainder were mostly built around WWI. Two are newer "Vancouver Specials" (F13)—one of the many innovative house-types explored in this chapter. Unlike Point Grey's uniform 24-foot setbacks, several houses are 10 feet or less from the sidewalk, leaving large rear yards for gardens. South Vancouver was a collection of scattered settlements. This area, known as Hillcrest, has seen mild gentrification in recent years, perhaps best revealed by the coffee houses and new businesses on Main Street. East 28th Avenue, like most South Vancouver streets, had a name before it joined Vancouver; portions were called Horne Road and Alves Road.

F3 Nat Bailey Stadium
4601 Ontario Street
1951

This perfect little ballpark was built and donated to the City by Sick's Capilano Brewery and called Capilano Stadium. Subsequent owner Molson's, which bought Sick's, named the team the Canadians after their own beer and renamed the 6,500-seat stadium to honour

F

Nat Bailey, an ardent baseball promoter who founded the White Spot restaurant chain. The Vancouver Canadians used to be a Triple-A team, but Vancouver lost the franchise to Sacramento in 2000 and now fields a Class A affiliate of the Toronto Blue Jays. Just west of the stadium is the **Vancouver Olympic Centre at Hillcrest Park** (4575 Clancy Loranger Way, Hughes Condon Marler 2009), built as the venue for Olympic and Paralympic curling and converted to a community centre, ice rink, curling club and library. The **Aquatic Centre at Hillcrest Park** was built adjacent to it by the City (Hughes Condon Marler 2011). The cleanly modernist **Millennium Sports Centre** (4588 Clancy Loranger Way, Walter Francl Architecture 2005) hosts gymnastics and indoor bowls.

F4 Bloedel Conservatory
Queen Elizabeth Park
Underwood, McKinley, Cameron,
Wilson & Smith, Thorson & Thorson structural
engineers 1969

A tropical rainforest and chattering birds thrive beneath the "triodetic" dome, 140 feet in diameter, assembled from aluminum pipe triangles and 1,500 Plexiglas bubbles. Lumberman and benefactor Prentice Bloedel donated the pavilion and Henry Moore's *Knife Edge—Two Piece*, which stands on a redesigned plaza (Perry + Associates 2007). The same architects designed the nearby **Seasons in the Park** restaurant (1973). The glazed, circular **Celebration Pavilion** (Henriquez Partners Architects 2007), adjacent to the parking lot, is a wedding venue. The plaza's "dancing fountain" (Perry + Associates with Vincent Helton & Associates 2007) and the parking lot sit atop a municipal reservoir. The structures crown 150-metre-high Little Mountain, the highest point in the city. Below, two abandoned quarries have been transformed into marvellous gardens. The north slope is an arboretum. All form part of Queen Elizabeth Park, officially opened in 1939 by King George VI and Queen Elizabeth. The Park Board threatened to close the conservatory as a cost-saving measure, but in 2010 it was taken under the wing of the VanDusen Botanical Garden (K42).

F5 Cowie Row Houses
4875–4887 Cambie Street
Eikos Planning 2010

British Columbia's *Land Title Act* does not permit true row houses, a relatively inexpensive house-type found throughout the world, since separately owned ("fee-simple") units cannot share a party wall without resorting to strata (condominium) ownership, with its shared communal spaces and monthly fees. Planner and politician Art Cowie, who devoted much of his life to exploring better ways

F

to design housing (κ9), developed these three prototype fee-simple row houses within the law by separating them with 1-inch gaps between two concrete walls—estimated to have added $250,000 to the construction cost. Each has a small "nanny suite" over the lane-facing garage, providing six units on an 80-foot lot.

The tour passes along "Cambie Heritage Boulevard," with its generous landscaped median recommended by the Bartholomew Plan (G1). This portion and the area south of King Edward were cut and filled for construction of the Canada Line rapid transit system. The original boulevard trees remain between King Edward and West 29th Avenues; the trees along the full route have been protected. Cambie Street from 16th Avenue to the Fraser River was rezoned in 2011 to allow five-storey buildings, an illustration of how transit lines spawn development and higher densities; see also D14.

F6 Mountain View Cemetery
5445 Fraser Street, between
East 31st and 43rd Avenues
John P. Lawson, City Engineer 1887;
many later additions

Vancouver's municipal cemetery is located on what was in 1887 remote, unincorporated land along the North Arm Wagon Road (now Fraser Street). The valley that runs most of its length is believed to be the former channel of Brewery Creek (D3), which had its source in marshland near here and emptied into False Creek. The cemetery has grown over the years from 25 to 106 acres and holds the buried or cremated remains of nearly 150,000 people. Many cultural groups have their own sections within the larger cemetery. The most visible are those for Jews (surrounded by a fence, as required by Jewish law), Chinese (with a ceremonial altar), Freemasons (with many fine monuments and a stand of mature horse chestnuts) and military personnel (in an official Commonwealth War Graves Commission site). Several buildings stand in the central area. Noteworthy are the privately owned Art Deco **Vancouver Crematorium** (1935) and the City-owned **Celebration Hall, Courtyard & Columbaria** (Phillips Farevaag Smallenberg, Birmingham & Wood, LEES + Associates 2009), a serene gathering place with an adjacent administration building within geometrically clean andesite-clad concrete walls. The evocative columbaria feature a sequence of andesite and granite walls along intersecting pathways, with individual niches and family urns lining the paths and fountains and ponds at the ends.

F7 Memorial Park South Field House
Near East 41st Avenue and Windsor Street
c. 1932

Dedicated in 1927, Memorial Park South features a grand boulevard entrance from 41st Avenue and fine stands of trees. A cenotaph commemorating the soldiers lost in WWI stands in the boulevard; it was moved here from the former South Vancouver Municipal Hall at 41st and Prince Albert after amalgamation with

Vancouver (1929). The picturesque field house reflects the English rustic manner adopted by the Vancouver Park Board. It features board-and-batten siding, a steep roof, whose broad eaves are supported by posts, and attractive woodwork in the gables.

F8 South Community Health Centre
6405 Knight Street
Duncan McNab & Associates 1955, 1960

International Style architecture had been considered radical for public building in the late 1940s (A22); within a decade it was the paradigm. Exposed steel columns divide the glass-and-brick infill into small units, creating a comfortably human scale. The lower entrance leads to a landscaped courtyard. Operated by Vancouver Coastal Health, which also runs full-service hospitals, the facility provides basic health care at the community level. This neighbourhood, centred on Fraser Street between East 41st and 49th Avenues, was originally called South Hill.

F9 Value Village
6415 Victoria Drive
McKee & Gray 1960

Now a thrift store allied with local charities, this was built as a supermarket in the SuperValu chain. Six graceful glued-

F

laminated (glulam) timber arches provide a broad interior space uninterrupted by columns. The astonishingly small metal connectors where the arches meet the concrete footings transfer the weight of the roof structure to the ground. The street-front glazing (a showy modernist grid) was designed for curb appeal. Archrival Safeway offered an alternative arched design (K37).

F10 **Corpus Christi Church** ↓
6350 Nanaimo Street
W.R. Ussner 1962

Sculptor Jack Harman's 16-foot-high welded bronze apostles (along the south side) and the resurrected Christ with three angels rise above ironstone-clad

arches on this neo-Byzantine, concrete church. A scalloped lantern sits above the porch; the serene, top-lit, arcaded interior features murals of the life of Christ, also by Harman. Contemporary with the church are a school, auditorium and priest house serving the parish, which began with a small log church by the Fraser River built by Oblate fathers in the early 1900s.

F11 **Laneway House**
6570 Knight Street (seen from rear lane)
Birmingham & Wood 2010

The City of Vancouver continues to permit housing of ever-diminishing size as it seeks to increase density in accordance with Metro Vancouver's Regional Growth Strategy and its own EcoDensity Charter. In 2009 the City enabled construction

of laneway houses, affordable and free-standing rental units that remain part of the larger property and do not disrupt the look and feel of a neighbourhood. This house, built by laneway house specialists Smallworks, provides 500 square feet of living space (plus garage), including a loft bedroom beneath a high, vaulted ceiling. The exterior finish is vinyl siding secured by metal strips.

F12 **6288 Windsor Street**
Henry Whittaker 1919

This mansard-roofed Dutch Colonial residence was one of ten in the neighbourhood built by the provincial Department of Lands under the federal Better Housing Scheme to provide affordable housing for veterans and widows of WWI. Another is across the street at **6273 Windsor**. All cost $2,500 or less. In all, 153 houses were built or improved in Vancouver over five years. The need to accommodate returning vets from WWII prompted a similar initiative (F21).

F13 **Vancouver Specials** ↑
6100-6200-blocks Windsor Street
Various builders 1970s

Around 1970, builders found a new efficient model for mass-market housing that maximized floor area and site coverage at an attractive price. The main living spaces are one floor up, with garage, laundry facilities and sometimes a "granny suite" on the ground floor. There is no basement, avoiding costly excavation and separating the bedrooms from the damp ground. The "Vancouver Specials," as they came to be called, are indeed special in that they achieved widespread popularity then suffered a backlash for their uniform flat fronts, boxy shapes and low roofs (K20). These adjacent houses on Windsor Street (with many others throughout the neighbourhood) offer variety in their ersatz materials, pastel colours, metal railings and window details. Now, a generation later, focus has shifted to their suitability for sustainable makeovers (E12). They supplanted small stucco boxes from the 1950s, many of which remain on these two blocks, and all are being replaced with newer, larger designs as the allowable density increases.

F14 Pope House
6306 Prince Albert Street
1912

This precious red-and-buff frame cottage, first occupied by fireman Ennis Pope, is a delightful survivor of old South Hill. Its octagonal corner verandah with a ball finial at the peak of its conical roof transforms it into a toytown château. The entrance is set at an angle to fit the street corner. Original leaded glass graces many windows. The garden is lush and the house lovingly maintained.

F15 Universal Buddhist Temple
525 East 49th Avenue
Vincent Kwan 1978

The temple was founded by C.C. Lu in 1968 to serve a group of lay Buddhists. The colourful cubic building, built a decade later, is finished in pink stucco with red columns, capped by a characteristically Chinese two-tiered gold-tiled roof. Ceramic tiles below the entrance offer a lesson from the Buddha.

F16 Langara College Library
100 West 49th Avenue
Teeple Architects, IBI/HB Architects 2007

Opened in 1965 at the former King Edward High School (D17) as a program of Vancouver City College, Langara College moved to this site—part of the CPR's Langara golf course—in 1970. It has been an independent post-secondary institution since 1994 and provides courses to more than twenty thousand students annually. "Langara" was the name the Spanish explorers gave to the local coast. The bold, monochrome form of the library has an appealing, crisp directness that is complemented by rectilinear reflecting pools (Phillips Farevaag Smallenberg landscape design). The same design team prepared a master plan for the campus in 2004, recommending this and other new buildings (including the Teeple-designed, Y-shaped **Students' Union Building**). The original **Classroom Building** to the east (Ronald B. Howard with Allan B. Wilson 1970), finished in textured concrete and red brick, reflects the brutalism of its time.

F17 Punjabi Market
Main Street and East 49th Avenue

South Vancouver contains new villages as well as old ones. The commercial and residential district centred at East 49th Avenue and Main Street, also called Little India, is dominated by immigrants from India and the Punjab and also includes Ismailis from Africa, Persians, Filipinos, and many more. People come from all around the Lower Mainland to shop at the Indian fabric, jewellery and spice outlets and to nosh at the restaurants and bakeries. South Asians were attracted here by job opportunities offered by sawmills and "truck gardens" along the Fraser River. Migrants from India have not always been welcome to Vancouver. In

1914, the Asiatic Exclusion League and other groups prevented the landing of the steamer *Komagata Maru*, which tested immigration laws by bringing three-hundred-odd East Indian passengers. The would-be migrants spent nine miserable summer weeks anchored in Burrard Inlet before being forced to return to Asia.

F18 Sunset Community Centre †
6810 Main Street
Bing Thom Architects 2008

This striking Park Board facility has quickly become a landmark along Main Street. It accommodates a preschool, gymnasium, exercise rooms and a host of other community activities. The building flaunts the landscaped contours of the site, emphasized by the curvilinear steel roof that spreads like petals, an allusion to the City's adjacent Sunset Nursery. The main spaces branch off an internal skylit stem and are defined by forty-six structural "tilt-up" concrete panels, also free-form, cast flat on site and tilted into position by a crane (Fast + Epp structural engineers). A bridge at the second level provides cross-circulation. Curtain walls are variegated with transparent, translucent and opaque glass panels for views, natural light and solar shade. "Sunset" is the name given by the City to the western portion of the former Killarney district (F25). En route to the Ross Street Sikh Temple (see next entry), just south of Marine Drive (accessible from Fraser Street), is the City's **Materials Testing Facility** (900 East Kent Avenue, Busby + Associates, Fast + Epp 1999), a budget-conscious eco-experiment built with salvaged "junk."

F19 Ross Street Sikh Temple
8000 Ross Street
Erickson/Massey 1970

Vancouver's Sikhs commissioned this architectural gem, their main *gurdwara*, or house of worship. The design was inspired by the formal geometry of Indian religious symbols. A massive, yet simple, white block (originally unpainted concrete) is capped by stepped diagonal squares and crowned by an open steel dome. The temple is operated by the Khalsa Diwan Society, which was founded in 1906 to support the small but growing Sikh population.

F20 Sir James Douglas Annex
7668 Borden Street
Allan B. Wilson 1957; Colborne Architectural Group Pacific, Pomeroy Consulting Engineers 2009

The Vancouver School Board built a number of fine early modern schools in the late 1940s and the 1950s in order to keep up with postwar development (see next entry) and the baby boom. In 1945 VSB architect E.D. King issued guidelines for new schools calling for simplicity of design and economical materials. Primary annexes such as this were to be of frame construction with plywood interior walls; larger schools, of reinforced concrete. Douglas Annex, originally Walter Moberly Annex B, is one of the best preserved of the small auxiliary schools. The architect was Allan B. Wilson, King's successor. A mostly flat roof, wood siding and broad windows parallel the design of early modern houses of the day. Douglas Annex was seismically upgraded in 2009 as part of a provincially led retrofit program. Walls were tied to the foundation and the roof, which was reinforced.

F21 2015 Fraserview Drive
1950

This Fraserview subdivision, commanding fine views of the Fraser River, was built between 1949 and 1951 as a "workingman's Shaughnessy Heights." The federal government's Central (now Canada) Mortgage & Housing Corporation expropriated 450 acres to accommodate returning WWII vets. Built mostly by private builders, Fraserview consisted of 1,100 houses on curving streets. This small 1½-storey home with side gables was typical; few remain today. The contrast between a postwar society that was

grateful for what it had and one that can't be satisfied could not be more striking: the curving streets are packed to the max with new larger and showier residences built in the 1990s and 2000s.

F22 Fraserview Golf Course Clubhouse
7800 Vivian Street
1938; rehabilitated by Matsuzaki Wright Architects 1998

One of three municipal golf courses in Vancouver, Fraserview occupies 225 acres overlooking the Fraser River from stands of Douglas-fir, hemlock and hardwoods. Part of the site was farmed from 1868 by former Royal Engineer (N17) W.H. Rowling, reportedly the area's first non-native settler. The sensitively rehabilitated clubhouse, with its steeply pitched roof and residual Arts and Crafts feel, rounds off

the course, begun in 1930. Labour for the first nine holes, designed by Major H.L. McPherson and opened in 1934, was provided by federally funded "relief" workers. The present course was completed in 1997 by Thomas McBroom Associates. As the names suggest, both respected the Scottish roots of course design.

At the base of the south slope, between Southeast Marine Drive and the river and well worth a detour, are Riverside (near the foot of Victoria Drive) and the Fraser Lands (further east), the names given to an immense swath of former industrial land along the North Arm of the Fraser River. Industrial marine uses were removed and residential developments built in their place in the 1980s and 1990s with townhouses and medium-rise multiple dwellings. Yet further east, between Kerr Street and Boundary Road, are the East Fraserlands, a 130-acre "sustainable, complete community" with a variety of housing-types and a central office and retail "high street," to be built out over the next two decades. It replaces several lumber mills, including what was the largest plywood mill in Canada. Despite all this development, the Fraser remains a working river with continuous marine activity, particularly tow boats pulling sawdust barges.

F23 La Petite Maison Housing Co-op
Talon Square (off Matheson Crescent)
Hawthorn Mansfield Towers Architects 1978

Champlain Heights was developed in the 1970s as a showcase residential community. The City of Vancouver retained ownership of the land, leasing it to developers. Each development is conceived as a separate little village accessed from a circular drive. Inspired by European townhouses set around a square, this stucco-and-wood co-op is typical of the neighbourhood's gentle

urbanism, humanist scale and generous landscaping. The first co-op was DeCosmos Village (East 49th Avenue at Boundary Road, Francis Donaldson 1972). Other projects include subsidized rentals (e.g., 3200-block East 58th Avenue, David Crinion/CMHC, Downs/Archambault 1973) and market condos.

F24 Brittany
East 54th Avenue at Mont Royal Square
Burrowes Huggins Architects 2006

What a difference a generation makes! Brittany and the adjacent Bordeaux and Champlain townhouse complexes, which together comprise Champlain Gardens, are a world away from Champlain Heights (see previous entry) in their increased height and density, reduced open space and decidedly big-city feel. The development, by PCI Group, accommodates

116 units. All break away from South Vancouver's tradition of single-family residences. Brittany's picturesque silhouettes, wood siding and Craftsman-like decorative gables produce a B.C.-flavoured neo-traditional design that a promotional blurb describes as being "Whistler-inspired."

F25 Killarney Community Centre Pool
6260 Killarney Street
Hughes Condon Marler Architects 2006

More an aquatic centre than just a pool, the building shows how to make a simple shed spacious and structurally exciting. Huge windows and a roof that angles upwards provide views of Killarney Park and the North Shore mountains. The Killarney district originally comprised the south slope of eastern Vancouver and 3.5 kilometres of Fraser River shoreline, including the future Champlain Heights

and Fraser Lands. Construction of the interurban railway in 1891 sparked development, and the street grid spread towards the river from No. 1 Road (which became East 45th Avenue, next to Killarney Park) and No. 2 Road (now East 54th Avenue). Today's Killarney neighbourhood is the northern portion of that district.

F26 Cooper House
5872 Wales Street
1919; 2005

This large half-timbered house is a survivor of the former Cooper farm, reminding us that the Killarney district used to be agricultural. The farm was sold and subdivided in 1941; more recently the house was moved to the street corner and five infill dwellings built beside it. The **Avalon Dairy**, opened in 1906 by transplanted Newfoundlander Jeremiah Crowley, operated its retail outlet across the street in the former family farmhouse (5805 Wales Street, 1908) until the Crowley descendants sold the property for redevelopment in 2011. An enduring reminder of the former rural landscape is the **Vancouver School Board grounds nursery** (5905 Wales Street).

F27 Sir Guy Carleton Elementary School
3250 Kingsway
Begun 1896; many additions to 1950

South Vancouver's rapid growth before WWI is evident in this cluster of school buildings. A frame schoolhouse at McKinnon Street (1896; damaged by fire in 2009) was East Vancouver School and survives as the oldest extant school building in Vancouver. The smaller structure next to it was added in 1907. The robust yellow wood building (W.T. Whiteway 1908) and the large classical red brick block (J.H. Bowman 1912) are types that reappear in schools throughout South Vancouver. A concrete gymnasium wing (E.D. King 1950) completes the complex. Kingsway—before 1913 called the Westminster Road—was a military trail that connected New Westminster with today's Vancouver. A block east of here stood the Collingwood Inn, a roadhouse that catered to stagecoaches. Collingwood was also the name of the larger village that grew around the roadhouse. The coaches were upstaged by the interurban tram (F31) in 1891 and then by automobiles in the twentieth century.

F28 Collingwood Branch Library
2985 Kingsway
Semmens & Simpson 1951

One of Vancouver Public Library's first suburban branches, and the most visited modernist building in Vancouver when completed, Collingwood demonstrates the use of modern forms to produce a regional style. The rectilinearity and industrial products are tempered by large expanses of glass (steel-sash windows from England), rough fieldstone and vertical wood siding (originally stained, not painted), which respond to the local climate and materials. Busy, built-up Kingsway now overwhelms the building, which fit the small-scale environment of its day. The same architects designed the former central library downtown (H46). An earlier modernist library was the Dunbar Branch Library (4515 Dunbar Street, McCarter & Nairne 1947–50).

F29 Purdy's Chocolate Factory
2777 Kingsway
Walter Monroe Cory, McCarter Nairne & Partners 1948–55; 1982

Richard Carmon Purdy opened a chocolate shop on Robson Street in 1907. The business, run since 1963 by Vancouver's Flavelle family, has expanded to more than fifty stores in three provinces. The factory moved in 1982 from 7th Avenue and Spruce Street in Fairview—the former location is remembered in tiny Choklit Park (D22)—to this former Canada Dry bottling plant. The early modern brick-and-glass structure, conceived by Canada Dry's New York–based architect W.M. Cory and designed by Vancouver's McCarter & Nairne, is uncompromisingly rectilinear, a tribute to postwar modernism.

F30 2400 Court
2400 Kingsway
1947

The last best remnant of the car culture that shaped mid-twentieth-century Kingsway, the 2400 Court (later styled "Motel") is a rare, unaltered period piece, from the vintage neon sign to the plain stucco boxes to the immaculate lawns. The "motor court" offers sixty-five units in eighteen detached cottages spread over 3 ½ acres. White stucco, green siding and hipped roofs provide a domestic

look, while the two-storey, flat-roofed office is a more modernistic, commercial affair. With the completion of the Pattullo Bridge in 1937, Kingsway became a link in the Pacific Highway connecting Vancouver to the U.S. and Mexico and the main thoroughfare leading into Vancouver (until succeeded by the Massey Tunnel and Oak Street Bridge in the 1950s and then by Highway 1). Accordingly it developed after WWII as a strip of gas stations, motels and drive-in restaurants. The nearby Eldorado Motor Hotel (2330 Kingsway, c. 1960) represents the next generation of motorist accommodation. The 2400 and the Eldorado both stand in the way of the City's intended Norquay Village Neighbourhood Centre—a South Vancouver village of tomorrow—and so their future is uncertain.

F31 **Earles Station**
4590 Earles Street
Robert Lyon 1912; Linda Baker 1989

This was built as an electric substation to power the B.C. Electric interurban railway that ran from downtown Vancouver to New Westminster and Chilliwack. The right-of-way is now used by SkyTrain. Architect Lyon produced a number of designs for the BCER. The massive concrete structure, a landmark in a neighbourhood of bland, low buildings was superbly converted into twelve loft units (four per floor), with a new wood "building within a building." The changes, such as the steel balconies, respect the original design.

F32 **Renfrew Branch Library** †
2969 East 22nd Avenue
Hughes Baldwin Architects, C.Y. Loh Associates 1996

Angular planes and knife-edge corners recall the modernist tradition of the old central and branch libraries (H46, F28) in this neo-expressionist design. It responds to the steeply sloping site and the scale of its setting, all bungalows and Vancouver Specials. The floor plan shadows the triangular roof, which alights with a whisper like a hang glider. The entrance is announced by the roof's projecting point. A small piazza animates the sidewalk. The interior is a model of spatial planning. The building's spine, an exposed truss on a row of concrete columns, leads the eye past stacks, computer stations and a children's section (where the ceiling drops gently to the young borrowers' stature), to a reading area with a view of Renfrew Park and the North Shore mountains. Daylight is supplemented with soft artificial light, and colour used to highlight structural columns and spaces. Directly across Nootka Street is **Fire Hall No. 15** (3003 East 22nd Avenue, 1915), a significant local landmark whose shell is intended to become part of a redevelopment with a new three-bay fire-truck hall designed by Hughes Condon Marler Architects (a successor to Hughes Baldwin).

F33 St. Joseph's Roman Catholic Church
1612 East 18th Avenue
Harry LeBlond & Associates 1982;
later alterations

The distinction between walls and roof is obscured in this spirited church, whose sloping sides (supported by glulam rafters) are gently curved in a tent-like form. They don't quite meet at the top, allowing the dramatic entry of light from the apex—a device seen in some Quebec churches of the day. This bold exaggeration of the modernist vocabulary is characteristic of late modernism.

F34 St. Mark's Evangelical Lutheran Church
1573 East 18th Avenue
1911

This stucco and half-timber church, formerly shingled on the lower walls, was originally the Robson Memorial Methodist Church and was revived by a German-speaking ministry. It was built to serve the Cedar Cottage neighbourhood, once a rustic stop on the interurban between Vancouver and New Westminster, and named after a neighbourhood nursery. The hill and nearby Trout Lake (now John Hendry Park, named after the lumberman father of Aldene Hendry Hamber, who, with her husband, Eric Hamber, was the land's last private owner—see J18) attracted well-to-do homeowners, but few big houses remain.

False Creek

"FALSE Creek" was just that—a shallow tidal inlet off English Bay that led nowhere. It was named by Captain G.H. Richards on his survey of 1859. First Nations used the south shore as a trail and established a village near today's Granville Island. Despite being a rich and diverse ecological marshland estuary that supported salmon streams, Europeans lamented False Creek for having no economic value. The City was obsessed with making it "useful," either by deepening it or filling it in. The latter was chosen, and considerable landfill occurred.

The largest initiative "reclaimed" the portion between Clark Drive and Main Street (which crossed the flats on a bridge), by 1917 consuming nearly one-third of False Creek's 1,000 acres. The City created the land for the station and yards of the Canadian Northern Railway (G16). Under the leadership of the City and the federal government, land was created on both shores of the Creek for heavy industry. What remained was occupied by log booms and barges and lined with smoke-belching mills and other heavy industry.

Values change, and a half-century later False Creek was dismissed as a "stinking industrial cesspool." In the 1960s and '70s, guided in part by the vision of Mayor Art Phillips and planning

Above: Emily Carr University of Art + Design (G4)

director Ray Spaxman, the City removed nearly all industry west of Cambie Street. In its place, partly on new fill, a residential community grew along the south side of the Creek displaying a new approach to "livable" multiple housing (G7–G9). More fill along the north shore in the 1980s accommodated Expo 86 (G14), the world's fair that launched Vancouver as a global destination. Southeast False Creek was cleared of industry and further filled at the beginning of the present century to accommodate the athletes' village for the Vancouver 2010 Winter Olympic Games, which has since been marketed to the public as a model sustainable community (G11). The survivor is Granville Island (G3–G6), redeveloped by the federal government in the 1970s for specialty retail, marine facilities and the arts. By the late twentieth century, False Creek had shrunk to about one-quarter of its original size.

The City's emerging status is best revealed in Concord Pacific Place (G19), developed on the Expo Lands developed by Hong Kong's Li Ka-shing and admired internationally for its livable density, which has come to be known as "Vancouverism," a term coined by American planners. Local architectural critic Trevor Boddy and English architect Dennis Sharp define Vancouverism as "an urbanism of density and public amenity."

Today's False Creek is a recreational waterway. Around it has risen a diversity of residential and mixed developments, with walking and bicycle paths at water's edge. Only the northeast portion remains undeveloped. It includes the Georgia Viaduct (1972), which replaced an earlier overpass (1915) and was the only part of a freeway plan to be built. The viaduct may be demolished for the valuable land below or could be "greened" as a promenade, as has been done successfully with redundant elevated rail lines in Paris and New York.

This chapter explores the perimeter of False Creek, beginning and ending at the narrows spanned by the Burrard Bridge (G1). The route meanders inland at the end to explore Yaletown, originally a CPR community and now a gentrified neighbourhood. This finale to the tour reiterates the transition from industry to residential, from local to global.

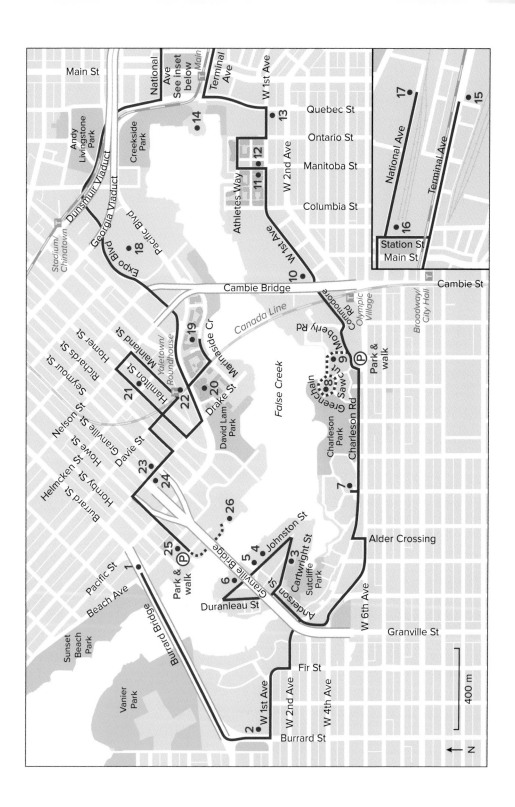

G1 Burrard Bridge
J.R. Grant engineer, Sharp & Thompson 1932

The Burrard Bridge was proposed as a new crossing over False Creek in an ambitious plan for Vancouver (1928) by American planning consultant Harland Bartholomew. He also suggested a large civic centre on the Kitsilano side, but the new City Hall was built elsewhere (D15). The bridge was designed with two levels, the upper one for cars and a lower one for trains and streetcars. At the behest of the Town Planning Commission, which insisted on omitting the rail deck, G.L.T. Sharp "architected up" engineer Grant's steel structure in the Art-Deco-ized Spanish Colonial style fashionable at the time. In 2008 the City considered a controversial widening of the bridge for dedicated bicycle lanes but solved the problem and respected the heritage by simply eliminating one automobile lane. Below the south approach is the **government fish dock** (accessible from Granville Island), where people can buy fish fresh from the boat.

G2 Seaforth Armoury
1650 Burrard Street
McCarter & Nairne 1936

This landmark Scots Baronial castle, rendered in poured-in-place concrete, wears a fanciful yet appropriate uniform for the Seaforth Highlanders. Two round towers guard the entrance, crenellations and turrets imply defensive strength, and cast thistles on the finials allude to the regiment's spiritual home. The coat-of-arms above the entry is by sculptor Charles Marega. Plans have been made to upgrade the structure to serve as a post-disaster facility (Colborne Architectural Group Pacific); work may begin in 2012. The Jericho Garrison plans to move just east on 1st Avenue so that its extensive Point Grey lands can be sold for development. En route to Granville Island (G3) is the **Waterfall Building** (1540 West 2nd Avenue, Nick Milkovich Architects, Arthur Erickson, Fast + Epp engineers 2001), an urbane, mixed-use, courtyard development featuring a "waterfall" at the entry.

G3 Arts Umbrella
1286 Cartwright Street
Henriquez Partners Architects 1987, 1998

Arts Umbrella, which attracts more than forty thousand children a year, was co-founded by Carol Henriquez in 1979 as a non-profit arts institute for youth. Her son Gregory Henriquez's first project after graduation from Carleton University's School of Architecture was the present east wing, which "represents a fragmented oversized face." Concrete blocks are capped by a bold superstructure whose large, leaded-glass "eye" looks out from beneath a corrugated metal "cosmic eyebrow" (some might call it an umbrella). The school's success required replacing an adjacent former nail factory—a survivor of industrial Granville Island—with a three-storey cubic block. The resulting contrast creates a playful dialogue. A short distance west is the **False Creek Community Centre** (1318 Cartwright Street, c. 1920; Henriquez Partners Architects 1991, 2001), initially accommodated in a recycled industrial building and enlarged with two recent additions. To the north is the restored **Travelling Crane** (c. 1925; 2001) and **Sea Village**, a community of funky float homes.

G4 Emily Carr University of Art + Design
1399 Johnston Street
1918 and later; Howard/Yano 1980
1400 Johnston Street
Patkau Architects, Toby Russell
Buckwell & Partners 1994

Attracting cultural and institutional tenants was essential to Granville Island's success. Emily Carr University (originally the Vancouver School of Art) is now the island's largest tenant. For the north building, which contains studios, offices, concourse and the Charles H. Scott Gallery, architect Ron Howard linked the former Westex Manufacturing and British Ropes buildings with new con-

struction featuring the corrugated metal siding, skylights and exposed timber beams characteristic of Granville Island's architectural vocabulary. The impressive and unconventional south building by Patkau Architects (page 104) is a contemporary incarnation of Granville Island's past, though built to a larger scale to include a three-storey parkade—"the big, dumb core," as the architects described it. The smart part of the building accommodates a library, lecture theatre and studios, stepping down from a skylit concourse to Johnston Street in a precipitous spatial sequence.

G5 Ocean Cement
1415 Johnston Street
1917 and later

Ocean Cement (originally Diether's Coal & Building Supplies) is the last big industry left on man-made Granville Island. Ocean Cement contributes to Granville Island's now-trendy sustainability. Barges bring limestone, sand and gravel, and trucks haul cement; the materials are stored in the elevators and mixed to produce concrete, with the consequent short trips for ready-mix trucks reducing carbon emissions. Granville Island's blend of industry, commerce and culture creates its vitality. Just west is **Creekhouse** (1551 Johnston Street, c. 1920; Brian Johnston 1972) one of the first rehabilitation projects on the Island, adapted from an abandoned Monsanto chemical warehouse.

G6 Granville Island Public Market †
1689 Johnston Street
1917; Hotson Bakker 1979

The bustling public market, with its fresh produce and wares, is the heart of highly successful Granville Island. It was among the first waterfront revitalization schemes to recycle industrial buildings, setting the tone for similar projects around the world. The land was reclaimed from False Creek for heavy industry, was redeveloped for specialty retail and the arts by the federal government in the 1970s and is operated by Canada Mortgage & Housing Corporation (CMHC). The market building best illustrates the

overall design approach by coordinating architects Norman Hotson and Joost Bakker. These timber-framed, tin-clad sheds that once housed Wright's Ropes and B.C. Equipment were recycled, emphasizing their lofty open spaces. Overhead gantry cranes are reminders of the past. Outside, the brick-paved roadways retain the railway tracks, and the street furniture consists of no-nonsense benches, posts, metal rails and lights, with no separation between pedestrians and cars. Behind and west of the market are mini-ferry docks, which serve False Creek.

G7 False Creek Co-operative Housing
918–1072 Scantlings,
951–99 Lamey's Mill Road
Henriquez & Todd 1977

In the 1960s and '70s the City of Vancouver removed all industry from this part of False Creek, increased the land mass through reclamation and developed a new residential community intended to accommodate a variety of income levels in a "livable" paradigm. The red roofs identify townhouses developed by the False Creek Co-operative Housing Association. The award-wining False Creek Elementary School (900 School Green, Henriquez & Todd 1978; DA Architects + Planners 2011) is integrated into the complex. The road passes under a mirrored and landscaped pedestrian bridge

(Hawthorn Mansfield Towers 1977) that links the False Creek development with the Fairview Slopes (D20–D22). The former CPR tracks along 6th Avenue comprise the first leg of a streetcar service being developed by the City of Vancouver. Currently used by two restored interurban cars, it will eventually acquire new equipment to link Kitsilano Point with Stanley Park. Motorists should park in the public lot across from 655 Moberly Road and visit the eastern portion of False Creek on foot.

G8 Heather Point
800–844 Millbank, 846–864 Greenchain, 807–831 Sawcut
Thompson, Berwick, Pratt & Partners 1977

This cluster of townhouses best expresses the vision for False Creek expressed by coordinating architects Thompson, Berwick, Pratt & Partners in their plan for the neighbourhood, whose street names come from the sawmill industry. A village-like intimacy is achieved by breaking up the composition with advancing and retreating walls, varying roof heights and the interplay of rooflets, chimneys and fences. The same architects also designed the buildings that define nearby **Leg-in-Boot Square** (named for the severed leg that once washed ashore), which was intended as the retail focus for False Creek but never succeeded commercially.

G9 682–698 Millbank

Rhone & Iredale 1977

These aluminum-and-glass condominiums, with their long planar façade, uniform roofline, straightforward use of modern materials and high-tech detailing, depart from the overall design concept for False Creek. Architect Peter Cardew gave the project a particular urbanity and stylish seaside feeling, inspired by the row housing of his native England.

G10 False Creek Energy Centre

Beneath south approach of the Cambie Street Bridge

Walter Francl Architecture, Pechet & Robb 2009

Part public art, part sustainability made visible, five stainless-steel stacks rise above the Cambie Street Bridge to announce the Energy Centre, the first urban power plant in North America to produce hot water from sewage. Heat pumps recover thermal energy from the sewage before its treatment at the Iona plant in Richmond. Low-emission natural-gas boilers supplement the sewage at peak times. The building (Francl) is parked under the bridge; the futuristic LED lights on the fingertips of the stacks (Pechet & Robb) morph from blue to red to indicate energy demand from the adjacent community (see next entry). The plant generates 70 per cent of Southeast False Creek's annual energy needs, the balance from rooftop solar-panel installations.

G11 Olympic Village/
The Village on False Creek
*Between West 2nd Avenue and
False Creek, from Columbia Street
to Ontario Street*
Merrick Architecture, Gomberoff Bell Lyon
Architects Group, Walter Francl Architecture,
Nick Milkovich Architects + Arthur Erickson,
Lawrence Doyle Young + Wright Architects,
Hotson Bakker Boniface Haden, Stantec
Architecture, VIA Architecture 2009

The City's planners recommended in 1991 that Southeast False Creek become a model sustainable community to showcase leading-edge environmental and social design. Millennium Development won the contract to build the community, initially called Millennium Water. Developers Peter and Shahram Malek asked the architects to create a "modern classic" of "quiet sustainability" that "would not become dated." The complex contains 1,100 units of market and "affordable" housing, complemented by commercial and public space and parkland. The result is a tight street grid somewhat European in appearance, scale and density. Green roofs and many other eco features (see previous entry) gained the Village LEED Plati-

num certification and the buildings LEED Gold. The urban realm (PWL Partnership, Phillips Farevaag Smallenberg, Durante Kreuk), public art, a waterfront walkway (with an elegantly engineered "canoe bridge") and an "eco-island" respond to the creek's West Coast context. The buildings were used first as the athletes' village for the Vancouver 2010 Winter Olympic Games, then returned to Millennium. The New York–based hedge-fund lender defaulted, and the City responded with a $750 million bail-out and subsequent repossession of the entire property, actions that have taken their toll on municipal programs. Marketing guru Bob Rennie (B6) rebranded the site as The Village on False Creek and offered the many unsold units at a discount. The developed area, which includes Creekside Community Recreation Centre (Walter Francl Architecture, Nick Milkovich Architects + Arthur Erickson 2010), represents only one-third of the land intended to be built out over the next decade or two. The project has stimulated redevelopment on the private lands south of 1st Avenue.

G12 **Vancouver Salt Company**
85 West 1st Avenue
c. 1930; 1955; Acton Ostry Architects,
Commonwealth Historic Resource Management
2010

This survivor of the many workplaces that once dominated Southeast False Creek was once squeezed between two lumber operations, part of the immense industrial community that developed here, mostly on reclaimed land. The Vancouver Salt Company "semi-refined" raw salt from San Francisco Bay into a coarse product first used as a preservative for the local fishery, particularly by Japanese-Canadian fish-packers, then also as road salt and for cold-storage plants. The utilitarian exterior conceals the spacious interior, with its remarkable heavy timber trusses supporting the roof, cupola and "monitor" windows. The building expanded north in 1955 (Wright Engineers) and was converted for use as a paper-recycling plant in the 1980s. The building has pride of place facing the main plaza of the new neighbourhood ("Shipyard Square," Phillips Farevaag Smallenberg), whose sinuous lamp standards recall the ribs of boats that used to dock here. The

rehabbed structure was used first as a gathering place for Olympic athletes and is intended to become a bakery, bistro and brewpub. It meets LEED Gold standards for sustainability while also ensuring respect for the original design.

G13 **Amato Gelato Cafe**
78 East 1st Avenue
Hadfield & Turner Architecture 1998

Mario LoScerbo came to Vancouver in the 1960s from Amato, Italy, with ice cream-making skills learned from his father and grandfather. He and his father expanded their business, making Mario's Gelati into an international enterprise

with this large production and retail facility, topped by a six-hundred-seat ballroom called "Villa Amato." The concrete structure's breezy personality features a north-facing glass curtain wall, a rippling sidewalk canopy and a transparent corner staircase tower that has become a neighbourhood landmark. Just south is **Opsal Steel** (East 2nd Avenue between Ontario and Quebec Streets, T.H. Bamforth 1918; IBI/HB Architects, McGinn Engineering and Preservation, estimated completion 2013), a heavy-timber structure built for Columbia Block and Tool, whose salvaged remains will be flanked by two tall residential towers.

G14 Science World
1455 Quebec Street
Bruno Freschi 1986; Boak Alexander Architects 1989; Cannon Design 2011

The shimmering "golf ball" is a geodesic dome—an iconic form invented by American R. Buckminster Fuller and featured at the U.S. Pavilion at Expo 67—made from 766 aluminum triangles covered with vinyl and supported by an outer frame of white steel. A legacy of Expo 86, the world's fair that launched Vancouver as a global destination, it served as the Expo preview centre. After extensive retrofitting it became Science World, a popular attraction. An OMNIMAX Theatre fills the dome. Recent renovations produced a greener building and added outdoor science experiences.

G15 Former Canada Packers Plant
750 Terminal Avenue
Eric R. Arthur 1937

International Style meets moderne in this striking and influential former meatpacking plant, a landmark along the reclaimed False Creek flats (see next entry). It is the only Vancouver building by New Zealander Eric Arthur, who came to Canada via Europe. As a popular professor at the University of Toronto's School of Architecture, he introduced Ned Pratt, Bob Berwick and other talented young Vancouver architects to modernism. Arthur was also a committed architectural historian who had his students study early Ontario buildings. This structure has met with hard times, but despite a fire and a series of new uses—most recently as self-storage—its class shows through in a sea of bland boxes on the reclaimed False Creek flats. SkyTrain, the automated light-rail transit system constructed in conjunction with the transportation-themed Expo 86, runs on an elevated guideway along Terminal Avenue on its way to Surrey.

G16 Pacific Central Station
1150 Station Street
Pratt & Ross, John Schofield 1919; Phillips
Barratt Engineers & Architects 1993

This classical creation, with its bold central arch and colonnaded wings, was built as the western terminus of the Canadian Northern Railway, Canada's second transcontinental line after the CPR (H28). All the land from Main Street (which formerly crossed the water on a bridge) eastward for about a mile to the bluff at Clark Drive had been the tidal flats of False Creek. The City filled the flats' more than 300 acres to accommodate the railway's yards and station in return for extensive pledges, including the construction of a large downtown hotel (the Hotel Vancouver, H51). The terminus of the American-owned Great Northern Railway (now Burlington Northern Santa Fe) was built first, immediately north, in 1917; it was demolished in 1965. The Canadian Northern went bankrupt and was absorbed in 1919 into the government's Canadian National Railways, now privatized. Since 1993 the station has accommodated both

trains and buses and is close to SkyTrain and city buses. The historic "Canadian National" roof sign was controversially changed to "Pacific Central." An attractive high-tech bus-bay canopy was added next to the tracks and the interior rehabilitated in an old character. Thornton Park, in front of the station, provides respite for neighbourhood denizens. It features *Marker of Change* (Beth Alber 1997), a circle of fourteen granite benches remembering the women who were massacred at Montreal's École Polytechnique in 1989. Across Main Street is **City Gate** (Perkins & Company 1992–2007), a high-density development that defines the eastern edge of today's False Creek.

G17 City of Vancouver National Works Yard
701 National Avenue
Omicron 2004

The City moved its primary engineering operations facility from Southeast False Creek, just east of Cambie Street, to a 12-acre site on the False Creek flats next to the rail yards. Omicron provided

architectural, engineering and construction management services, with Scott Kemp the architect of record for this administration building. The vigorous industrial vernacular design clearly reveals the wood roof structure and its steel supports inside and out. A glass-and-metal exterior skin encloses the building. The building achieved LEED Gold certification for sustainability.

G18 B.C. Place Stadium
777 Pacific Boulevard
Phillips Barratt Engineers & Architects 1983; Stantec Architecture 2011

This 55,000-seat (originally 60,000-seat) downtown stadium—a North American municipal status symbol—was conceived for Expo 86 by the Provincial government, which owns and operates it. The choice of site ignored planning logic in freeway-free Vancouver, whose population is exceeded by that of its suburbs. A SkyTrain station, another Expo legacy, addressed the transit issue. The stadium is the venue for the CFL B.C. Lions and Major League Soccer's Whitecaps. The original Teflon roof, held aloft by air pressure and the largest of its kind in the world, defied gravity until a winter storm in 2007 tore a panel and deflated it. Temporarily repaired, it was replaced in 2011 with a retractable cable-stayed fabric roof (the opening the size of the field below and supported by thirty-six steel masts, each 47-metres tall), the largest of its type.

Memorable events included the opening and closing ceremonies of the 2010 Winter Olympic Games. The adjacent **Rogers Arena** (800 Griffiths Way, Brisbin Brook Beynon Architects, Baker McGarva Hart 1995) seats 20,000 for NHL hockey and more for rock concerts. Just west of the stadium, at the foot of Robson Street, is the **Terry Fox Memorial** (Douglas Coupland 2011), which replaced a symbolic triumphal arch (Franklin Allen 1984) that introduced postmodernism to Vancouver but that few people liked.

G19 Concord Pacific Place
North shore of False Creek, between the Granville and Cambie Street Bridges
Concept architects (Pacific Place Design Consortium): Baker McGarva Hart, The Hulbert Group, Downs/Archambault, Davidson Yuen Simpson Architects

Principal architects (with the above): Hancock Brückner, Busby + Associates Architects, Roger Hughes Architects, Hewitt + Kwasnicky Architects, IBI Group, Henriquez Partners Architects, Neale Staniszkis Doll Adams Architects, James K.M. Cheng Architects

Landscape architects: Don Vaughan & Associates (concept), Philips Wuori Long (detailed design) 1989–2011

The handover of Hong Kong from the U.K. to China in 1997, announced formally a dozen years earlier, led to an exodus from the colony of residents—and serious money. Many came to Vancouver, whose emerging global status following the success of Expo 86 (G14), superb setting, stable government and underexploited real estate made it an attractive home and investment. The new immigrants provided a primary market and source of financing for the Expo lands, which were bought for a song from the provincial government in 1988 by Hong Kong developer Li Ka-shing. Li's Concord Pacific Developments unveiled a startling plan for the site, which would have included a financial centre, a mixed-use "international village" and residential towers on a string of islands in a lagoon off Pacific Boulevard. The megaproject alarmed planners and citizens, in part for its elite aloofness. The City took the opportunity to implement development objectives

for livable urbanism established in 1982 under Ray Spaxman, the planning director. Concord Pacific agreed to work with the City to mutual advantage. The lagoon islands were rejected as anti-social, and the replacement plan followed author Jane Jacobs's philosophy of respect for the street grid, pedestrian-friendly neighbourhoods, mixed uses and sufficient density, expressed here as point towers set back from low podiums, softened by landscaping, water features and public access to a new seawall—the mix that has come to be known internationally as "Vancouverism."

QuayWest Resort Residences (1033–1067 Marinaside Crescent, James K.M. Cheng Architects 2002) typifies this manner. Two concrete-and-glass condo towers exploit views of the water and the mountains, while townhouses (and midrises elsewhere) flush to the sidewalks satisfy planners' preference for clearly defined urban streetwalls. A private, landscaped courtyard disguises the density. Architect James Cheng became an adept navigator of this complexity. Spaxman called his buildings "beautifully controlled," in keeping with the overall development, micromanaged by the City's planners. Spaxman's heir, Larry Beasley, oversaw Concord Pacific Place, ensuring that public benefit was gained in tandem with developers' profits. Concord Pacific Place includes more than ten thousand residential units, interleaved with parks, schools, the Roundhouse Community Centre (see next entry), retail and commercial services and a rapid-transit station (G22). This high-density livability achieved by public amenities, efficient (if unexciting) architectural design and recycling industrial land and heritage buildings respects Jacobs's teachings and has stimulated interest from urban planners worldwide.

G20 Roundhouse Community Arts & Recreation Centre
Davie Street and Pacific Boulevard
CPR Engineering Department 1888; Baker McGarva Hart Architects, Forma Design landscape design 1990s; Nick Milkovich Architects, Phillips Farevaag Smallenberg 2011

The Roundhouse is a relic of the city's origins as the CPR's Pacific terminus and of its busy yards and workshops, which covered this north shore of False Creek. Following a standard plan, the Roundhouse was built around a turntable, from which tracks radiated to locomotive service bays in the post-and-beam interior. After closure in 1981 it was stabilized (Hotson Bakker Architects) for use during Expo 86, whose theme was transportation. Redevelopment of the Expo lands led to its retrofit and expansion as a community centre in the 1990s, after the City rejected Concord Pacific's idea that it become a shopping mall. Performance spaces, an exhibition hall, studios and a café occupy the former locomotive repair shop. Additions include a gymnasium. The architects were committed to

the principle that "history should not be too precious; some ruggedness should be kept; a strong and simple order would tell the architectural story." The project was completed with a glazed pavilion (1997) that displays Engine No. 374, which hauled the first transcontinental passenger train into Vancouver in 1887. "Heritage bricks" inscribed with the names of donors to the engine's restoration pave the pavilion's floor. The Roundhouse Turntable Plaza has been upgraded with a high-tech tent-like structure, designed to make the plaza more user friendly.

G21 Former Canadian Westinghouse Company Warehouse
1090 Homer Street
c. 1910; Novam Development 1992

Yaletown was originally the site of the CPR yards (G20) and home to its workers. Some early houses were barged down the Fraser River from the previous yard complex at Yale—hence the name. In the early twentieth century the surrounding area was built out with warehouses served by CPR tracks. The name "Yaletown"

has been extended in the last generation to include this district, as many warehouses were adapted for fresh commercial and residential uses, supplemented by new condo towers and townhouses around the perimeter. Yaletown's warehouses are consistent in scale and character, many built before WWI. They have formal if utilitarian façades, often brick faced. Commercial rehabilitation of this building retained the wood posts and beams and the brick internal walls to create the trendy, semi-industrial look. Cantilevered rear canopies over the retained raised loading docks along Hamilton and Mainland Streets, which had train tracks, fit design guidelines that renovations should reference the past. Nostalgia signalled Yaletown's makeover as a latte-lifestyle, hipster haven (the sheltered loading docks provide perfect café patios). The **Stall Building** (1014 Homer Street, Dominion Construction 1931; 1986), originally used by General Motors, moderne in style, was one of the first rehabs, prompted by post-Expo euphoria and cheap real estate. **The Opus Hotel** (322 Davie Street, Paul Merrick Architects, Hancock Brückner Eng + Wright, Architectura 2002), one of the few new buildings, fits perfectly into the Yaletown ambiance.

G22 Yaletown–Roundhouse Canada Line Station
Bill Curtis Plaza, 200 Davie Street
VIA Architecture 2009

The Canada Line's no-frills design resulted in a utilitarianism so severe (and refreshing) that it might have been imported from North Korea. The stations, mostly underground, are concrete, glass and steel, accented as here with wood on the surface. The architects brought SkyTrain experience to the job. This station is a clever solution to a tight site below and above ground, sidestepping buildings, an underground parkade and a pocket park (Bill Curtis Plaza). The entrance, essentially a glass box, is a contemporary foil to the nearby Roundhouse (G20). In front stands *Equestrian Monument* (David Robinson 2009), a temporary installation that was part of the Canada Line public art program. Just east, at the foot of Davie Street, is *Street Light* (Bernie Miller & Alan Tregebov 1997), whose image-infused, perforated glass-and-metal panels hang from I-beams, another of many art installations in the area. The City of Vancouver's public art program was established in 1990; it requires developers to contribute money for rezoned land to beautify the city. Across the plaza, the rehabilitated **Yaletown Building** (1152 Mainland Street, 1913) displays its street number painted large on the side elevation, a reminder that the district's warehouses were once festooned with painted business signs.

G23 Federal Motor Company Building
1295 Seymour Street
Bedford Davidson 1920; Gower Yeung
& Associates 1995; Merrick Architecture,
Commonwealth Historic Resource
Management 2008

Extensive glazing, an exposed concrete frame and a strong cornice on this former truck showroom have been retained in a careful rehabilitation, which reinforced the building's original luminosity and structural clarity. The X-shaped seismic braces (1995) were allowed to show. This is the heritage tail that wagged the development dog, since its conservation gave the adjacent Élan condominiums bonus height and density.

G24 Yale Hotel
1300 Granville Street
N.S. Hoffar 1890

Developer and alderman J.W. Horne, whose land holdings were reportedly exceeded only by those of the CPR, built this as the Colonial Hotel, rebranded as the Yale in 1911, in an area of railway workers' bunkhouses. The building's style is a watered-down French Second Empire, seen in the mansard roof and arched win-

dows. At full strength the style was popular for government buildings in Canada and the U.S. Next door was the site of the Cecil Hotel, latterly a strip bar, where the *Georgia Straight* newspaper was christened in 1967; Greenpeace activists also met there. The site was rezoned in 2008 and the hotel razed for a condo tower (The Rolston, IBI Group), with the Yale, the "home of Vancouver's rhythm and blues," as the heritage riff. A 1990s neon saxophone above the hotel's 1950s sign adds a jazzy visual note.

G25 888 Beach
888 Beach Avenue
James K.M. Cheng Architects 1993

Distribution of this development's volume is enlivened by a sloping site with views across False Creek. 888 Beach and the lower **Ocean Tower** (also by Cheng;

1501 Howe Street, 1992) exploit the marine theme with curving elevations like 1930s ocean liners. Scaled over a city block on the Granville slopes, with townhouses, mid-rise flats and landscaping, this was a prelude to the full orchestration of Vancouverism that was performed just east at Concord Pacific Place (G19) and later at Coal Harbour (135–138). An alternative typology was **Anchor Point** (1330 Burrard Street, Waisman Architectural Group 1978, 1981). This adopted the continuous streetwall and internal courtyard form common in Europe, updated at The Village at False Creek (G11).

G26 False Creek Yacht Club †
1661 Granville Street
Bing Thom Architects 1990

A one-block walk from the foot of Howe Street, this building is emblematic of the new False Creek, cleaned up but with a residue of industrial and marine iconography. High-tech masts and stays, gangway access, a wrap-around deck and a corrugated metal superstructure with portholes and picture windows give it a cheerful nautical personality. Supported at the creek's edge on dock-like cylindrical steel posts, it is aligned off grid for views of Granville Island (G3–G6), whose industrial vernacular it recalls, and of English Bay seen through the Burrard Bridge (G1). The private club is also emblematic of the new downtown Vancouver—a recreational resort as much as a working city, defined by its views and views of it, and by its waterfront.

Downtown

A BRONZE plaque at the southwest corner of Hastings and Hamilton streets marks the spot where CPR Land Commissioner Lauchlan Hamilton began, in 1885, "to measure an empty land into the streets of Vancouver." This is today's downtown, part of the generous land grant that had accompanied the relocation of the CPR's western terminus from Port Moody to Burrard Inlet in 1886. District Lot 541 extended from Cambie Street west to Burrard Street, between the inlet and False Creek. Vigorous land promotion—and the location of the CPR's station and steamship wharf at the north foot of Howe and Hornby Streets—shifted the nineteenth-century downtown from Main and Hastings to Georgia and Granville, where the railway opened the first Hotel Vancouver in 1887. The Edwardian boom confirmed the permanence of the new downtown with an imposing array of office buildings, stores and banks, the latter in the manner of Greek and Roman temples. The CPR Station of 1914 (H28) remains the prime symbol of that era and of the railway's role in Vancouver's rise "from mill town to metropolis."

Construction of the Art Deco Marine Building (H34) shifted the central business district farther west to Burrard Street. The Depression and WWII prevented further development until the postwar recovery in the 1950s. That optimistic period saw the

Above: Robson Square (H50)

introduction of modernist architecture to Canada, including Vancouver, which was recognized nationally for its progressive architectural culture. Construction of the Vancouver Public Library (H46) and the B.C. Electric office building (H48), both on Burrard Street, gave the city fine examples of both the International Style and its softer West Coast variant. Both survive, although they were stripped down to their concrete frames and reclad in new, if old-looking, curtain walls. Burrard Street boasted other modernist landmarks as well, now demolished or changed beyond recognition.

Vancouver narrowly escaped the comprehensive redevelopment and freeway mania of the 1960s when the CPR's Marathon Realty unveiled Project 200, approved by City Council in 1968, which would have replaced most of Gastown's historic buildings with neo-Corbusian cityscape. The project, conceived when suburban sprawl and auto dependency were acceptable, needed a freeway from Strathcona to Stanley Park, which provoked fierce opposition. The freeway was not built, partly because the federal and provincial governments could not agree to the costs in time. Project 200 was stymied by market forces, the freeway failure and popular disenchantment with grand plans like Pacific Centre.

For a while it seemed as if Vancouver's developers were aiming for new heights, as at the forty-storey Toronto Dominion Tower of Pacific Centre (H2), accompanied by its underground mall and Eaton's department store. But reaction to that trend saw the introduction of enlightened urban planning, taken to an experimental, horizontal extreme in the 1970s at the three-block Robson Square development, a skyscraper tipped on its side (H50).

Nevertheless the physical limits of the downtown peninsula and the demand for growth insist on verticality. Buildings have risen higher and higher, with One Wall Centre (H49) and the Shangri-La (H44)—both residential on the upper floors—eclipsing the previously tallest towers. City planners have done their best to ensure that intense recent densification on and around the downtown peninsula has created a "livable city" with civilized public space and amenities that complement the wonderful natural setting, but the objective remains a challenge. For example, in the mid-2000s, the condo economy's distortion of mixed-use zoning was blamed for a decline in commercial real estate (and tax dollars)—and Coal Harbour seems a resort city for a wealthy elite of Canadians and international investors. The irony here is that few of the heirs of those who fought the freeway find the livable city affordable.

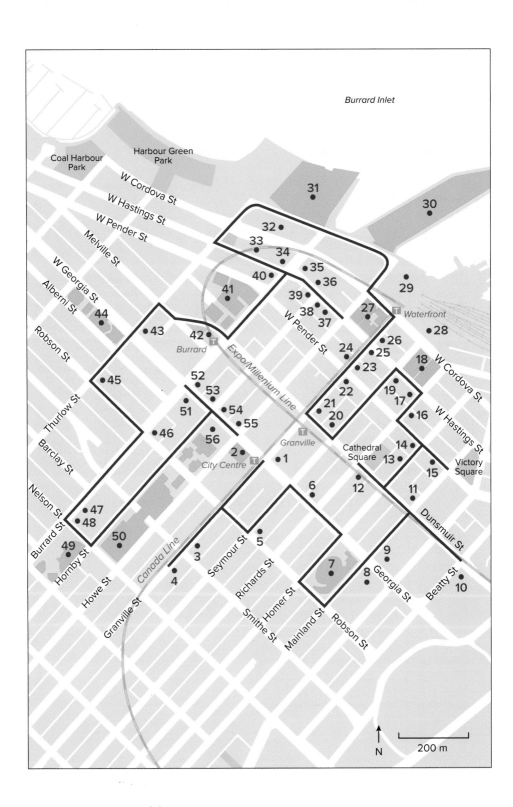

H1 Hudson's Bay Company
674 Granville Street
Burke, Horwood & White 1913; 1926

The Hudson's Bay Company (HBC) helped establish the Georgia and Granville intersection as Vancouver's retail centre when it built a new store (C.O. Wickenden 1893). The Bay's first store had been on Cordova Street (T.C. Sorby 1887). The relocation reflected the shift of business from Main and Hastings, swayed by the arrival of the CPR, its marketing of its land holdings and the developing West End.

The HBC was founded in 1670 in London, and the plans for the present store were approved at the company's head office there, the venture from fur trading into department stores having been recommended by Richard Burbidge, managing director of Harrods, who sat on the HBC board from 1910. Construction started at Georgia and Seymour and extended, replacing Wickenden's building in 1926. The façades are terracotta, similar in appearance to the company's stores in Calgary and Victoria. The Selfridges Department Store in London (Daniel H. Burnham, Francis S. Swales 1909) was the inspiration for their neoclassical style.

The Bay joined the Vancouver Block (Parr & Fee 1912) and the eleven-storey Birks Building (Somervell & Putnam 1913) to form a big-city streetscape, now haunted by the ghost of Birks. The terracotta-clad beauty was demolished in 1974 despite gutsy grassroots opposition, which mobilized the City to initiate its heritage conservation program. Birks's sidewalk clock ("Meet me under the clock," as people used to say) survived

(H25). The Birks Building and the adjacent Georgian Revival Strand Theatre (C. Howard Crane, E.G. Kiehler, C.E. Schley 1919) were replaced by the banal **Scotia Tower** (650 West Georgia Street, Webb, Zerafa, Menkes, Housden Partnership 1977).

The Bay acquired a link to Granville SkyTrain Station in 1985, above which the façade of the **Hunter Brothers Block** (1892), revealed as part of the Hudson development (H21) when modern cladding was removed in 2004, evokes the Bay's 1893 store.

H2 Pacific Centre
701 West Georgia Street
César Pelli, Victor Gruen & Associates, McCarter Nairne & Partners 1976; Zeidler Roberts Partnership 1989; Musson Cattell Mackey Partnership 2002; IBI Group 2008

Derived from the TD Centre, Toronto, master-minded by Ludwig Mies van der Rohe, this three-block development, much of it an underground shopping mall, was begun in 1969. It included the **Toronto Dominion Tower** (1971), Eaton's (1972)—now **Sears** department store—both by Pelli, and the **IBM Building** (1975). All were unadorned, informed by Mies's "less is more" dictum. The architecture was either admired for its austerity (particularly the TD Tower, the city's tallest at the time) or loathed for its look and corporate hubris. The tower and podium design of the **Four Seasons Hotel** (791 West Georgia Street, Webb, Zerafa, Menkes, Housden Partnership 1976) was made less severe, after public criticism of TD's "black tower" led to political intervention by Mayor Art Phillips. More recent attempts to soften the scene are the glazed rotunda (1989) on the plaza at Georgia and Howe and the see-through elevations of Holt Renfrew (2008) at Dunsmuir and Granville.

Pacific Centre consolidated Georgia and Granville as a prime location. It is

connected to the Vancouver Centre beneath the Scotia Tower to the Bay, SkyTrain and a vast underground parkade. The centre's subterranean shopping seemed alien to Vancouver, being similar to those in Toronto and Montreal, which were developed to allow consumers comfort in freezing weather. Pacific Centre suppressed street life, not helped when Granville became a transit mall in the 1970s. The street has revived north of Georgia with up-market retail (H25) and south of Robson as a renewed "entertainment district" (see next two entries). The **Canada Line station** (VIA Architecture 2009) at Georgia and Granville was named Vancouver City Centre, reflecting the intersection's preeminence.

H3 Orpheum Theatre

884 Granville Street/601 Smithe Street

Benjamin Marcus Priteca 1927; Thompson, Berwick, Pratt & Partners 1975–77; Paul Merrick Architects 1983; Aercoustics Engineering, Proscenium Architecture + Interiors 1995, 2010

This lavish western outpost of the Chicago-based Orpheum vaudeville circuit was the largest (2,800-seat) theatre in Canada and the Pacific Northwest. Born in the vaudeville mecca that was Glasgow, Priteca moved to Seattle in 1909, where he became star designer for impresario Alexander Pantages. An early sketch of the Orpheum's façade is stage-set Gothic, not Beaux-Arts as built. That elevation is a prelude to a fantasia of Iberian baroque plasterwork in the multi-level foyer and magnificent auditorium.

By 1973, the theatre had become a tired movie house, threatened with multiplex conversion by Famous Players. A popular campaign prompted the City to buy it and adapt it for the Vancouver Symphony Orchestra. The auditorium was restored and the stage enlarged. The silent movie-era Wurlitzer organ was saved. Octogenarian painter Tony Heinsbergen (Priteca's collaborator) was engaged to return to the Orpheum and paint an "Orpheus" mural in the auditorium's dome. Neon Products restored the 1948 exterior sign. Subsequent work by Vancouver Civic Theatres opened up the Smithe Street façade in 1983, as an extended foyer. Award-winning acoustic improvements (notably the convex sound reflectors) and other alterations commissioned by Rae Ackerman, Civic Theatres' long-serving director, have kept the house and heritage alive. Backstage enlargement and space for the VSO School of Music (843 Seymour Street, Bingham Hill Architects 2011) was gained with a density transfer in 2006 to the same architects' Capitol Residences, an adjacent condo tower on the former Capitol cinema site.

H4 Vogue Theatre

918 Granville Street

Kaplan & Sprachman 1941; 2010

The neon-lit heyday of "Theatre Row" is revived in this Art Deco delight, built for live performances and movies, rehabilitated by Gibbons Hospitality Group. The façade is classic Hollywood deco, a billboard for the fantasy promised inside, with neon and bold typography on a vertical sign topped with a stylized figure of the goddess Diana. It was restored to the original colours; the foyer and auditorium also echo the streamlined styling of the era. The Vogue was the fancy of the Reifel brewing brothers (K36), who also built the **Commodore Ballroom** (868 Granville Street, Henry Herbert Gillingham 1929) with an icing of Art Deco on its brick façade. The revival of Granville Street's entertainment district is illuminated by neon signs, now encouraged; a 1967 bylaw effectively banned displays in the "neon capital of North America," as Vancouver was known (D23).

H5 Telus House
555 Robson Street
1947; Busby + Associates Architects, Read Jones Christoffersen engineers 2007

Begun in 2001, this telecom centre "reused, recycled, went green" to make the 1940s William Farrell Building a model of sustainability. A double-glazed wrap was suspended from the existing elevations to create a double-wall, triple-skinned green building, the first in Canada. The void between the old brick walls and the envelope acts as a ventilation stack and provides insulation. Transparent and fritted glass panels respectively allow

solar gain in winter and shade in summer. Natural ventilation is aided by photovoltaic/battery-charged fans. The retrofit created a healthier workplace. A steel-framed atrium was added directly north. The commitment to sustainability will be advanced in an architecturally and structurally ambitious plan for a corporate headquarters called **Telus Garden** (Henriquez Partners Architects), announced in 2011. The massive commercial and residential development will abut Telus House and fill the city block.

H6 Cavelti Building
555 West Georgia Street
Townley & Matheson 1928;
Blewett Dodd Ching Lee 1991

Formerly the Randall Building, for S.W. Randall, horse-racing promoter and one-time owner of Exhibition Park (E17), this building on a site zoned for higher density was saved by the enthusiasm of jeweller Toni Cavelti. The successful restoration of the neo-Gothic terracotta above renovated storefronts, and the additional floor on the roof (the increased density, set back to respect the original façade) created a showpiece for the City's heritage

density bonus program. Application of the program, which also can bank and transfer unused density from heritage sites to new buildings, has since become standard procedure. City heritage designation (legal protection) is mandatory in such agreements. Designation here was flexible enough to allow the addition of a mural, of medieval goldsmiths at work (Kitty Mykka 1993).

H7 Library Square ↑
350 West Georgia Street
Moshe Safdie & Associates,
Downs/Archambault 1995

Architect Safdie denied any resemblance to the Colosseum in Rome in this international competition-winning entry, typical of postmodernism's selective, often arbitrary, use of the past. The jury, chaired by Mayor Gordon Campbell, gave it the thumbs up after a public vote—based on the three finalists' models, exhibited anonymously—favoured the concept. The competition prospectus excluded upcoming talent. UBC architecture students with placards reading "West Coast style?" turned up at the grand opening dressed in togas—a private joke, as architect Safdie once remarked of postmodernism, in a public place.

Safdie's original schematic was breathtaking. A top-glazed, curving galleria within a faux-classical precast wrap enclosed a modernist library block. The project was to be festooned like the Hanging Gardens of Babylon. As built, it does not look like them, but a green roof was planted (Cornelia Hahn Oberlander 1995), inaccessible to the public because two floors were added to the library on a twenty-year lease to the provincial government. A tower for federal government offices also helped finance the project.

Library Square's design rejected the assumed elitism of traditional public buildings. The public flocked to see its Piranesian spaces. Cafés and retail make the venue inclusive like a mall, a gathering place for new users the VPL attracted in record numbers. That interior focus came at a cost to the perimeter, which disregards the downtown grid, although the south-facing plaza proved popular. More significant than the urban design, or whether or not Library Square's exterior should have referred to its predecessor's West Coast modernism (H46)—was that the VPL board anticipated the downtown residential boom and built a facility for it, centered in the heart of a cultural precinct that includes the Queen Elizabeth Theatre, the Playhouse Theatre and the CBC.

H8 CBC/Radio-Canada Vancouver
700 Hamilton Street
Thompson, Berwick, Pratt & Partners 1975;
Hotson Bakker Boniface Haden 2009

The 1970s building is now a backdrop for a bright CBC news centre. The former, an example of "brutalism"—coined from the French *béton brut*, referring to concrete left raw, as poured—was nicknamed "the bunker" because it looked like one and the studios were underground, for acoustic reasons. The aesthetic was championed by architects, but the public (and CBC staff in this case) was less receptive. This building's mechanical systems were on the top floors from where six ventilation ducts—set outside to prevent transmission of vibrations to the studios—plunged to a plaza, creating an effect that, while invigorating, was more industrial than cultural.

In 2009, the news centre brought the basement to the plaza to give the corporation a more friendly face. The new building is sleek, largely transparent, allowing the public a glimpse of news broadcasts as they happen. The plaza (PWL Partnership landscape design 2009) includes *The Wall*, a Vancouver Heritage Foundation public art initiative. To help fund the new centre, CBC sold its parking lot to Concord Pacific Developments, which built the residential **TV Towers** at 788 Hamilton Street and 233 Robson Street (Hotson Bakker Boniface Haden 2009).

H9 Queen Elizabeth Theatre
649 Cambie Street
Affleck, Desbarats, Dimakopoulos, Lebensold, Michaud & Sise 1962; Erickson/Massey Architects 1986; Aercoustics Engineering; Proscenium Architecture + Interiors 2009

Designed by a stellar group of Montreal architects, who would later be known as Arcop (Architects in Co-partnership), this major investment was the result of an open competition held by the City in 1954. The theatre's massing and its foyer's transparency and relationship to the plaza resembled the new and highly acclaimed Royal Festival Hall, London (1951); the theatre was opened by Queen Elizabeth II. A long-awaited renovation fixed the building's seismic, mechanical and acoustic deficiencies. The foyer was

heightened, and 1980s "improvements" were dismantled to revive the original character. The adjoining **Vancouver Playhouse** (1962), an integral part of the original complex, was also renovated.

From the same era, on a gigantic scale, is the **Vancouver Main Post Office** (349 West Georgia Street, McCarter Nairne & Partners, Department of Public Works 1958), the world's largest welded steel structure when built. The vast postal hall is one of the city's finest modern public spaces, comparable with that at Waterfront Station (H28). A tunnel connected the post office to the station, but airmail forced its closure in 1965. In 2011, Canada Post announced a future move to YVR. First Nations claim the post office block (and many other federal sites), based on the fact that no treaties to settle land claims on mainland B.C. were signed in the nineteenth century.

H10 **Beatty Street Drill Hall**
620 Beatty Street
David Ewart, Department of Public Works 1901

This pseudo-medieval fortress, home of the British Columbia Regiment, has granite foundations, 3-foot-thick brick walls,

battlements and twin turrets to express its military function. When built, it faced a parade ground (Larwill Park) across the street; an escarpment drops at the rear. The drill hall would have been a landmark in a visionary plan by Bing Thom in 1996 to construct the Vancouver Convention & Exhibition Centre (H31) under the escarpment, with the old parade ground above as a public plaza and Georgia Street as a Champs-Élysées. In 2011, City Council agreed to reserve two-thirds of Larwill Park for a proposed relocation of the Vancouver Art Gallery (H56).

H11 Del Mar Inn
553 Hamilton Street
William P. White 1912

To clear this site for the **B.C. Hydro Building** (333 Dunsmuir Street, Musson Cattell Mackey Partnership 1992), the company acquired and tore down properties in the way—except this one. George Riste, owner of the Del Mar Hotel, had provided affordable digs for Downtown Eastsiders for two decades. He put social conscience before profit and refused to sell. Comment was irresistible. The Contemporary Art Gallery, located at the Del Mar at the time, installed a typographic frieze (Kathryn Walter 1990) above the ground floor: *Unlimited Growth Increases the Divide*. The B.C. Hydro tower cascades with postmodern design clichés—a decline in the quality of patronage from its elegant predecessor (H48).

H12 Holy Rosary Cathedral
646 Richards Street
Thomas Enner Julian 1900

The cornerstone of this splendid cathedral for the Roman Catholic parish (founded in 1885) was laid in 1899. The style is French Gothic, popular in Catholic parishes in Quebec, with asymmetrical spires to have been more elaborate: flying buttresses at the base of the taller one were not installed. The plan is conventional, cruciform. Ribbed vaulting accentuates the nave, transepts and altar. Stained glass by Charles Champigneulle of Paris and Guido Nincheri of Montreal is exceptional, as is the full peal of bells. The building and steeples were re-roofed in 1995, with zinc imitating slate. The adjoining rectory is attractive, with contextual stonework.

H13 The Salvation Army Belkin House
555 Homer Street
Neale Staniszkis Doll Adams Architects 2004

The "Sally Ann" calls this facility a "home for the homeless," and the design gives those who use it dignity. The communal main floor is spacious and maximizes available daylight. Rooms above all have views, some inward over a raised courtyard. The building acknowledges the existing streetscape, picking up the proportions of the West Pender Building

(see next entry) but in a modernist manner. To the north is **Central City Lodge** (415 West Pender Street, 1995), slightly more heritage conscious, another shelter by the same architects.

H14 West Pender Building
402 West Pender Street
Henry Sandham Griffith 1912

This Chicago Style block, composed like a classical column with base, body and cornice, and elevations expressing the modern structural frame, was built for British Columbia Securities and the Dominion Trust. The period interior is remarkable, including the old banking hall, which Henriquez Partners Architects converted for their office. The basement housed what the press had once called the "safest armour steel vaults in the West." They were until January 1977, when a Montreal gang broke in from the fire escape in the alley on a Friday night, drilled through concrete and steel plate and ransacked 1,200 safety deposit boxes, before being nabbed at the airport.

The Edwardian boom gave Vancouver a clutch of similar buildings—the **Lumbermen's Building** (509 Richards Street, J.P. Matheson & Son 1911; Gair Williamson Architects 2008) for example, built for another of Vancouver's early financial institutions (the North West Trust Company) riding the pre-WWI building boom—that shot up ten storeys or more on narrow lots.

H15 300-block West Pender Street
1906–29; 1997

The frankly contemporary **Covenant House**, formerly Vancity Place for Youth (326 West Pender Street, Nigel Baldwin Architects 1997), achieves a similar contextual fit to Belkin House (H13), on a smaller scale. It incorporates the

Georgian Revival **McBeth & Campbell Printers & Binders** (J.S.D. Taylor 1929) and complements, without pastiche, the chunky Richardsonian Romanesque **Lyric Theatre** (300 West Pender, 1906), a Royal Canadian Legion branch after WWII, and the **B.C. Permanent Loan Company** (330 West Pender Street, Hooper & Watkins 1907). The latter is a Beaux-Arts bauble displaying the hallmarks of the style: symmetrical plan and elevation, paired classical columns and a pediment framing an arch, spandrel and columned entrance. Its Tiffany-style stained-glass dome by Henry Bloomfield & Sons in the former banking hall is a treasure.

Across the lane is the old **Bank of British Columbia** (490 West Hastings Street, Thomas Charles Sorby 1889), one of the few downtown buildings surviving from the first generation of commercial construction. Traces of past elegance remain on this much-abused Italian Renaissance Revival structure, arcaded (with finely carved capitals) on the Richards Street ground floor. Its English-born architect arrived in Vancouver in 1886, aged fifty, at the height of his powers. His ability was not given full rein by his "colonial" clients, including the CPR for whom he designed the first Hotel Vancouver (1887; demolished 1913).

H16 Century House
432 Richards Street
John Smith Davidson Taylor 1912

A pediment topped with beavers is the Canadian content on this curiosity, built as the Canada Permanent Mortgage Building. Taylor trained in Aberdeen, the Scottish "Granite City," before he opened an office in Vancouver in 1909. The façade is granite, the feel is Greek and the blend of old world elements eccentric, unconstrained by precedent other than the Scottish Greek Revival and the idiosyncratic neoclassicism of Taylor's hometown.

H17 Standard Building
510 West Hastings Street
Russell & Babcock 1914

Vertical emphasis and spiky Gothic terracotta since removed from the top floor showed the influence, without a spire, of the Woolworth Building (1912) in New York. The architects were a Tacoma firm, best known as the designers of Gover-

nor's Mansion at Olympia, Washington. The surviving ornamentation is classical and heraldic. The lobby—complete with a vintage Cutler Mail Box and chute—is exuberant, and the former banking hall retains its period plasterwork. **The Seymour Building** (525 Seymour Street, Somervell & Putnam 1912) introduced skyscraper Gothic to Vancouver.

H18 Harbour Centre †
555 West Hastings Street
McCarter & Nairne 1928; Webb, Zerafa, Menkes, Housden Partnership, Eng & Wright 1977

An office tower with a revolving restaurant accessed by exterior elevators looms above this city block. More significant than the flying saucer–shaped restaurant (aspiring "world-class" cities had to have one) was the adaptive reuse of the Art Deco Spencer's Department Store (515 West Hastings Street) by Simon Fraser University as a downtown campus (Aitken Wreglesworth Associates 1990). This brought out-of-office-hours activity to the city centre at a time when planners sought ways to redirect the drift to

suburbia and revive declining downtown cores. Spencer's, a rival of Woodward's (A25), was established in Victoria in 1873 by Welsh immigrant David Spencer. Eaton's took over the chain in 1948 and later vacated the Hastings Street store for a move uptown to Pacific Centre (H2), prompting this block's redevelopment.

H19 Morris J. Wosk Centre for Dialogue †
580 West Hastings Street/ 438 Seymour Street
Somervell & Putnam 1920; Architectura 1999

The centre occupies the former Toronto Dominion Bank building, now part of Conference Plaza, a mixed-used development of condos, shops, offices and a hotel covering most of a city block. The developer, Allied Holdings, donated the bank, which had been vacated, to SFU. The building was a late flowering of neoclassicism, Edwardian in spirit and Greco-Roman in inspiration; its American architects had designed some of Vancouver's best architecture of the pre-WWI era. It is now an international conference

centre, entered off Seymour Street where a glazed addition steps out to a courtyard, once the alley. The banking hall was reconfigured (with the original coffered ceiling retained) as a circular forum and named Asia Pacific Hall (a legacy of Canada's Asia Pacific Conference in 1997).

H20 British Columbia Institute of Technology ↑
555 Seymour Street
Architectura 1997

Billed as Western Canada's first "smart" building, with all systems computer controlled, this downtown campus (the main campus is in Burnaby) shimmers with a techno glow. The facility fits a tight site but has spatial clarity. The entrance is a glazed bay, with a steel staircase (George Third & Son fabricator) suspended from a top-floor truss, from where it seems to float above the foyer. Concrete columns are exposed as they ascend through the building; the aluminum-and-steel exterior is softened inside with blond wood; lighting is an adjustable blend of solar

and artificial sources. BCIT's students, like those attending SFU (H18), the Vancouver Film School and numerous English language (ESL) schools, add street life and sociability to the area.

H21 Shoppers Drug Mart ↑
586 Granville Street
McCarter & Nairne 1958; 2006

The corner was cut away for a retail entrance to this CIBC branch after its closure in 2005. Exterior integrity was lost, as was the original banking hall. A superb mosaic mural by B.C. Binning was preserved in situ after Heritage Vancouver argued it should be retained and be visible. Binning—whose star was sparkling in decorative designs for the B.C. Electric Building (H48)—spent four months in Venice to oversee its preparation. The client was the Imperial Bank of Canada, which commissioned it to celebrate B.C.'s no-limits, resource-based economy. Its confident iconography now seems poignant. Across Dunsmuir Street are the façades of the former **B.C. Electric Show-**

room (Hodgson & Simmonds, McCarter & Nairne 1928), with faux-Mediterranean window bays in cast bronze, retained, with the Hunter Brothers Block (H1), as a heritage trade-off for **The Hudson** condominium (610 Granville Street, Stantec Architecture 2006).

H22 Segal Graduate School of Business †

500 Granville Street

Somervell & Putnam 1916; Kenneth Guscotte Rea 1925; Merrick Architecture, Donald Luxton & Associates 2005

Built for the Merchants Bank of Canada, this neoclassical palazzo was enlarged by the Bank of Montreal as its main branch after it acquired the Merchants Bank in 1921. Montreal architect Rea added three bays up Granville Street and included a Corinthian-columned entrance and the bank's coat-of-arms above the cornice. He also continued Somervell & Putnam's subtle neoclassical ornament, much of it terracotta. SFU continued as a savior of downtown heritage architecture (H18, H19), with an adaptive reuse of the building as a business school after the bank moved out in 2001. The façades and banking hall were restored. Coffered ceilings flow through and unify space subdivided as meeting and event rooms. A seismic upgrade and state-of-the-art systems were required, de rigueur on heritage rehabs of this size and quality.

H

H24 Toronto Dominion Bank Building

499 Granville Street/717 West Pender Street
McCarter & Nairne 1951; Musson Cattell Mackey Partnership 2008

H23 Rogers Building

470 Granville Street
Gould & Champney 1912

Seattle architects, drawn to B.C.'s economic boom, designed this handsome, reinforced-concrete structure, clad with white terracotta tiles reportedly shipped from Chicago. Marble columns frame the entrance. Glazed terracotta withstands—indeed, shines in—the wet climate of the Pacific Northwest. When Augustus Warren Gould returned to Seattle, he designed the similar Arctic Building (1917), with ornamental terracotta walrus heads instead of the numerous lions here. His client in Vancouver was Jonathan Rogers, developer, alderman, public benefactor, who arrived on the first passenger train from Montreal in 1887. Vancouver's legendary chronicler, Chuck Davis, had an office in the building in the mid-1990s.

Canada Permanent Building

455 Granville Street
McCarter & Nairne 1951; Musson Cattell Mackey Partnership 2008

The five-storey Canada Permanent Building (above) is stripped-back classicism with a marble and stone façade, indicating a conservative client. The other, built for the Dominion Bank of Canada, is more progressive with horizontal emphasis and finned solar shading (*brise soleil*, popularized by Le Corbusier) in a manner that was—and still seems—entirely modern. The Canada Permanent's modernity was its vault, claimed to be the only atomic bomb-proof one in Canada—a relic of the Cold War. The buildings symbolize post-WWII economic recovery and the beginning of Vancouver's transformation to a "post-industrial" economy. Corporate mergers resulted in both buildings' being owned by TD Bank.

H25 Birks Building
698 West Hastings Street
Darling & Pearson 1908; Oberto Oberti 1994

The Toronto-based architects of this temple bank (originally the Canadian Bank of Commerce) deployed massive fluted Ionic columns and an imposing cornice. The effect is severe, more Greek than Roman with deeply modelled elevations. The building was refurbished by Novam Development for Henry Birks & Sons, the Montreal-based jeweller. Birks's famous cast-iron clock, manufactured by E. Howard & Company of Boston, was moved from the previous location at the base of the Scotia Tower (H1). Retail visibility required heritage-style canopies and display windows, with flashings like false eyelashes, punched into the bank's solid base (the brass doors are original).

H26 Royal Bank Building
675 West Hastings Street
Sumner Godfrey Davenport 1931; Blewett Dodd Architecture 2000

The Royal Bank influenced the business district's shift from Hastings and Main when it built Vancouver's first temple bank at 400 West Hastings (Dalton & Eveleigh 1903). That building was downgraded to branch status when the Royal moved to this palatial tower. Architect Davenport had worked with the New York firm York & Sawyer on the design for the Royal Bank's headquarters, a neoclassical skyscraper in Montreal completed in 1928. The style here, with neo-Romanesque exterior details and a splendid Florentine banking hall, is similar to the contemporaneous Canadian Bank of Commerce tower in Toronto (York & Sawyer, Darling & Pearson). The Vancouver building's half-finished appearance was due to the Depression. It was repaired externally in 2000.

POST OFFICE BUILDING

FEDERAL BUILDING

WINCH BUILDING

H27 Sinclair Centre

757 West Hastings Street
Henriquez & Partners, Toby Russell Buckwell &
Partners 1986

POST OFFICE BUILDING
David Ewart, Department of Public Works 1910

FEDERAL BUILDING
T.W. Fuller, Department of Public Works;
McCarter & Nairne 1937

WINCH BUILDING
Hooper & Watkins 1911

CUSTOMS EXAMINING WAREHOUSE
David Ewart 1913

Sinclair Centre, identified by the Post
Office Building's clock tower at Hastings and Granville, is the only downtown
block to retain all its heritage architecture. Its four heritage buildings were rehabilitated in this imaginative retail and
office project for the federal government,
which owned the site. The intervention

CUSTOMS EXAMINING WAREHOUSE

was focused behind the façades, where an atrium was inserted, separated from the old alley-facing elevations (the alley's alignment was retained as a covered passage between Granville and Howe Streets). The atrium forms an inner public square in the glass-roofed manner of nineteenth-century European arcades, with varied levels animating the spatial experience.

The Beaux-Arts-style Post Office Building is an exuberant neo-baroque essay by Public Works' chief architect; the Winch Building at Hastings and Howe, designed for railway worker and cowboy-turned-cannery king and real estate magnate Richard Vance Winch, is Italianate, slightly stiff but well cut, reflecting Winch's social status; the brick-and-stone Customs Examining Warehouse is squat Chicago Style, stern; the Federal Building (the post office extension) at Cordova and Granville has classically derived elevations enlivened with Art Deco details.

H28 Waterfront Station ↑
601 West Cordova Street
Barott, Blackader & Webster 1914; Hawthorn Mansfield Towers Architects 1978

The CPR built three stations in succession here, each larger and more extravagant as rail services, and the company's steamship routes to Asia (H30), expanded. The first was a single-storey shed on a wharf (1886) at the foot of Howe Street; the second, a château-style terminal (Edward Maxwell 1898)—an offspring of the design survives at New Westminster (N23). This third essay has a spacious concourse decorated with salon-style paintings of the untamed landscape through which the railway builders triumphed. Its fusion of façade colonnade with grand hall is typical of Beaux-Arts stations, which were big enough to be adaptable after passenger rail services declined. Renamed Waterfront Station (the elegant CPR typography remains above the colonnade), it is now a transit hub for bus routes, SeaBus, SkyTrain and the West Coast Express commuter train, which runs along Burrard Inlet on the original CPR tracks (SkyTrain uses the CPR-built Dunsmuir Tunnel under downtown). The CPR's eloquent **war memorial** (Coeur de Lion MacCarthy 1922) stands outside.

H29 Granville Square
200 Granville Street
Francis Donaldson 1973

Built by the Canadian Pacific's Marathon Realty on a massive concrete podium constructed astride the CPR tracks, this was the only tall building to emerge from Project 200 (A8). A vast viewing deck was provided on top of the podium, to have been part of a network of walkways and plazas. Donaldson worked on the MacMillan Bloedel Building (H43), and his tower here has a similar muscularity. It was the tallest reinforced-concrete building in the country when completed. Harbour air traffic (mostly float planes) is controlled from the roof, where the world's highest air-traffic control tower, at 465 feet (141 meters), was commissioned in 1978.

H30 Canada Place
999 Canada Place
Zeidler Roberts Partnership, Musson Cattell Mackey Partnership, Downs/Archambault 1986; Musson Cattell Mackey Partnership 2003; Ledcor Group 2011

Built on the foundations of Canadian Pacific's Pier B-C (1927), this flagship opened as the Canadian pavilion for Expo 86. Its high-tech, cable-stayed, sail-like roof was conceived, like the Sydney Opera House, as a harbour icon. It was designed to combine a hotel, cruise ship terminal and the Vancouver Trade & Con-

vention Centre (as it was called, in the former pavilion under the "sails"), and is the headquarters of Port Metro Vancouver—Canada's largest and busiest port.

The complex is a megastructure, a building-type predicted in the 1960s by the Archigram group in London but never actually built. Archigram's megastructures were futuristic, multifunctional and modular; one was designed to move on mechanical stilts. Canada Place looks as though it too could move, sail off to Asia like the CP's Empress liners, which once docked at Pier B-C. But although there are many buildings in Vancouver whose departure would be welcomed, this is not one. Its promenade decks are a gift to the public realm. It was built partly on air rights above rail tracks, like Place Bonaventure in Montreal (1967), also a trade and convention megastructure. It was elongated (2003) at the prow, to berth more Alaska-bound cruise ships. A roof rehabilitation (2011) replaced the "sail" fabric. Its Heritage Horns, which boom out the first four notes of "O Canada" at midday from the roof of the Pan Pacific Hotel, were acquired from the B.C. Hydro Building in 1994 (H48).

H31 Vancouver Convention & Exhibition Centre

1055 Canada Place

DA Architects + Planners, Musson Cattell Mackey Partnership, LMN Architects, Glotman Simpson Consulting Engineers, PWL Partnership landscape design 2009

A decade of debate culminated in this expansion of Canada Place, led by B.C. Premier Gordon Campbell and Tourism Vancouver. Hosting conventions is big business that requires correspondingly big spaces. The new centre more than tripled the capacity, to 466,500 square feet. It maintained the existing brand identity and its waterfront location's marketing advantages. Huge cost overruns were justified by the projected economic benefits and its use as the media centre for the 2010 Winter Olympic Games (the Olympic cauldron remains on nearby Jack Poole Plaza, named for the chair of the Vancouver Organizing Committee).

The building is massive, with function rooms and foyers (clad with local Douglas-fir and hemlock) above a low-level exhibition hall. It is supported on 826 steel piles, with 40 per cent of its precast concrete deck and steel-trussed upper structure built over water. Seawater heating and cooling, an artificial-reef fish habitat built into the foundation, and a 6-acre, slanted "living roof" (grassed like a West Coast cliff-top coastal meadow) are among the sustainable features that gained the facility LEED Platinum certification in 2010, a world first for a convention centre. Security prevents public access to the green roof, but a walkway continues the Coal Harbour seawall around the structure. The plaza, also massive, is given humour by Douglas Coupland's *Digital Orca* artwork (2010).

H32 Fairmont Pacific Rim
1038 Canada Place
James K.M. Cheng Architects 2010

Shaw Tower
1067–1077 West Cordova Street
James K.M. Cheng Architects 2004

A creative collaboration between the architect and developer Ian Gillespie produced these assertive towers, whose vertical multi-use is a concept common in Asian cities from Singapore to Shanghai. The Fairmont Pacific Rim (forty-four storeys; by floor space the largest downtown building), somewhat triangular in plan, has luxury residences above a five-star hotel that benefits from being adjacent to the new Convention Centre (see previous entry). The forty-one-storey Shaw Tower's sixteen lower floors are commercial (twelve for Shaw Communications and one for Westbank Projects, the developer of both buildings), bucking the trend that was converting downtown Vancouver to a residential zone. The upper floors have 130 live-work condo units within an arrowhead-shaped plan with set-back landscaped terraces. The Shaw Tower's nightscape features a vertical light sculpture (Diana Thater 2004) to bring "pizzazz," as Gillespie put it, to the city's public art scene; the Fairmont has a poetic typographic artwork (Liam Gillick 2009).

H33 Guinness Tower
1055 West Hastings Street
Charles Paine & Associates 1969

This vintage high-rise, with glass-and-aluminum curtain walls composed with Miesian minimalism, lightness and clarity, is Vancouver's purest example of the International Style, although the TD Tower (H2) gives it a run for its

money. The only decoration is in the lobby, where a surrealist ceramic artwork, *The Fathomless Richness of the Seabed* by Catalan-born Quebec artist Jordi Bonet, relates the tower to its setting (and echoes the decor at the Marine Building; see next entry). **Oceanic Plaza** (1066 West Hastings Street, 1977), was a distinguished follow-up in the same style by the same architects.

H34 Marine Building
355 Burrard Street
McCarter & Nairne 1930; Paul Merrick
Architects 1988

Called "the best Art Deco office building in the world" by poet laureate and architecture aficionado Sir John Betjeman, the Marine Building celebrates seaborne trade and transport with a decorative scheme of astonishing variety. Terracotta trim drips with stylized sea life, ships of exploration and symbols of transportation; star signs of the zodiac on the floor of the lobby represent navigation. The decor was designed in house, and by Ernest A. Batchelder, prominent in the Arts and Crafts movement in California. Batchelder-style terracotta can also be seen on the Marine Building's only regional rival, the Northern Life Tower (1929) in Seattle. The *Chicago Tribune* architectural competition of 1922 and the Exposition des Arts Décoratifs held in Paris in 1925 were the sources of both structures' set-back form and style of ornamentation.

McCarter & Nairne's vision was described in *The Vancouver Sun*'s opening-day supplement (October 7, 1930): "The building suggests some great marine rock rising from the sea, clinging with sea flora and fauna, tinted in sea green, flashed with gold, at night a dim silhouette piercing the sea mists." Ron Nairne was the poet-artist, J.Y. McCarter the hard-nosed engineer—a perfect partnership. The promoter was Lieutenant Commander J.W. Hobbs, an expat Englishman; the developer was Stimson's Canadian Development Company, Toronto. They sought to exploit the port's position on the imperial "All Red Route" and to tap into trade to Europe via the Panama Canal.

At twenty-one storeys of steel frame, with concrete floor slabs and brick cladding, it was the tallest building in the British Empire. It had the fastest elevators on the continent west of New York (and a private one to the penthouse, occupied for a time by A.J.T. Taylor, whose British Pacific Building Company bought the mortgaged masterpiece in 1933). McCarter & Nairne leased space, along with the Vancouver Merchants Exchange and marine-related businesses for which it was intended.

Upgrades in the 1980s maintained the landmark's status but replaced the "battleship linoleum" lobby floor (imported from Scotland, now in the Vancouver Museum); the Merchants' Exchange (on the main floor) became a harbourview restaurant. McCarter & Nairne's vision, of the building "rising from the sea," has since been obscured by recent towers. In a city obsessed with views, that vision should have been protected.

H35 AXA Place
999 West Hastings Street
Musson Cattell Mackey Partnership 1981; 2009

Daon Developments was a major player and needed a built image to show it. This elegant tower, originally called the Daon Building, accomplished that, although not in the form intended. The project was a test case for a civic-oriented approach to development approval that was formulated after the 1974 municipal election. The objective was not to discourage development but to steer it to provide community benefit as well as profit. Density incentives were floated to persuade developers to respect the local context and enhance the public realm. In effect, architects and their clients were encouraged to learn good manners. A brutalist hulk proposed here was rejected, its bulky massing eliminated in this alternative. Floor plans were cut at the edges (most have fourteen corner offices); the tower's light footprint on the site was oriented for a landscaped plaza. The plaza respects the Marine Building, which the Daon Building's glazing reflects, and preserved a view (now obscured) across Coal Harbour to Stanley Park. An energy-efficient retrofit was completed in 2009.

H36 Vancouver Club
915 West Hastings Street
Sharp & Thompson 1914; Musson Cattell Mackey Partnership 1992

Established in 1889, the club's first building was located here in 1891, close to the CPR pier and station, the emerging business district and members' mansions in "Blueblood Alley." Sharp & Thompson, recently arrived from England, transplanted a London gentlemen's club, a social environment with which the Van-

couver Club's then all-male, all-white members were familiar or to which they aspired. The style is Italian Renaissance, with Edwardian posturing. The brickwork and stone trim add a Georgian Revival aura. A 1992 exterior makeover carried the façade treatment around the east side to the north elevation. Sharp & Thompson also designed the Spanish Colonial Revival, long-defunct **Quadra Club** (1021 West Hastings, 1929), the heritage pawn in a high-rise gambit that intrudes between the Marine Building and the Guinness Tower.

H37 Jameson House
838 West Hastings Street
Foster + Partners, Walter Francl Architecture,
Robert Lemon Architect 2011

The 2008 recession and financial restructuring delayed this big-name addition to the skyline, designed in 2004. The big name was Sir Norman Foster, leading light of British high-tech and founder of an international practice whose buildings range from the Hongkong & Shanghai Bank headquarters in Hong Kong (1986) to the revitalization of the Reichstag in Berlin (1999).

Jameson House is a mixed-use retail, office and residential project, each element expressed in vertical composition. A heritage density bonus preserved the terracotta façade of the **B.C. & Yukon Chamber of Mines** (built for the Royal Financial Company; J.C. Day 1927) and the Georgian Revival **Ceperley Rounsefell Building** (Sharp & Thompson 1921). These form a traditional streetwall; the office floors are set back above this to create an illusion of heritage volume, disguising the façadism of the Chamber of Mines and Ceperley Rounsefell buildings. Neither compromises the modernity of the new structure, which also acknowledges the adjacent Crédit Foncier Building (see

next entry), from whose cornice level Jameson House's quadruple shafts of curved condos rise. Foster is one of the handful of "starchitects" whose name alone can elevate a project from trite to trophy. Vancouver's aesthetically circumspect planning culture has not exactly embraced big foreign names; the achievement here (lead architect Nigel Dancey) is a building that fits its context as much as it does the Foster brand.

H38 Crédit Foncier Building
850 West Hastings Street
Barott, Blackader & Webster 1914

Built for the Montreal-based Crédit Foncier Franco-Canadien, this reinforced-concrete commercial palazzo reworks classical themes with just the right blend of flamboyance and refinement. Façades rise from a Corinthian-columned entrance and pilastered arcade to a two-storey eaves gallery and a decorative

copper cornice. Then, as now, construction was labour intensive. Contractor H.L. Stevens & Company assigned a dozen stonemasons to cut the stone blocks and carve the thirty-six Corinthian capitals (more than on any other city building).

H39 Bank of Canada Building
900 West Hastings Street
Thompson, Berwick, Pratt & Partners 1965

Precast concrete panels add texture to this tower above a foursquare street-level podium, built to the same height as the Hudson's Bay Insurance Building (William A. Doctor 1912), which stood directly west until demolished (c. 1985). The old building's façade, salvaged and fastened to the podium, demonstrates the folly of façadism—buildings are understood from their plan. The Bank of Canada's is cruciform, projected up to allow views from eight (rather than the conventional four) corners. The abstract precast pattern created a futuristic rather than "New Formalist" (H41) effect, but

the intent was the same: to soften the International Style's austerity (H33). In 1999, the podium was opened up for retail space.

H40 Douglas Jung Building
401 Burrard Street
Architectura 2002

This federal government building is the successor to its former Customs Building (C.B.K. Van Norman 1954; demolished 1993), one of Vancouver's mid-century modern landmarks along Burrard Street either torn down or defaced. Its demolition prompted the creation of the City's Recent Landmarks Program, which can award heritage status if a building is at least twenty years old. The new design recycled the Customs Building's

black granite and nods to its predecessor's scale and relationship to the Marine Building. It is eco-friendly and its public realm more open. It was named for Howard Charles Green, a minister of public works in the 1950s, but renamed in 2007 to reflect a changing social recognition. Douglas Jung, who became the first Chinese-Canadian MP in 1957, was a soldier in a special forces unit in Asia in WWII. His service, with other Chinese Canadians, won the right to vote that had previously been denied.

H41 Bentall Centre
500-block Burrard Street
Frank W. Musson & Associates 1969, 1974, 1981; Musson Cattell Mackey Partnership 2007

Charles Bentall arrived in B.C. from England in 1908 as a draftsman, worked for steel fabricator John Coughlan & Sons when the firm built the Sun Tower (A23) and became president of Dominion Construction, which he steered to success that culminated in this flagship development. White precast concrete fluting and rooftop epaulettes on the first two towers created the effect of an attenuated classical temple in the "New Formalist" manner. A miniature temple of finance was provided for the Bank of Montreal at the corner of Dunsmuir and Burrard. The third and fourth towers continued the theme with less aplomb. **Bentall Five** (550 Burrard Street), all glass with a trendy twist to the curtain wall, ignored it. A bronze sculpture by Seattle-born artist George Tsutakawa survives as a period piece on the original plaza. The more assertive **Royal Centre** (1055 West Georgia Street, Dirassar, James, Jorgenson & Davis, Webb Zerafa Menkes 1972) expanded Bentall's "city within a city" concept (H2).

H42 **Burrard Station**
625 Burrard Street
Allen Parker & Associates, Baker McGarva Hart,
Don Vaughan landscape design 1986

Architects Baker McGarva Hart (now
VIA Architecture) established the design rationale for the Expo, Millennium
and Canada Line stations and completed
detailed design for some. This Expo Line
station is bright, spacious and easy to
navigate despite its several levels. A mini-
plaza was provided on Burrard Street,
from where the transition from street
level to the station's skylit concourse
and the trains below is seamless. Like
all apparently simple solutions, this one
required attention to detail. Considered
integral was the leftover part of the triangular site, where the public realm was
enhanced with a layered pocket park,
named for Captain George Vancouver's
ship, HMS *Discovery*.

H43 **MacMillan Bloedel Building**
1075 West Georgia Street
Erickson/Massey 1969; Arthur Erickson
Architects 1993

Forestry giant MacMillan Bloedel was, as
Erickson put it, "a pretty rough company
needing a gutsy building." J.V. Clyne,
CEO, was the perfect client. He told Erickson, "I don't know anything about
architecture; I leave it up to you." The
structure has been likened to an old-

growth tree—it tapers from eight feet
thick at plaza level to eight inches on the
top floors—but that was the consequence
of Erickson's decision to build it with
poured-in-place, load-bearing concrete.
The result is monumental and elegant.
Erickson called it his "Doric façade." Two
slabs are offset, a dynamic that optically
reduces the bulk; deep-set windows add
texture. MacBlo was a lord of the forest,
but the industry became besieged by environmental protest. The company sold
the building, decamped to Cathedral
Place (H53) and later sold out to a U.S.
corporation. Erickson was consultant for
an upgrade that deferred to the building's powerful personality.

H44 Shangri-La Vancouver
1128 West Georgia Street
James K.M. Cheng Architects, Jones Kwong
Kishi engineers, Phillips Farevaag Smallenberg
landscape design 2009

Developed by Westbank Projects, this shimmering skyscraper succeeded One Wall Centre (H49) as Vancouver's tallest building. With sixty-two-storeys of glass and reinforced concrete, it was also the heaviest. Its carbon footprint included thousands of truckloads of spoil excavated for the foundation, the deepest dig in the city (more than 25 metres below grade). The mixed-use development, with live-work units and condos above the hotel, includes restaurants, retail and **Coastal**

Church (First Church of Christ, Scientist; Matheson & De Guerre 1918), which was restored, and reinforced with seismic buttresses. Saving the church, and providing a sculpture garden for the Vancouver Art Gallery, gained Westbank density.

The Shangri-La's high-rise modernism is arresting and inventive (1,340 "buttons," designed to color-shift depending on the light and viewing angle, conceal each unit's vents). The tower was squeezed to a triangular floor plate on the site's northeast corner to sidestep one of the city's view corridors, which runs through the centre of the block. The triangular theme is repeated over the site, an echo of Crown Life Plaza (I41), which did triangles first and did them better, but Cheng's tower meets the ground in a similarly pleasing way; viewed close-up the height seems inconsequential, a result of thoughtful urban design. This includes a diagonal promenade with a carbon-compensating bamboo forest and "floating" steps to West Georgia.

H45 The Manhattan
784 Thurlow Street
Parr & Fee 1908; Norman Hotson Architects,
Thompson, Berwick, Pratt & Partners 1982

Industrialist W.L. Tait (J15) built this apartment building, one of the first in Vancouver. It was a mixed-use corner building, with retail on Robson Street and a top-floor restaurant. Its bay windows and plan, with a deep courtyard for daylight, influenced other projects (I6). In the 1970s, an anti-demolition protest squat led to its conversion as a housing co-op with funding from CMHC, on a thirty-two-year lease from the owner, who had sought to tear it down for a one-storey commercial building and parking lot. The rehab included a hydraulic elevator, steelwork to replace the wood frame on the ground floor and a seismic upgrade

(one of the earliest to a heritage structure in the city). At that time, Robson Street still had some of the stores and cafés, run by immigrants from post-WWII Europe, that had given it the sobriquet "Robsonstrasse." The name of Tait's novelty foreshadowed the future "Manhattanization" of Vancouver and the rise in property values that changed the street and the city. A sign of that arrived in the 1990s when the intersection of Robson and Thurlow achieved prominence for its two Starbucks, one in the Manhattan, the other kitty-corner.

H46 750 Burrard Street
Semmens & Simpson 1957;
James K.M. Cheng Architects 1996

Vancouver's former Central Library was the result of the Library Board's vision to relocate from the old downtown's Carnegie building (A35) to a new library on a more prominent site. Funding was voted by the public in 1945; the City bought the site in 1952. The new Central Library was the most significant public building of its time, a symbol of post-WWII optimism. It was designed in the progressive idiom that modernized Vancouver in the 1960s. It was inclusive, easily navigated and informal, but it became overcrowded

and unsuitable for the expanding service. It closed in 1995 after the City sold the building to fund Library Square (H7).

Despite heritage designation having been agreed, it was stripped down to its concrete structure—nothing but columns and slabs—to prepare it for a retail and media makeover. The granite base on Burrard Street was altered, the glass curtain wall removed and replaced with a replica; automated aluminum sunscreens on Robson were removed and transparency obscured by signage. A Venetian glass mosaic inside (Lionel A.J. Thomas 1956) was sacrificed; a bronze installation (1960) by Thomas survives on the Burrard Street elevation. A TV station's paraphernalia appeared on the roof, above a new top storey. A semblance of the building's sophistication remains along with an inscription in the granite recording the library's inauguration. With both this and The Electra (H48), the City created a new program to preserve "recent heritage" yet allowed the two most iconic buildings to be entirely rebuilt.

H47 Dal Grauer Substation
950 Burrard Street
Sharp & Thompson, Berwick, Pratt 1954

Architect Ned Pratt persuaded B.C. Electric to plug into the modernist mode after the utility proposed a boxy brick substation—which Pratt said would look like a

mausoleum for the churches across the street (I1). The resulting transparency—with a steel-and-glass curtain wall composed with the geometry of a Mondrian painting—revealed the electrical plant's purpose: to bring power to the people and show them how that was done. Unfortunately, several explosions occurred inside. In 1977, the windows were covered with Mylar to prevent the glass from shattering. The recession in 2008 delayed a restoration plan (Busby Perkins + Will, Robert Lemon Architect 2006).

H48 The Electra
989 Nelson Street
Thompson, Berwick & Pratt, Otto Safir engineer
1957; Paul Merrick Architects 1994

TBP, having no experience with skyscrapers, designed B.C. Electric's new headquarters after Ned Pratt engaged Otto Safir to engineer it. The team included designer Ron Thom and artist B.C. Binning, whose abstract mosaics in a West Coast palette derive from the building's lozenge-shaped floor plan. It was B.C. Electric chairman Dal Grauer who (despite being in the business of selling electricity) insisted that every desk be within 15 feet of a window. This determined the floor plate. Safir's solution was to have all systems distributed via a central concrete shaft off of which floors branch out, cantilevered, column

free with daylight and a view for every worker.

The tower is particularly civilized in the way it meets the ground. That spatial encounter and Binning's period details were preserved during condo conversion—the first major change of use from office to residential in Vancouver. The City insisted on heritage designation, the first for a post-1940s building in the city, but agreed that the original porcelain, aluminum and glass curtain walls could be replaced with facsimiles with operable windows. Vertical light features on both ends of the tower were restored. The musical horns on the roof, a B.C. Hydro Canadian Centennial project, were relocated to Canada Place (H30).

H49 One Wall Centre

938 Nelson Street

Busby + Associates Architects, Glotman
Simpson engineers, Phillips Farevaag
Smallenberg landscape design 2001

When the design for this iconic sky-scraper—to be the tallest in Vancouver (H44), on the highest point downtown—was unveiled in 1997, it breached the City's 300-foot height guideline and provoked a debate about high-rise buildings. City Council, the Urban Design Panel and public review endorsed it, after a sky-line study (Spaxman Consulting Group, Jankovic Consultants) proved it would not block view cones and corridors, which protect views of the North Shore mountains from locations that include City Hall.

One Wall Centre stepped respectfully aside from the B.C. Electric Building (see previous entry), whose structural ingenuity it matches, with concrete-and-steel "core and outrigger" construction and two water-filled "tuned liquid column dampers" on the top levels to counter wind sway. The view of the earlier icon was enhanced by generous landscaping.

The energy-efficient, forty-eight-storey elliptical hotel-condo combo became *cause célèbre* when the curtain wall was halfway up. The planning department alleged that the glass was darker than approved. The City requested a stop-work order until the issue could be resolved. The architect and developer, Peter Wall, argued the glass (similar to the existing Wall Centre's two towers; Bruno Freschi, Chris Doray 1994) had been approved. Another architect, James Cheng, was called in as an arbiter, and he recommended the lower half stay dark and that the upper half be lighter. The hotel had committed to major conferences; the two-tone compromise allowed it to open on schedule. That solution suggests the tower's hotel and condo split but at considerable aesthetic cost.

H50 Robson Square

800-block Robson Street

Arthur Erickson Architects, Bogue Babicki Associates engineers, Cornelia Hahn Oberlander, Raoul Robillard landscape design 1974–82; Clive Grout Architects, Nick Milkovich Architects, Hughes Condon Marler Architects, Arthur Erickson, Phillips Farevaag Smallenberg, Cornelia Hahn Oberlander 2004–11

The Social Credit provincial government planned a blockbuster fifty-five-storey office tower for this site. The New Democratic Party won the 1972 election and changed the architects and architectural program. The outcome was this linear, multi-use development—essentially the tower laid on its side—covering three city blocks. It combined the Provincial Law Courts, a media centre (now UBC at Robson Square) and provincial government offices.

The Law Courts step down to a concourse covered by a sloping steel space-frame, glazed for daylight and to sym-

bolize judicial transparency—the perspective from the entrance on Nelson Street pinpoints a bronze statue: *Themis, Goddess of Justice* (Jack Harman 1982). A canal-like water feature leading to a cascade bridges Smithe Street to establish a relationship with the old Provincial Courthouse, an emblem of British imperial justice at the north end of the site. That structure was rehabilitated for the Vancouver Art Gallery (H56) and integrated with Robson Square's urban design. This includes a sunken plaza with an ice rink; its domes were renewed for the 2010 Winter Olympic Games, for which it was a civic star.

Concrete was Erickson's muse and material of choice. It spreads across the site, which is saved from severity by terraced, landscaped public spaces: "a linear urban park, importing nature into the city," as he and Cornelia Oberlander described it. The provincial government began the Robson Square Repair & Renewal Project in 2004, to upgrade the exterior of the entire complex, with a commitment to maintain this uniquely West Coast fusion of architectural and landscape design.

H51 Hotel Vancouver
900 West Georgia Street
Archibald & Schofield 1928–39

The CPR was the first to build hotels in the image of Loire châteaux with a dash of Sir Walter Scott that reflected Canada's French and Scottish heritage and established the "château style" that became a national symbol. (The Château Frontenac in Quebec comes to mind.) Renaissance detail, gargoyles and relief sculpture are

capped here with a steep copper roof, the style's signature. Stonework is crisply carved, concealing a modern steel frame. This hotel, designed for Canadian National Railways, part of a land deal between the CNR's predecessor and the City (G16), was delayed by the Depression and rushed to completion in 1939 for the royal visit of King George VI and Queen Elizabeth. The rival CPR had co-operatively closed its own Hotel Vancouver (1887; Francis S. Swales 1916; demolished 1949) two blocks east, lent the name and entered into a joint-management contract. Subsequently, the hotel became part of CP's national chain (now Fairmont Hotels & Resorts).

H52 Christ Church Cathedral
690 Burrard Street

Charles Osborn Wickenden 1895; Twizell & Twizell 1930; Iredale Group Architecture, Proscenium Architecture + Interiors, Durante Kreuk landscape design 2006

Downtown Vancouver's oldest religious building (a cathedral since 1929, when a chancel was added) was built in what was then a residential neighbourhood, on a fragment of the land granted to the CPR as an inducement to build the transcontinental railway. Parish member Henry John Cambie, chief engineer of the CPR's Pacific Division, helped negotiate acquisition of the property. The architect was born in England, and the exterior's pointed-arched windows, buttresses and steep gabled roof radiate nostalgia for the cozy parish churches of the old country, as does the traditional stained glass. Frontier craftsmanship is preserved in the forest-like hammer-beam, cedar and Douglas-fir roof structure.

All was nearly lost when the diocese proposed an office tower, underground sanctuary and campanile (Arthur Erickson 1971). A happier solution—the first of its type in Canada—was found in the transfer of unused density rights to the adjacent site to the north, now **Park Place** (666 Burrard Street, Musson Cattell Mackey Partnership 1984) whose tower is higher and bulkier as a result. The diocese gained cash for social programs and an ongoing restoration program, seismic upgrade and public realm redesign begun in 1998, completed in 2006.

H53 Cathedral Place
925 West Georgia Street
Paul Merrick Architects, Christopher Phillips & Associates, Cornelia Hahn Oberlander 1991

Developer Ron Shon asked his architect to imbue Cathedral Place with "timelessness." The response was a postmodern potpourri from the immediate urban context: the name from the adjacent church, griffins and a château-style chapeau from the Hotel Vancouver (H51), a lobby inspired by the Marine Building (H34) and setbacks and sculpted nurses (L20) in memory of those on the Art Deco Georgia Medical Dental Building (McCarter & Nairne 1929), which this tower replaced. A cloister was provided at the back of the tower, where a faux-French pavilion (for the Canadian Craft Museum), since 2008 the Bill Reid Gallery of Northwest Coast Art, was clad with Art Deco panels reproduced from the Medical Dental Building's upper floors.

H54 Hongkong and Shanghai Bank
885 West Georgia Street
Webb, Zerafa, Menkes, Housden Partnership 1986

The immense atrium of this postmodern tower is thrust out to the street, but the tower is set back with courtesy to its neighbours, almost symbolically so. The building represents HSBC's sudden high profile in B.C. following its acquisition of the Bank of British Columbia in 1986; it is also symbolic of Vancouver's increasing significance on the Pacific Rim. The atrium is animated by the structural misbehaviour of sculptor Alan Storey's *Broken Column* (1987).

H55 Hotel Georgia
801 West Georgia Street
Robert T. Garrow, John Graham 1927; Endall
Elliot Associates, IBI/HB Architects 2011

Now named the Rosewood Hotel Georgia, this is a classically proportioned building with Georgian-style façades in the American manner. The hotel's interior decor was flapper-era fantasy, with a faux-Renaissance wood panelling in the foyer and an "Aztec Ballroom." The building's traditional elevations and some interior features were preserved during a 1998 rehab, and in the recent luxury make-over (Robert Lemon Architect, heritage consultant for both). A condo tower, the **Private Residences at Hotel Georgia**, rises from the site of the old hotel's parkade.

H56 Vancouver Art Gallery
750 Hornby Street
Francis Mawson Rattenbury 1906; Thomas
Hooper 1912; Arthur Erickson 1983

Judicial rectitude and respectability are expressed in the neoclassicism of this former provincial court house. The style was commonly chosen for its lineage from ancient Rome, in this case to flatter a British dominion's institution. There are porticos and a rotunda, which became the internal focus of the Vancouver Art Gallery when it opened here in 1983, following the transfer of court facilities to the adjacent Robson Square (H50). The entrance facing the **Centennial Fountain** (1966), on a piazza at Georgia Street, was sealed, and its two lions (John Bruce, sculptor 1910, modelled after those in London's

H

Trafalgar Square) orphaned. The rear elevation acquired a covered concourse (entered from Hornby and Robson Streets), part of the rehabilitation by Arthur Erickson for the VAG.

The piazza is a popular public space, used for demonstrations, multicultural festivals and much more. Proposals (originally by Erickson) that it be excavated and roofed for an extension to the building have come to nothing, although they may do if the VAG moves and a new use for the building is found. The gallery's present regime plans an "iconic" new facility, twice the size of the existing one, on a different site (H10). The idea that the VAG vacate its heavily used and historic downtown venue is controversial.

The West End

OFFICERS from the Royal Navy survey ship HMS *Plumper* found coal, potentially suitable for steamships, on the shore of Burrard Inlet, in 1859 at the foot of what is now Bute Street. A syndicate formed by local investors to exploit the mineral failed to find workable reserves, so Coal Harbour, as the water east of Stanley Park came to be called, was never mined. John Morton, an English potter in New Westminster, learned of the discovery and knew that coal might also mean clay for bricks. In 1862 he, his cousin Samuel Brighouse and friend William Hailstone pre-empted 550-acres of Crown land—the present West End—for around a dollar an acre. Brick-making for construction came to nothing on an inlet with abundant timber, but "The Three Greenhorns," as they were mocked, were sitting on what became some of the most valuable real estate in Canada.

Two decades later, their land was a bargaining chip for the business community to persuade the Canadian Pacific Railway to locate the transcontinental terminus in Vancouver. The Three Greenhorns donated one lot in every three, knowing the rest would soar in value. The land west and south of Morton's cabin (located at the foot of Burrard Street) was developed by the CPR and became known as "Blueblood Alley" for its homes for the city's elite (142).

Above: Alexandra Park Bandstand (121)

The survey had noted that the peninsula at the western tip of the future downtown Vancouver was suitable for harbour defence against American expansion. Consequently it became a military reserve. In 1886 the City of Vancouver Council tabled its first resolution: to ask Ottawa to release the 1,000-acre government reserve to the City for a park, named Stanley Park after the governor general. This was far-sighted and altruistic, as well as good business. Keeping the park off the market enhanced the value of land held by those who voted for the park. From the start, the economics of real estate influenced council decisions and how the city would develop.

The West End was laid out as a grid after the forest was cleared by contractor John McDougall (who had cleared the right of way to bring the CPR from Port Moody). Streets near downtown filled with frame, gable-roofed family homes of the type preserved at Mole Hill (14), while big houses on large lots with views of English Bay and Stanley Park were built after Coal Harbour had been industrialized with mills and boatyards. After 1900, commerce along the streetcar lines on Davie, Denman and Robson Streets, and the appearance of apartment buildings such as the Beaconsfield (16), persuaded the well-to-do to flee to Shaughnessy Heights and the West Side.

The West End evolved as a cosmopolitan inner-city suburb with an eclectic mix of architecture. The many churches, social centres, cafés and corner groceries on leafy West End sidewalks complemented the residences and maintained livability—although prostitution, usually seen as a Downtown Eastside problem, provoked Concerned Residents of the West End (CROWE) to challenge streetwalkers in the 1980s.

High-rise apartment buildings began to appear after rezoning in 1956. Planning reforms in the 1970s led to discretionary zoning. In the West End, guidelines were adopted by Council in 1989, partly to prevent demolition of rental housing. These allowed high-rise development on a case-by-case basis while encouraging the creation of green space and heritage preservation. The glut of condominiums in the 1990s and 2000s is being tempered by the City's introduction of Short Term Incentives for Rental Housing (STIR) in 2009. Much of the West End's beloved ambience has been lost, especially on Robson Street, once famed for its German shops and character and now just another venue for high-end global retailers.

The neighbourhood's vitality and density (said to be the highest in Canada), if not its variety, informed the massive developments at Coal Harbour (by the CPR's realty wing) and False Creek in the 1990s. Now as then, the Canadian Pacific Railway exploited the best spots: the company's redevelopment of Coal Harbour as a resort city, unaffordable to the majority of people in Vancouver, is the salient recent example.

Coal Harbour and False Creek took development pressure off the central, non-waterfront land, at least temporarily. Heritage conservation incentives rescued many old homes and selective zoning significant older apartment buildings. But now that the two areas have been built out, the West End's relative affordability and livability—and its underappreciated modernist architecture—are once again threatened by redevelopment.

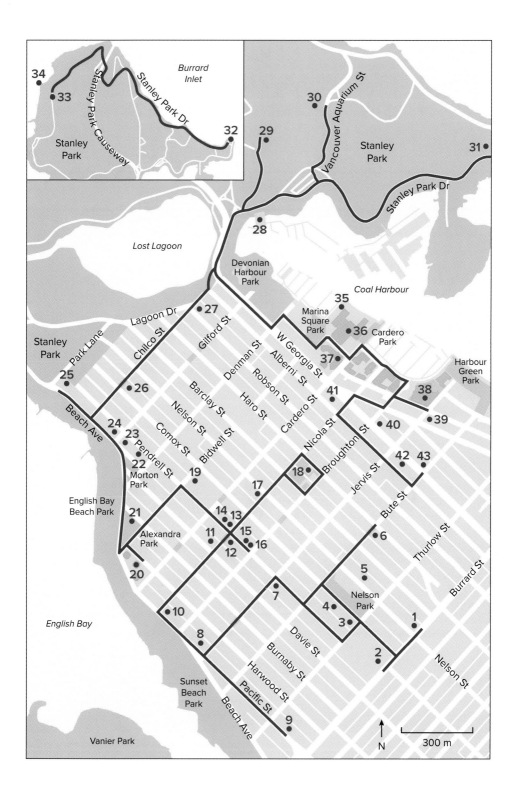

11 First Baptist Church
969 Burrard Street
Burke, Horwood & White 1911; 1931

St. Andrew's–Wesley United Church
1022 Nelson Street
Twizell & Twizell 1933

Brothers Robert Percival and George Sterling Twizell were provincial society architects with a big-name client. St. Andrew's–Wesley was a union of St. Andrew's Presbyterian and Wesley Methodist churches; the two denominations (and Congregationalism) merged to join the United Church of Canada in 1925. The new congregation celebrated with a revival of Perpendicular Gothic in the High Anglican manner, although some parishioners thought it was pretentious and inappropriate for Protestant denominations to follow an Anglican model. The exterior stonework conceals a reinforced-concrete structure, with a timber roof covering an aisled, arcaded nave. The windows, with stained glass by Morris & Company, England (1937), and *dalle de verre* by Gabriel Loire of Chartres (1969, 1981), are superb.

Edmund Burke was a Baptist and senior partner in a prestigious Toronto architectural firm. First Baptist Church, also Gothic Revival like its neighbour, follows earlier Medieval examples, with

lancet windows and rusticated load-bearing granite. Pioneer and church member John Morton laid the cornerstone in 1910. The sanctuary was gutted by fire in 1931 but rebuilt with a coffered ceiling evoking the interior that had been destroyed. The contrasting yet thematically parallel churches converge in unplanned urban design: a Gothic Revival gateway to the West End.

12 St. Paul's Hospital
1081 Burrard Street
Robert F. Tegen 1913; Gardiner & Mercer 1931; 1983; 1991

The first St. Paul's Hospital was three-storey wooden building (1894) by architect manquée Mother Joseph Pariseau, who led five missionaries of The Sisters of Providence (founded in Montreal in 1843) to the Pacific Northwest in 1856. St. Paul's is considerably expanded since Mother Joseph's "cottage hospital" for twenty-

five patients. This brick-and-terracotta Italianate design from Portland-based Tegen was expanded in 1931 with two wings, sympathetic to Tegen's design, and modern buildings in 1983 and 1991. Operator Providence Health Care's options to close the complex and move its services out of the neighbourhood have been opposed by the Save St. Paul's Coalition, in favour of renewal on this site.

13 Dr. Peter Centre West End
1110 Comox Street
Neale Staniszkis Doll Adams Architects 2003

The Dr. Peter AIDS Foundation was founded by Dr. Peter Jepson-Young shortly before his death in 1992, after he broadcast a two-year CBC TV diary about living with HIV/AIDS. This building, which provides community day and residential care, was designed so that its users should not feel or be shut away from society. It mediates another divide, a visual one between the bulk of St. Paul's Hospital and the residential scale of Mole Hill (see next entry) on the east edge of which the centre sits. It makes a contextual reference to the siding and eaves of a heritage house (1906) that was refurbished as offices and linked to the new building by a glazed passage. The centre also complements **Strathmore Lodge** (1086 Bute Street, 1909), a bookend on the west edge of the block.

14 Mole Hill
Comox and Pendrell Streets, between Thurlow and Bute
1888–1908; Sean McEwen, Hotson Bakker Boniface Haden Architects, Donald Luxton & Associates, Durante Kreuk landscape design 2003

New Urbanism, which critiqued modernist planning (C2), was inspired by traditional neighbourhoods like Mole Hill, with leafy sidewalks and heritage houses. Most of those here were rental units, acquired piecemeal by the City to make way for a long-standing plan to expand Nelson Park. In 1994, residents formed the Mole Hill Living Heritage Society to oppose the park expansion and save the homes. They named the block for Henry Mole, an early settler. Activist Blair Petrie documented the history of each house in a book, which won a city heritage award. At the time, the City was completing a $3 million city-wide study called City-Plan. Among its conclusions, it favoured community-based planning and the new urbanism of walkable, mixed-use and mixed-income neighbourhoods and was adopted in 1995. Council voted reluctantly to reprieve the Mole Hill properties.

Work to revitalize twenty-six houses began in 1999. They were rehabilitated by the City, in partnership with B.C. Housing Society and the Mole Hill Community Housing Society, to provide 170 units, from studios to three-bedroom (40 for families). Tenants were not displaced. Fair rents were set. No distinction was made between subsidized and market rental units—all were polished to the same high-quality finish. Boarded-up porches and columns were exposed and restored; every heritage feature that could be salvaged was. Seismic upgrades to code were made. All units tap into geothermal heating; there are community gardens in the lane. Much of the Benjamin Moore/Vancouver Heritage

Foundation's "True Colours" heritage palette was created from original exterior colours identified here.

The streetscapes are almost as the Edwardians saw them, but "living heritage" did not mean that the block should be frozen in time. This is a $28 million, twenty-first-century showpiece of sustainability. Competing agendas were addressed and resolved without compromising housing, conservation and community objectives.

15 Nicholson Tower
1115 Nelson Street
Erickson/Massey 1969

This multi-storey building was a joint federal–provincial government project to provide 223 seniors' units. The structure is concrete, brutalist, more thoughtfully designed than it looks. Three thin slabs are joined in a sandwich, the two outer slices offset to reduce the apparent bulk. The tower's relatively small foot-print created green space in the Le Corbusier manner fashionable at the time (120). Erickson/Massey continued the brutalist theme at **1230 and 1260 Nelson Street** (1970), two rental apartment towers built to an economical plan, astride landscaping.

16 The Beaconsfield

884 Bute Street
John Smith Davidson Taylor 1909

This is one of many apartment blocks in the West End that adopted a plan with a deep entrance courtyard, similar to the Manhattan (H45), to provide light and air to all rooms while maximizing floor space. This version, with brick elevations and bay windows with pale trim, has the look and feel of a Victorian "mansion" block (an apartment building, often faced with brick) in London. The twin Arts and Crafts wooden balconies, each in a four-storey bay, are wonderful, unique in the city. A Palladian window graces the entrance court. The **Rand House** (995 Bute Street, 1896; Birmingham & Wood 2006), now suites, was one of the large family homes built after a street-car service began on Robson Street in 1895. The house next door, **989 Bute Street** (1899) became a B&B in 1986, like the **"O Canada" House** (1114 Barclay Street, 1897; 1996), where Ewing Buchan penned a version of the national anthem. The area's continuing evolution can be seen at **1235 and 1277 Nelson Street**. The former is a jazzy Art Deco walk-up (Ross A. Lort 1931); the latter an elliptical tower (Henriquez & Partners 1995) that replaced a twin walk-up, a fragment of which was incorporated as a memory into the garden design.

17 St. Paul's Anglican Church

1130 Jervis Street
William Henry Archer 1905

This replaced St. Paul's Mission Church (1889), which served CPR workers in Yaletown until 1896, when it was winched on skids up Davie Street to serve the growing parish in the West End. A steeple planned for the street corner was not built. No matter, because the building preserves its predecessor's pioneer Gothic charm and is atmospheric inside. Corinthian columns support a scissor-truss roof. There is wood panelling and stained glass, some by Henry Bloomfield & Sons, and two windows, reputedly by Tiffany, New York, sponsored by B.T. Rogers (111). The organ, by Casavant Frères, Quebec, is said to be the company's oldest west of the Rockies.

18 Tudor Manor

1311 Beach Avenue
Townley & Matheson 1928; Paul Merrick Architect 1988

Tudor Manor was a *cause célèbre* in the West End. The original apartment building was highly valued by the community, as was the setback that provides green space in front. The developer could have demolished it for a three-storey building covering most of the site. In order to preserve the linear footprint and the open space, the tower solution was chosen: it

19 Pacific Heights Housing Co-operative
1035 Pacific Street
Roger Hughes Architects 1985

Heritage on a sloping site posed a challenge to this development, which took a different form from that at Tudor Manor (see previous entry) but without postmodern pastiche. A linear composition of contemporary units was built as backdrop to eight rehabilitated Edwardian homes, which were moved forward and regrouped as four pairs above parking entered at grade; a glazed elevator tower anchors the old and new components. This pragmatic arrangement now seems to have been ahead of its time: a laneway infill helping to preserve a traditional streetscape of heritage homes.

110 Kensington Place
1386 Nicola Street
Phillip Julien 1914

One of the first properties in Vancouver to become a "strata-title" condominium, the Kensington evokes the posh neigh-

interrupted fewer views, cast fewer shadows and ensured the original building could be rehabilitated economically. The Tudor Revival style conveyed Vancouver's upper-crust British heritage. References to the style were applied to the tower in the postmodern "contextual" fashion.

bourhood in London, but the style is Italian, Belle Époque, a vision from the shore of Lake Garda on English Bay. Suites (four per floor) were lavishly appointed. The structure is concrete and old-growth timber with a stuccoed exterior. The entrance is baroque, in cast concrete (the metal-and-glass door is contemporary; the cast-iron lamp posts are original). Classically derived columns define recessed loggias that rise to top-floor exterior decoration somewhat reminiscent of Italian "Liberty Style" Art Nouveau. The cornice was rebuilt following a restoration study (Iredale Partnership 1988), since implemented periodically and extensively.

111 Gabriola
1531 Davie Street
Samuel Maclure 1901

B.T. Rogers commissioned this Queen Anne mansion to match any in Montreal's Square Mile, which Rogers would have seen before he arrived in Vancouver (C15). Maclure was the leading architect of luxury homes on the West Coast, but Gabriola is not typical of his oeuvre, which was Tudor Revival/Arts and Crafts (J3). Sandstone quarried on Gabriola Island is textured around the porte cochère in the Richardsonian Romanesque manner, with friezes carved in the Italian "gro-

tesque" style. A baronial interior boasted a grand staircase with a pre-Raphaelite stained-glass window designed by James Bloomfield, positioned to catch the morning sun. Rogers died in 1918, his aristocratic yearnings not satisfied. His widow moved to the 10-acre Shannon estate (K39) he was developing. The interior is much altered. Gabriola was subdivided as Angus Apartments in 1924 and later became a restaurant.

112 The Beaufort
1160 Nicola Street
1932

Tudor Revival's enduring appeal is evident in this picturesque walk-up, composed with a prominent half-timbered, gabled bay above the entrance, leaded glass and faux heraldry as if part of an English country estate. Half timbering runs the full length of the front and side elevations. Incongruous but attractive Art Nouveau tiles decorate the entrance

recess. The street was closed to traffic as part of a program of public realm enhancement and traffic calming, and a mini park was created, one of many rolled out east of Denman in the 1980s, following a trial traffic diverter in 1973 at Robson and Chilco (127).

113 The Queen Charlotte
1101 Nicola Street
Dominion Construction 1928; 1996

This reinforced-concrete Spanish Colonial Revival apartment building is a survivor from an era of gracious living and maid service. Its semicircular gables, stucco and imitation tile eaves are typical of the style. The strata council commissioned a study (Robert G. Lemon Architecture & Preservation 1991) to restore its heritage features, which include a Moorish tiled vestibule and Art Deco details in the lobby. The original Turnbull elevator (by the same company that made the Marine Building's lifts (H34) was saved by an "equivalency" agreement with provincial inspectors after safety features were retrofitted. Stucco was repaired and repainted in period colour; metal window boxes and balcony railings above the entrance were replicated from a Dominion Construction drawing.

114 Charlotte Gardens
1525 Pendrell Street
1987

This is a California-stucco-style, wood-frame apartment building on a concrete slab above a parkade. In the mid-1990s, it became a statistic in B.C.'s "leaky condo crisis" and was stripped and "rain-screened." By 2002, approximately fifty thousand units in similar properties in B.C.—most in Metro Vancouver—were affected. This was the consequence of a hot market where selling lifestyles overlooked the longevity of the buildings. Slapdash construction, a National Building Code that ignored climatic variations across the country and a federal National Energy Program that mandated airtight insulation (trapping moisture inside exterior walls) contributed to the "disaster," as it was called by the provincial government's Barrett Commission. The commission's report blamed everybody and therefore nobody, passing the buck for "building envelope failure," as the jargon euphemized it, and remedial costs to owners.

115 Pendrell Suites
1419 Pendrell Street
Claude Percy Jones 1910

Pendrell Apartments (the former name of this boutique apartment hotel) gained cult status as FBI agent Dana Scully's Washington, D.C., digs in *The X-Files*. From 1993 to 1998, the show was produced and shot in Vancouver, a.k.a. "Hollywood North." *The X-Files* exploited the city's moody climate and forests, film noir–style architecture and alleys and the spooky potential of its Shaughnessy mansions. Spooky is not how Pendrell Suites looks (even if Scully was abducted there). It is a bow-windowed Georgian Revival walk-up that would fit comfortably on the streets of London, the architect's hometown.

116 Thomas Fee House
1401 Pendrell Street
Parr & Fee 1904; Marshall Fisher Architects 1994

Wrap-around infill respects this house and the immediate heritage context. The house was moved closer to the corner to make room for the infill, one of the first times this had been done in Vancouver, the move and the added density enabled by the Heritage Program. The entrance to

the underground parking is discreet. A brick bay on Pendrell adopts the style and scale of the adjacent Pendrell Suites; setbacks and balconies meet the Fee house with a clarity that makes clear what is new and what is old.

Fee was born in Quebec to Irish parents. He arrived at Port Moody on the CPR in 1886 "without a dime" and became one of the city's most successful architects of his era. He built an elaborate villa at 1029 Gilford Street (1907; demolished c. 1960), for which this was a model; the turret is off centre and gave him a view of English Bay.

117 Fire Hall No. 6
1001 Nicola Street
Honeyman & Curtis 1908

This was the first fire station in North America built to accommodate "self-propelled" (motorized) fire engines. The modernizer was fire chief John Howe

Carlisle, who ordered three unproven American units from Ohio, the first imported to Canada. The building was fitted out and equipped as a state-of-the-art operation in everything but the image of its architecture. The style is Italianate, with a tiled roof with shady eaves for that Mediterranean sun and a hose tower that would suit a Tuscan village skyline. The building was rehabilitated and upgraded in 1988 (Henry Hawthorn).

118 Barclay Square Heritage Park
Barclay, Nicola, Haro and Broughton Streets
1890–1908; Downs/Archambault, Iredale Partnership, Allan Diamond Architect c. 1985

The Vancouver Historical Society and the Community Arts Council blazed a "living heritage" trail (14) after the Park Board bought the dwellings on the block in 1966 for demolition. Some were torn down. The campaign to save those remaining led to this blend of two-thirds park and one-third heritage preservation in the 1980s. The City of Vancouver, Heritage Canada and B.C. Heritage took on the project.

Nine heritage homes were saved by adaptive reuse: six rehabilitated for housing, two for community services, and the Roedde House (1893) as a museum, where the story of the block and its early residents is told. The museum was the home of Leipzig-trained bookbinder and printer Gustav Roedde. The style is Queen Anne, distinguished by a turret, some say from Francis Rattenbury's

pen (Rattenbury worked in Vancouver in 1892, preparing a competition-winning design for the B.C. Parliament Buildings in Victoria).

119 Lord Roberts Elementary School
1100 Bidwell Street
William Tuff Whiteway 1907; Downs/ Archambault 1996

Residential growth in the West End prompted the replacement of the first school on this site (1901) with this larger edifice. Like others of its era, it was built with unreinforced load-bearing brick and stone. It was upgraded to meet seismic safety and modern educational requirements, one of the first such interventions by the School Board to address the shortcomings of its stock of heritage structures. Postmodern "gates" were added as memory of the "boys" and "girls" entrances, no longer used. Top-floor arched windows are Renaissance; those on the main floor, with carved capitals, Romanesque—the overall appearance

is Italianate. Early Vancouver schools were named after famous British people, in this case Lord Roberts of Kandahar, imperial soldier and field marshal.

120 Beach Towers
1600-block Beach Avenue
C.B.K. Van Norman & Associates 1965, 1968

Built as a group of three, these are classic point towers, straight up, no fuss, by way of Le Corbusier's 1920s plans for utopias of orderly point towers in green spaces. That approach was taken up by planners around the world in the 1960s, and this is Vancouver's best example of it. Concave balconies relieve the brutalist concrete elevations, repeated on a fourth tower on Harwood Street. The breezy green spaces, with surface parking slabs, are crucial

to the cluster's cultural context. Despite their density, the towers' placement allows English Bay to be seen from street level: the floor plates give each of the six hundred units unobstructed views. A plan for infill at grade threatened the ensemble in 2011.

121 Alexandra Park Bandstand
1700-block Beach Avenue
E.E. Blackmore 1914; 1987

This octagonal cedar bandstand is identical to the first Stanley Park Bandstand (E.E. Blackmore 1911), which was replaced by Malkin Bowl in 1934. Alexandra Park, named for Edward VII's queen, overlooks the beach created when the Park Board replaced the rocks with sand and built a pleasure pier (1909; demolished 1939) at the foot of Gilford Street; Blackmore designed English Bay Bathing Pavilion (1909), which stood across Beach Avenue near the site of the present bathhouse (1932). The Park Board seeks to repeat the success of the Kitsilano Beach Restaurant (K3) with a new **English Bay bistro** here (Acton Ostry Architects). The bandstand was renamed the Haywood Bandstand after a donor to its 1980s restoration.

122 **Ocean Towers**
1835 Morton Street
Chow, Nelson & Reinecke 1959

Le Corbusier in Hawaii is the smile on the face of this resort-style slab block, blissfully unaware of the existing architectural context. It took advantage of re-zoning in 1956 that allowed high-rises in the West End. All sixty-eight apartments (four per floor, plus penthouse) have sea views. A 108-car underground parkade was provided. Horizontal fins on each level across the full frontage act as sunscreens and soften the slab, which is raised on concrete *pilotis*.

123 **Sylvia Hotel**
1154 Gilford Street
William P. White 1912

Built as Sylvia Court Apartments, designed by a Seattle architect who specialized in the building-type and named for owner Abraham Goldstein's twelve-year-old daughter, the Sylvia reigned as the tallest building in the West End until eclipsed by Ocean Towers (122). Converted to an apartment hotel in 1936, it preserved the old West End of chintz and afternoon tea until merchant navy crews moved in during WWII. A "dine in the sky" restaurant opened in 1949, and the city's first cocktail bar followed in 1954. A postmodern neighbour, **Sylvia Tower** (1861 Beach Avenue, Henriquez & Partners 1987) reconfigured the Sylvia's site, adding a bistro, patio and condos. The Virginia creeper that grows on the main façade—a proto-eco-friendly green wall, inhabited by raccoons—was planted by one of the original residents.

125 Park Board Offices
2099 Beach Avenue
Underwood, McKinley & Cameron 1960

Much of the peninsula called Stanley Park had been logged by the 1880s, when City Council resolved to create the park. The loss of the old-growth forest was not at odds with the romantic Victorian notion of "nature" in landscaped form, of which Stanley Park is an example. It was the City's first official green space, named for Lord Stanley, governor general of Canada. It set the tone for Vancouverites' engagement with the city's natural setting. It is now a forest park: twentieth- and twenty-first-century interventions have been directed at producing the appearance of the vanished pristine forest.

Architectural interventions in the park (which are increasing) traditionally defer to the setting. The asymmetrical plan of the Park Board Office is responsive to the park's informality, as the building's granite and wood is to the landscape. The glass entrance opens to a split-level interior framed with Douglas-fir and panelled with cedar and Japanese ash. On a granite plinth nearby is a **bronze bust of Mayor David Oppenheimer** (Charles Marega 1911), who opened the park in 1888. This was Italian-born and -trained Marega's first commission in Vancouver; among his many other works are the lions at the south portal of Lions Gate Bridge (M1).

124 Eugenia Place
1919 Beach Avenue
Henriquez & Partners 1990

The Eugenia steps back to preserve the Sylvia Hotel's prospect of English Bay. It was named for developers Caleb and Tom Chan's mother, but there is more to the narrative of this essay than a sentimental client and an allusion to how the Sylvia was named. The Eugenia is a metaphor, a memory of nature. The inverted cone-shaped entrance is like the root of a tree; the glazed bay that shoots up to the penthouse deck is the trunk. An Oregon pin oak grows from the deck. The historical precedent is the tree-topped, fourteenth-century Torre Guinigi in Lucca, Italy, but the memory evoked is of the old-growth Douglas-firs that covered the West End and the height to which they grew before the forest was logged in the nineteenth century; the concrete stumps in the garden symbolize what was left.

126 Hirshfield House
1963 Comox Street
Gamble & Knapp 1910

River stone in the garden, leaded-glass windows, half-timbered gables, big brackets and eaves under a shallow-pitched roof are Craftsman bungalow elements, composed here in a form that resembles a Swiss chalet. This rare relic of the old West End was built for real estate broker and businessman Alfred C. Hirshfield at a time when apartment buildings (16, 123) were densifying the district. After WWI, many older houses were torn down or converted to multiple-unit rental accommodation. Those that survived were besieged by redevelopment in the 1960s (120, 122).

127 Chilco Towers
710 Chilco Street
Kenneth Gardner 1958

Venetian glass tiles colourize this cool, modernist reinforced-concrete slab block. It was advertised as "the ultimate in luxurious living . . . every suite has a panoramic view of Lost Lagoon, Stanley Park and the North Shore mountains." Gardner also designed **Lagoon Terrace** (1960 Robson Street, 1960). A softer form of 1950s modernism is **1972 Robson Street**, in the manner of Semmens & Simpson, who designed numerous blocks like this in the area; **815 Chilco Street** (C.B.K. Van

Norman 1970) is more eccentric, with brutalist concrete, circular balcony parapets and abstract expressionist doors; **845 Chilco Street** (1972) has a vertical abstract installation by Jordi Bonet (H33).

Chilco was a through street to Beach Avenue, a shortcut for Lions Gate traffic until residents complained. The City closed the street in 1973 and created the first traffic calming of its type in North America—a mini park, the model for many in the West End.

128 Vancouver Rowing Club
450 Stanley Park Drive
James W. Keagey 1911

The club's origin dates from 1886. The sight of rowers exercising on Coal Harbour was a typical image of the British Empire at play. In 1891, the first game of cricket in the city was played at Stanley Park's **Brockton Oval**; an English village-style pavilion was added in 1927. Captain Edward Stamp began logging this area in 1865, but tidal currents made log booms unstable, so he built Hastings Mill (C19, K13) on the south shore of the inlet. The rowing club's clubhouse, built on a deck over the water, is Tudor Revival style,

another reference to the Empire. Nearby on Deadman's Island is **HMCS Discovery**, a navy reserve named for George Vancouver's ship. The headquarters building is Georgian Revival (1943). The island was a Squamish burial ground that became a quarantine station during an outbreak of smallpox in the 1880s, hence the macabre moniker.

129 Stanley Park Pavilion
610 Pipeline Road
Otto Moberg 1911; 1924

The picturesque pavilion displays typical "rustic" features: frontier-style stonework, cedar shingles and a jigsaw-cut wooden balcony, all completely at home in this setting that includes a backdrop of North Shore peaks. It is an example of the rustic style deemed appropriate for natural settings, such as mountain parks like Banff, established in 1885, managed by Parks Canada. The CPR, which played a role in the creation of Banff National Park, had adopted a Swiss chalet style— with pitched, gabled roofs to shed snow— for its small stations and early hotels in the Rockies. The pavilion is reminiscent of them. A south wing was added in 1924.

130 Aquaquest: The Marilyn Blusson Learning Centre
845 Avison Way
Stantec Architecture, Sharp & Diamond
landscape design 2006

This addition to the **Vancouver Aquarium and Marine Science Centre**, Canada's first public aquarium when it opened in 1956, adds gallery and display space, classrooms and offices. Its architecture is West Coast contemporary, with a glued-laminated (glulam) timber roof and concrete walls. There is a living wall irrigated by rainwater harvested from the roof; sea water from Burrard Inlet is circulated for exhibits and for radiant heat and cooling.

The building's form is arranged to maximize solar gain, natural light and ventilation, while minimizing its footprint in the park. It achieved LEED Gold certification. The Aquarium is one of Vancouver's most visited attractions. Its Pacific Canada Pavilion (Bing Thom Architects 1999) reconfigured the original spaces and oriented them to the outdoor sea mammal pool. The symbolism of ocean creatures for First Nations people is illustrated by *The Chief of the Undersea World*, the bronze Orca by famed sculptor Bill Reid on the plaza at the entrance.

131 Brockton Point Totem Poles and Interpretive Centre
Stanley Park Drive, near Brockton Oval
Lubor Trubka Associates Architects 2001; 2009

Totem poles in the park were part of an unrealized 1920s plan to create an "Indian village"—and not one that would recognize the local Squamish band that had been forced out of the park. Four historic poles were brought from the Northwest Coast, displayed without explanation and eventually dispersed to museums. The oldest pole here now dates from 1955, was carved for Woodward's Department Store (A25) and is on loan from the Museum of Anthropology (L7). A redesign of the site included interpretative panels, landscaping to present the poles in an "authentic" setting and a pavilion in cedar, glass and concrete, butterfly roofed after its 2009 addition. Tree-like struts on concrete posts allow the roof to float above the structure. The effect is sympathetic to the park and the cultural setting.

132 Brockton Point Lighthouse
Colonel William P. Anderson 1914

Brockton Point was named by Captain G.H. Richards of HMS *Plumper* for ship's engineer Francis Brockton. The first light was placed at the point in 1890; the first lighthouse was built with wood (1902) to accommodate a keeper of the light who also rang a fog bell and fired the **nine o'clock gun**. The gun is a naval cannon cast in London in 1816, brought to the park in 1898, where it allowed ships' clocks to be set (originally it announced a 6 PM close of Sunday fishing in the harbour). The present lighthouse (automated in 1956) is concrete, castle-like, with arches at its base to allow passage on the seawall. The designer was Chief Engineer and Superintendent of Lighthouses for the Department of Marine & Fisheries (M36).

133 Hollow Tree
Stanley Park Drive, above Third Beach

Most of the park's remaining old-growth trees were cut and skidded down Prospect Point when a parkway was built from West Georgia Street to Lions Gate Bridge (M1). The Hollow Tree, a western red cedar about a thousand years old, indicates their girth, the oak on the roof of Eugenia Place (124) their height. The Hollow Tree, a leading attraction since the park opened, was hit by a windstorm in

2006, which destroyed about ten thousand trees. The Hollow Tree survived but began to lean dangerously. The Park Board would have removed it as a hazard to public safety, but a campaign by The Stanley Park Hollow Tree Conservation Society forced the Board to reverse its decision. The Conservation Society righted and stabilized the tree in 2009, the cost funded entirely by public donations.

134 Stanley Park Seawall

The 8.8-kilometre seawall symbolizes a century of Park Board and more recent City Planning Department objectives. It was begun in 1917, as an amenity and to prevent erosion. Between the wars, it was a "workfare" project for unemployed men. Construction was largely supervised by a Scottish stonemason, James Cunningham, for whom it was a life's work, and he is commemorated on a plaque near Siwash Rock. (The rock is the subject of a Squamish legend, made known more widely by writer Pauline Johnson, also memorialized in the park.) The paved circuit was completed in 1980. The seawall was

seriously damaged by the windstorm of 2006, and a reconstruction was completed in 2011. The seawall was the progenitor of Vancouver's 22-kilometre promenade from Kitsilano, around False Creek and Stanley Park to Coal Harbour and Canada Place (H30). The redevelopment plan for Coal Harbour (136) was conditioned by the desire to extend the park into the development.

135 Lift Bar & Grill
333 Menchions Mews
DA Architects + Planners 2004

This is a new building, not a rehabbed industrial relic, although it looks like one, sited on an existing concrete dock. The authentic survivors were erased to make way for the CPR's Marathon Realty's massive residential Coal Harbour redevelopment, between the Bayshore and Canada Place (see next entry).

The Lift's address is a memory of Coal Harbour's last shipyard, W.R. Menchions & Company (c. 1910), closed in 1990. Coal Harbour's developer and city planners felt such sites were untidy and limited public access to the waterfront, in contrast to the approach taken at Granville Island (G6). Menchions had potential as a historic resource, a reminder that this was a working waterfront lined with sawmills, boatyards, docks and rail tracks. DA Architects evoked that era in the Lift's form and materials: a curved wave of metal roof resembling an upturned boat hull, its shingles shaped like fish scales; an entrance canopy cablestayed like a mast; durable teak details. The use of teak is a practical reference to traditional ships' decking; the metal cladding refers to the Royal Vancouver Yacht Club's covered slips.

136 Westin Bayshore ↓

1601 Bayshore Drive
Douglas Simpson & Associates 1961;
Reno C. Negrin & Associates 1970;
Downs/Archambault Partners 2000

Built on the site of Pacific Coast Lumber Mills, the Bayshore Inn, as it was known, is intact where it meets the seawall but considerably altered at the entrance and inside. The inn has lost its Elvis-era vibe, which included one of Trader Vic's Polynesian-themed restaurants outside. The resort hotel—which promises guests "a stunning waterfront retreat"—was the obvious prototype for Coal Harbour's condos, which also seem disengaged from city life.

The planning process for them, begun in 1988, was interactive, following the precedent at False Creek (G19), with developer Marathon Realty and the planning department shaping the scheme to fit their broadly mutual, if not always shared, intentions. Numerous architects, landscape designers and planners were involved. Public input was solicited to form the guidelines, and over fifty public meetings were held. Public opinion said "no" to cars and commercial use of the waterfront and "yes" to residential, but not necessarily to the wealthy highrise suburb that resulted. Public access to the waterfront was gained on the seawall, which was extended from Stanley Park and integrated with the urbanism of the towers that face it, with strategic landscaping.

137 Performing Arts Lodge Canada Foundation

581 Cardero Street
DA Architects + Planners 2006

This multi-use project has subsidized housing for low-income, retired performing arts professionals, whom PAL assists, and market units. It includes a 100-seat theatre on the eighth floor of the structure and a roof garden, as well as space for child care, a playground and sidewalk retail. The tower, à la mode with an exposed concrete elevator stack and ship-like prow, maxes out the views

with little of the social sustainability that steered this project into the exclusive, elegantly landscaped Bayshore Gardens neighbourhood (not part of the Marathon site and more urban).

138 Coal Harbour Community Centre ✝
480 Broughton Street
Henriquez Partners Architects, Philips Wuori Long landscape design 2000

The centre was one of the amenities—along with the seawall extension, an extensive park and social housing—that the City gained from "development cost charges" embedded in the development permit approval process. The structure, which the architects liken to a submarine, seems to emerge like a hull from the edge of the harbour. The interior skylight is like a conning tower. Communal spaces are glazed to the seawall on one side of the conning tower's corridor, submerged on the other, which connects to an underground parkade. A spacious rooftop

that the market units get. Adjacent on Bayshore Drive, there is a typical street-wall of townhouses and an underground parkade. This tower and townhouse typology sails all the way to Canada Place,

park makes the most of available sunlight on a north-facing site overshadowed at times by condos. The centre primarily is concrete, on 1,200 piles necessary because the entire Coal Harbour strip below Hastings Street was reclaimed from the sea by the CPR around 1900.

139 Evergreen Building ↓
1285 West Pender Street
Arthur Erickson Architects 1980; Omicron, Arthur Erickson, Cornelia Hahn Oberlander landscape design, Donald Luxton & Associates 2007

Erickson's architectural response to this trapezoid site was to express its contrasting aspects in the building's arrangement of offices. Harbour-facing zigzag terraces with hanging gardens contrast with hard modernism on the city side. The corner projection at Pender and Jervis was cut away, supported on a concrete stilt to soften the structure's edge to the view. In

2005, the building was threatened with demolition for a condo tower. Heritage advocates supported its retention, and the Arthur Erickson Conservancy campaigned for it. The City protected the building with heritage designation, and Bentall Real Estate Services rehabilitated it as boutique offices, treating it with the esteem it deserved. The Evergreen's retention in its original form was one of the most significant outcomes in the effort to have the Vancouver's modernist heritage appreciated and conserved.

140 The Qube
1333 West Georgia Street
Rhone & Iredale, Bogue Babicki Associates engineers 1969; Musson Cattell Mackey Partnership 2005

Originally the Westcoast Transmission Building, this is as much a triumph of engineering as it is of architecture. Inspired by suspension bridges, it was

built from the top down from a concrete service core. Steel cables were hung from the top and steel-frame floors constructed one by one down to the fourth level, where the core is exposed as the entrance on an open podium. The core contains the elevators, electrical and mechanical systems, leaving floating floors with unimpeded views. The structural system was chosen for seismic safety (before the codes required it)—in a quake the building should shake like a leaf but not collapse.

The architects delivered it as a three-dimensional object in a volume of space and scenery to which it was specifically sensitive. The open podium was an inspired piece of urban design, minimizing the building's visual impact and obstruction of harbour views, now blocked. A lesser-known reason for no ground floor was that the marketing team told the developer that there was no market for ground-floor retail this far west on Georgia. Rehabilitation as the Qube condominium respected the building's unique qualities.

141 Former Crown Life Plaza †
1500 West Georgia Street
Rhone & Iredale 1978

This multi-storey office building opened as Crown Life Plaza. The International Style curtain walls and a concrete service core exposed on the roof are composed with expressive economy. The triangular plan is a response to the site, which was divided with an intuitive feel for urban form. The offices, a single-storey retail building and a reflecting pool's open space between them, were given individual expression over a city block, as triangular elements. The curtain wall angled

to West Georgia Street steps aside on *pilotis* to allow a view cone (now partly obscured) from Alberni Street to Stanley Park. The natural slope of the site was evoked by the reflecting pool's waterfall, a block-long cascade to the sidewalk on West Georgia. The design of the office building was informed by the progressive 1960s work of James Stirling in the U.K., from where project architect Peter Cardew immigrated.

142 Residences on Georgia †
1200–1288 West Georgia Street
1898; James K.M. Cheng Architects 1998

With rooftop beacons, clean lines and an art glass installation by Dale Chihuly, these are among the most stylish condos to "Vancouverize" the Georgia Street corridor. The largest single-phase residential complex in the country at the time, it exploited the demand for downtown living promoted by the City in its quest to increase density. The arrangement of two towers, row housing and landscaping is typical of Vancouverism. The typology has been replicated, not always with the modernist poise, formal plan and savvy urbanism here. Cheng also designed **The Palisades** (1996), twin elliptical towers across Alberni Street for the same developer (Westbank Projects).

Part of the Residences project was the **Abbott House** (1898) on Jervis Street, the last relic of Blueblood Alley, the choice residential enclave of the city's elite. Henry Abbott was the CPR's western superintendent, and this was his retirement home. Westbank converted it as five condos and gained a heritage density bonus for the towers and agreed heritage designation. Siding was deteriorated and could not have provided a waterproof envelope, so it was replaced (a fragment

of the old siding was retained, in front under the porch overhang). The hall and staircase were carefully restored (the prominent art glass window is original) during rehabilitation (Commonwealth Historic Resource Management). The makeover preserved the original's Queen Anne presence.

143 Banff Apartments ⬆

1201 West Georgia Street
Henry Barton Watson 1909

The Banff appropriates the name of the Scottish-inspired CPR hotel at Banff Springs, Alberta, but was originally called Florence Court, designed in Italianate style with a columned loggia at the entrance as if it were a Florentine palazzo. The interior once contained a skylit gallery. Plans show domes never built. Balconies and bay windows enliven the façades, which had pedimented lintels and a cornice balustrade removed in an undocumented "improvement." The original Banff is in northeast Scotland, the regional birthplace of George Stephen, the CPR's first president, and Donald Alexander Smith, Lord Strathcona, the financier who drove the "last spike" to complete the transcontinental in 1885. The building is a reminder, like the Abbott House (see previous entry), that Georgia Street west of Burrard was originally residential.

J

Shaughnessy Heights

THE Canadian Pacific Railway announced in 1907 that a 250-acre portion of its immense holdings south of False Creek would be developed as an exclusive residential area. The land had been logged in the 1870s under contract to Captain Edward Stamp of Hastings Mill. Strategically located on the crest of a hill, close to the proposed new Granville Street Bridge (opened 1909), the subdivision was to be named Shaughnessy Heights after CPR president Sir Thomas Shaughnessy (J23). The timing was perfect. Vancouver was entering a period of unprecedented growth and prosperity. The proliferation of small houses and apartments in the West End encouraged wealthier residents to flee to the new development.

The plan for Shaughnessy features tree-lined and boulevarded streets that follow the natural contours of the land. The centrepiece is The Crescent (actually an oval; J3–J8), close to Granville Street. The plan was produced for the CPR in 1907 by Montreal landscape architect Frederick Todd and Danish engineer L.E. Davick. Todd had trained with Frederick Law Olmsted, best known as the designer of Central Park in New York and Mount Royal Park in Montreal. Many streets were named after CPR officials: Angus, Marpole, Osler, Hosmer, Nanton and others.

Shaughnessy was promoted as an exclusive residential area with large lots, between ⅕ acre and 1½ acres. The CPR set $6,000 as the minimum price of any house and offered generous loans.

Above: Glen Brae/Canuck Place (J15)

Restrictions admitted only "racially appropriate" homeowners (servants aside; plans often indicate a small "Chinaman's room" in the basement).

The era preceding WWI was one of architectural revivals, the last flowering of traditions that emanated from classical antiquity, the Middle Ages and the age of Enlightenment. Architects offered their clients a choice of historical styles. The one selected defined a homeowner's values and aspirations. The Tudor Revival brought associations of English landed gentry, the Roman Revival symbolized power, and the Arts and Crafts manner implied embracing modern ideals. "Modernism" had not yet entered the Canadian architectural repertoire.

The aftermath of WWI brought a new order, including pressures for more affordable housing. In 1922, the provincial government responded with the *Shaughnessy Heights Building Restriction Act*, which limited the area to single-family homes and discouraged further division of properties. During the Depression, many residents could no longer afford to maintain expensive homes, and the area came to be known as "Poverty Hill" and "Mortgage Heights." Emergency legislation during WWII permitted conversion into rooming houses. Shared homes operating in 1955 could remain that way, but new rental suites were banned. The City of Vancouver's strict zoning (1959) continued to restrict change, although it permitted subdivisions as long as the new lots were at least 85 feet wide and 9,500 square feet in area—still very large by Vancouver standards.

Change was evidently necessary to meet the economic challenges of maintaining large houses and the new demographics that brought a variety of tastes. The First Shaughnessy Official Development Plan (1982) enabled one- and two-family infill dwellings, which provided revenue to the landowners. ("First Shaughnessy" is north of King Edward; "Second" and "Third" Shaughnessys are south of it and less exclusive.) Design guidelines for First Shaughnessy encourage "preservation of the Shaughnessy *character*." They encourage, but do not enforce, the preservation of authentic old buildings.

Property owners and their architects have interpreted the plan and its guidelines in different ways. The treatment of both infill dwellings and new principal houses includes some that are truly in the spirit of the historical sources (J11), others that try to do this but without success, those that adopt a gentle modernism that makes no waves (J22) and a few that are boldly contemporary (J10).

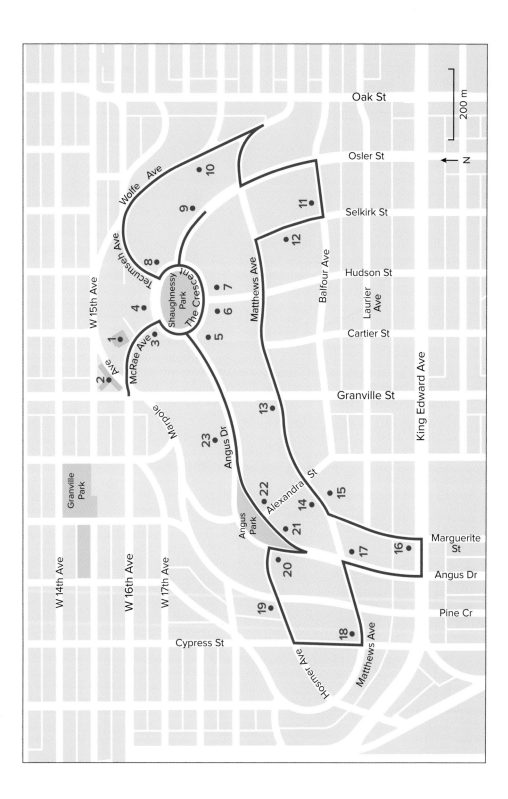

J2 **Hycroft Towers**
1445 Marpole Avenue
Semmens & Simpson 1951; later alterations

Marketed as "Canada's largest apartment house," this T-shaped building dominates the brow of South Granville. Its aggressive modernist treatment, with strip windows alternating with white spandrels, contrasts with the dignified historicism of Shaughnessy Heights, accessed just up McRae Avenue. The west wing was originally supported on *pilotis*, which gave pedestrians a view of the mountains. The ground floor has since been filled in and the original 158 suites increased to 180. The building was converted to strata title in 1973, reportedly the first in Vancouver to change from rental to individual ownership.

J1 **Hycroft**
1489 McRae Avenue
Thomas Hooper 1912; Gerald Hamilton & Associates 1963

General (and future senator) Alexander Duncan McRae was representative of the wealthy Vancouverites who chose to relocate to Shaughnessy Heights. McRae made his fortune in lumber, fishing, coal and real estate and built the district's most imposing mansion. Six majestic columns, repeated to the north overlooking an Italianate garden, support a grand porte cochère. The interior plasterwork, by sculptor Charles Marega, survived the building's stint as a veterans' hospital (1943–60), after McRae gave it to the federal government. Since 1962 it has been the home of the University Women's Club. Most of the gardens and outbuildings east of the house were replaced a year later with a number of unassuming brick townhouses that are well integrated into the topography. The townhouses required a special zoning change and were Shaughnessy's first infill development, built to provide the club with a revenue stream.

J3 **Miramar**
3333 The Crescent
Maclure & Fox 1913; Formwerks Architectural 2012

The Tudor Revival, characterized by ornamental "half-timbering" (mimicking the heavy-timber frame and stuccoed infill of buildings from the Tudor period), steep roofs, dormer windows and tall chimneys, was the favoured style in Shaughnessy Heights. It evoked visions of English country manors and their attendant culture, gentility and wealth.

The Province publisher (and later lieutenant governor) Walter C. Nichol chose Victoria architect Samuel Maclure and his Vancouver partner, Cecil Croker Fox, leading practitioners of the style and architects to high society. Fox died in action in WWI, ending the productive partnership and, in a broader sense, an era. The house was subsequently sold to mining tycoon William R. Wilson and then to Austrian refugee and future forestry magnate Leopold Bentley, who also bought the land on which Hycroft Towers (J2) now stands to protect his view. The gardens that extended to the north have recently been supplanted by fifteen townhouses with underground parking—the same revenue-producing solution adopted nearly fifty years earlier at Hycroft (J1) but in this case very visible from the street. The controversial development was approved in part because it ensured the protection of the historic house and its south garden. Maclure & Fox also excelled at middle-sized Tudor Revival houses, such as the nearby **Arthur Brenchley House** (3351 Granville Street, 1912), built for a wholesale grocer.

J4 Henry M. Leggat House
1363 The Crescent
c. 1911

Just east of Miramar (J3) is this attractive Georgian Revival house, with its characteristic central triangular pediment,

curved porch, hipped roof, wood clapboard siding with corner pilasters, bow windows and sash windows. All recall the eighteenth-century townhouses of New England. The porch wing to the left breaks up the symmetry, adding a more Canadian and Shaughnessy-specific picturesque composition.

J5 Frederick M. Kelly House †
1398 The Crescent
Townley & Matheson 1921

The houses around The Crescent—actually an oval—provide a catalogue of historical architectural styles popular during this revivalist era. The Dutch Colonial Revival swept Vancouver in the 1920s, with this house—now called "Crescent Falls"—an early example of the fashion. The second-floor windows are treated as an extended dormer in the characteristic double-sloped mansard (or gambrel) roof. Here stucco has graduated from half-timbering infill to status as a full-fledged facing material.

J6 The Hollies
1388 The Crescent
Gamble & Knapp 1912; 1940; 1982; 1992

The columned and pedimented portico, inspired by Roman temple fronts, flaunts grandiose classical airs that would not be out of place on a southern U.S. plantation (partner Jacob Knapp came to Vancou-

ver from Seattle). The client was George E. MacDonald, who had interests in timber and mining and was general manager of the Pacific Great Eastern Railway (M6). In 1922 he sold the house to rival A.R. Mann of the Canadian Northern Railway. A number of wings have been added and removed over the years, but the front retains its original form and grandeur.

J7 Bryce W. Fleck House
1296 The Crescent
Honeyman & Curtis 1929

This house for industrial supplier Fleck and the nearby **C. Carry House** (1232 The Crescent, attributed to Honeyman & Curtis 1929) show the persistence of the Tudor Revival a decade and a half after Maclure & Fox popularized it (J3). The association with English aristocracy was irresistible to local socialites and social climbers—its adoption by the latter

leading to the dismissive term "stockbro-ker Tudor." Stucco, beloved in the 1920s, is now the principal finish material. Care is revealed in the details, particularly the porte cochère, bay windows, stained glass and curved gable over the entrance.

J8 L.W. Shatford House
3338 The Crescent
1912

Politician and broker Lytton W. Shatford built this house, with its distinctive pro-jecting gabled wing over the porch. A love of wood is evident in the shingled

siding and the generous ornament. Pro-jecting rafters, eaves brackets, second-storey overhangs and the entrance piers all exploit the structural and decora-tive use of timber. Just south, **Villa Russe** (3390 The Crescent, Cleven Cox 1921; Ar-thur Erickson 1959) was built for Russian émigré financier and arts patron Misak Y. Aivazoff and was later owned by B.C. Electric president Dal Grauer.

J9 Iowa ✝
3498 Osler Street
MacKenzie & Ker 1914

Wood is again used to best advantage in this exquisite house for lumberman Frank L. Buckley. The three-bay façade looks back more than a half-century to the American Gothic cottages of Andrew Jackson Downing, whose published de-signs led in turn to the typical Ontario house of the later nineteenth century. Leaded-glass windows and decorative woodwork reveal a high level of crafts-manship. The house starred as the Soviet consulate in the movie *Russian Roulette* (1975), which ended with a helicopter shootout on the roof of the Hotel Vancouver. A number of recent houses have replaced the first-generation buildings along Osler Street. The one across the street at 3537 Osler Street is a big new "character house," whose elongated horizontal proportions, oversized windows and heavy-handed detail don't approach the gracious spirit of the originals (contrast J11).

J10 **1098 Wolfe Avenue**

Measured Architecture, Fast + Epp engineers, Elizabeth Watts landscape design 2008

To many, good contemporary architecture is preferable to mediocre character houses. The historic character of Shaughnessy is protected within the precinct, but bold new designs can be built on the periphery. After much debate, the Advisory Design Panel approved the plans for this house, noting that Shaughnessy "shouldn't be a time warp replica." With its foundation cut into the slope, green-roof camouflage and landscaped grounds that slope down from the heights, the house is unobtrusive to neighbours on the leafy lands above but emphatic from the street. The flat roof is dynamically cantilevered above minimalist, skylit interior spaces. Granite projects at front and rear, a reference to the area's traditional stonework (seen on the old retaining wall).

J11 **1163 Balfour Avenue**

John Hollifield 1995

Design guidelines for First Shaughnessy (1982) encourage "preservation of the Shaughnessy *character*." They encourage, but do not enforce, the preservation of authentic historic buildings. Many architects have interpreted the guidelines as license to make it seem that nothing has changed since 1920—at least on the outside. This residence is one of the better neo-heritage designs that have appeared in Shaughnessy as a consequence. It won a heritage award for its "compatible new design in a heritage context." Its approach contrasts with the one taken at the previous and following houses, one main house and one infill house, which adopt a fully contemporary manner. Both practices have their advocates, and the debate continues.

J12 Rosemary
3689 Selkirk Street
Maclure & Fox 1915; Henriquez Partners
Architects 2003

Lawyer and liquor magnate A.E. Tulk named this magnificent Tudor Revival house after his only daughter. The ochre-and-brown half-timbering is combined with beige shingles, brown clapboard and red brick to give the impression of a rambling English manor built over generations—perhaps similar to a house in Norfolk whose picture Tulk reportedly showed Maclure. It was later the home of Lieutenant Governor John William Fordham Johnson. From 1947 to 1994 it was a retreat operated by the Order of the Convent of Our Lady of the Cenacle. The subsequent owner, lawyer Gordon Shrum, maintained the house while reconfiguring the property. He moved the **Lando House** (1910), an early vernacular "foursquare" predating Shaughnessy's love affair with revivals, from Matthews Avenue to 3611–3613 Selkirk and duplexed it. He intends to build a new main house in its place on Matthews. And Richard Henriquez designed the large **Shrum Guest House** behind Rosemary, in keeping with the regulation that permits more efficient use of large Shaughnessy properties by adding infill dwellings. The concrete-and-glass guest house is designed entirely in a contemporary language yet remains respectful of the grand old house. The debate as to whether infill should look new or be in period dress parallels the discussion over replacement houses. Compare, for example, the attractive neo-Tudor Revival infill house and garage around the corner at **1470 Matthews Avenue** (Raymond Letkeman 1985), looking like a coach house and stables and built soon after infill was enabled by the First Shaughnessy Official Development Plan (1982).

J13 Rockland
3589 Granville Street
H. Murray 1912

Iron cresting—which survived WWII scrap-metal drives—caps the ridge of this stalwart stone-and-shingle residence, built for William Walsh. A broad,

J14 R.S. Lennie House ↓
1737 Matthews Avenue
Sharp & Thompson 1912

G.L.T. Sharp and C.J. Thompson, the English-trained partners of a firm that dominated Vancouver architecture for three-quarters of a century, began their fertile careers as confirmed revivalists, then led the way to modernism in the 1940s. Their Georgian Revival-cum-Italian Renaissance public buildings (H36), Gothic and Tudor Revival churches (K31) and this large Tudor Revival house for lawyer Lennie show the variety of traditional styles in vogue at the time and in which they were fluent.

hipped roof with flared and bracketed eaves provides a strong horizontal emphasis, while the corner turret, dormers and other projections offer picturesque counterpoint. For more than two decades the house was occupied by the John Westaway Society, a residential philosophical association. It has been returned to residential use, with a secondary residence inserted in the **coach house** (1533 Matthews Avenue). A stone garden wall, stone gateposts, wrought iron gates and a tall cedar hedge provide privacy.

J15 Glen Brae/Canuck Place
1690 Matthews Avenue
Parr & Fee 1910; Downs/Archambault 1995

Two voluptuous domed towers and a theatrical Corinthian-columned porch make this one of the most unforgettable of Shaughnessy homes. It was built by

lumber and real estate tycoon William Lamont Tait, who built his "Valley by the Mountains" ("Glen Brae") to remind him of the castles of his native Scotland. The superb cast-iron fence was manufactured by Walter MacFarlane of Glasgow, from where the glazed bricks were also imported. The third-storey ballroom had a sprung floor laid over a pad of seaweed. Briefly home to the local chapter of the Ku Klux Klan in the 1920s, Glen Brae was bequeathed to the City by a later owner in 1991. It has been lovingly rehabilitated to become a hospice and palliative care facility for sick children known as Canuck Place, a name that recognizes the ongoing support of the Vancouver Canucks hockey team.

J16 B.T. Lea House
4051 Marguerite Street
John A. Pauw 1930

Continuous horizontal lines and broad overhanging roofs reveal the influence of Frank Lloyd Wright and the Prairie Style. Transient Dutch architect Pauw selected a pleasing palette of materials with the variegated brick ground floor, wood upper storey and shingle roof. South of King Edward Avenue is the Second Shaughnessy subdivision, land. The lots are smaller and never achieved the exclusivity of the original section. Compare, for example, the **A.B. Weeks House** across the street at 1808 West King Edward Avenue (1923), a Mission Style house (see J21) somewhat smaller in scale.

J17 **John Hendry House**
3802 Angus Drive
Maclure & Fox 1915

Lumber magnate John Hendry was a native of New Brunswick who came to B.C. in 1873 to work at the Moodyville sawmill and rose to become president of B.C. Mills, Timber & Trading Company (C19). He left his large West End residence at Burnaby and Jarvis Streets (1902; demolished) for this larger Tudor Revival mansion. The former coach house at the south end of the original lot, also designed in the style, has been converted into a private home.

J18 **Greencroft**
3838 Cypress Street
Thomas Hooper 1913; Robert G. Lemon Architecture & Preservation, Birmingham & Wood 2002

Home for nearly a half century to industrialist, lieutenant governor and UBC chancellor Eric Hamber and his wife, Aldene, the daughter of John Hendry (J17), this impressive house features a steep hipped roof and a large château-style tower. The Hambers' many distinguished

guests reportedly included King George VI, Queen Elizabeth, Prime Minister Louis St. Laurent and President Franklin D. Roosevelt. Amidst massive controversy, two infill dwellings were added at the rear corners of the lot (1889 Matthews Avenue and 3818 Cypress Street; four new houses were originally proposed), the main house was divided into two units, and additional heritage density was transferred to another site.

J19 William Ditmars House

3637 Pine Crescent
c. 1913

This red-brick, classically derived Georgian Revival house is relatively unusual for Vancouver, where the more casual, romantically inspired Arts and Crafts and Tudor Revival styles were preferred. This design owes much to the Federal Style, a variant of the Georgian Revival in the U.S. The formal façade, with its porch and shuttered windows, is capped by a gable roof and dormers.

J20 W.F. Huntting House

3689 Angus Drive
Maclure & Fox 1913; Raymond Ching 1986

The horizontally proportioned roughcast façade, terminated at each end by a gable and topped by a steep roof, resembles houses by English Arts and Crafts architect C.F.A. Voysey, with whom Cecil Croker Fox had worked. Here Fox emerges from the Tudor shadow of his senior partner, Samuel Maclure. Two infill houses

(1695 Angus Drive and 1818 Hosmer Avenue) were inserted into the once-extensive grounds.

J21 W.F. Salsbury House

1790 Angus Drive
A.A. Cox 1912

The white roughcast walls, prominent shaped gables and deep balcony show the sunny allure of the Mission Style, a California import, whereas the picturesque massing and broad roofs betray the influence of old England. William F. Salsbury, who reportedly arrived in B.C. on the

first transcontinental train, was one of the many CPR officials who settled in the railway's Shaughnessy Heights.

J22 Angus Place
3610–3630 Alexandra Street, 1660 Angus Drive
Tanner/Kay 1973

The design of this "four-house village," somewhat Mediterranean in its enclosure and in its plain stucco walls, consciously combines modern and traditional elements. Shed roofs, panelled doors with fanlights, and whimsical arches offer a preview of the kind of playfulness and ironic juxtaposition of features that has come to be called postmodern. The four units face away from the street towards a communal pool.

J23 Sir Thomas Shaughnessy House
1551 Angus Drive
Honeyman & Curtis 1910; Benjamin Ling 1998

This was the Vancouver residence of Sir Thomas Shaughnessy, president of the CPR from 1899 to 1918, after whom the subdivision was named. Like many CPR executives, he owned a palatial home in Montreal's Square Mile. His Vancouver Arts and Crafts "cottage" (as plans described it) was one of the first houses built and was intended to set the tone for future development. Little did Shaughnessy know that it would appear small by comparison with the houses that would follow in the next few years. The house looked like a crumbling British hunting lodge when its significance was discovered in 1993. It had been bought in 1919 by C.W. Frazee of the Royal Bank, whose family still owned it. Subsequent infill behind the house produced the revenue (and the commitment) to ensure its retention.

The West Side

T HE principal land mass of Vancouver is a large peninsula that
terminates to the west as Point Grey. Coast Salish First Nations
used the land for centuries: the Musqueam Band in the south,
along the North Arm of the Fraser River, and the Squamish Nation
in the north, along English Bay.

The first Europeans to sight the sandy cliffs of Point Grey were
the crew of Commander José María Narváez, who explored the
Strait of Georgia for Spain in 1791. Captain George Vancouver visited the area a year later for Great Britain and named the point
after his comrade, Captain George Grey.

Two-thirds of a century passed before Europeans showed further interest in Point Grey. In 1859 land at the end of Point Grey
and at Jericho was surveyed and reserved for military purposes.
At about the same time, the McCleerys, Magees, Moles, Shannons
and other farming families settled along the fertile North Arm of
the Fraser River. The community of Eburne developed on both
sides of the river to serve the farms and some sawmills. The north
portion of Eburne became known as Marpole (K37), and the ham-
let to the south vanished, most recently as part of Vancouver International Airport (N1). Logging operations took place here as
throughout Vancouver.

Above: Ma House (K16)

Land from English Bay to 16th Avenue became a part of the City of Vancouver in 1886. Kitsilano (K4, K6) began to grow as a "streetcar suburb" in the early 1900s, enabled by the inauguration of the interurban trains in 1905 and by streetcar service along 4th Avenue in 1909. This, the West Side, became the residential area of choice for the economically and politically dominant professionals and managers who had originally settled in the West End. Much of the land comprised the CPR's immense District Lot 526, part of its land grant from the federal government. The CPR controlled the rate of development, ensuring orderly growth and maintaining a uniform level of quality.

In 1906, the area west of Ontario Street and south of 16th Avenue separated from the District of South Vancouver. Two years later, the breakaway community was incorporated as the Municipality of Point Grey, with its services concentrated in Kerrisdale (K29). A middle- and upper-income suburb from the start, Point Grey's status and healthy tax base got a boost from the development of Shaughnessy Heights within its borders. Citizens consistently voted for municipal improvements. In 1922, Point Grey enacted the first zoning bylaw in Canada, which separated land uses and encouraged parks and street beautification. Point Grey and working-class South Vancouver were reunited when they amalgamated with the City of Vancouver in 1929. Despite the supposed equalization of services, the original physical and economic differences are still evident.

As elsewhere in Vancouver, recent planning promotes densification—the replacement of single-family houses with multiple residences and the erection of ever-larger buildings with smaller and smaller living units. The zoning encourages new buildings with traditional architectural character—neither heritage conservation nor bold new design. In some cases, the results have been outstanding, but much of the time the design outcome is mediocrity. Ironically, many wealthier residents have relocated to luxury condominiums in the West End, reversing the migration of a century ago.

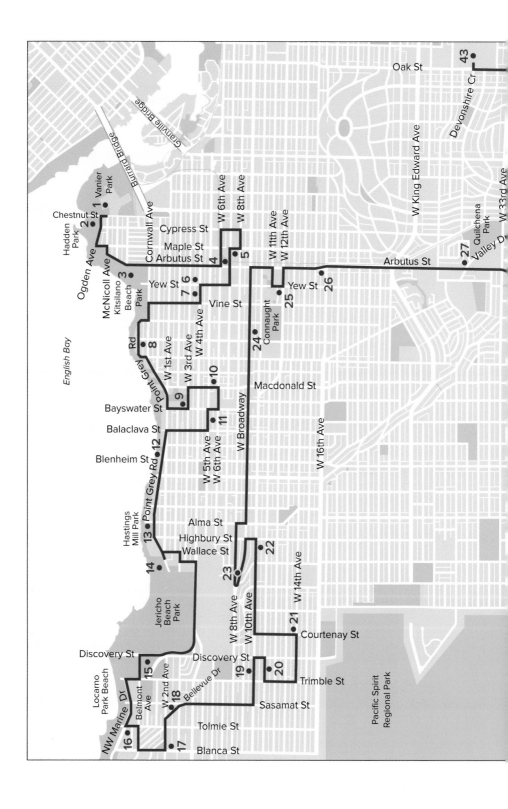

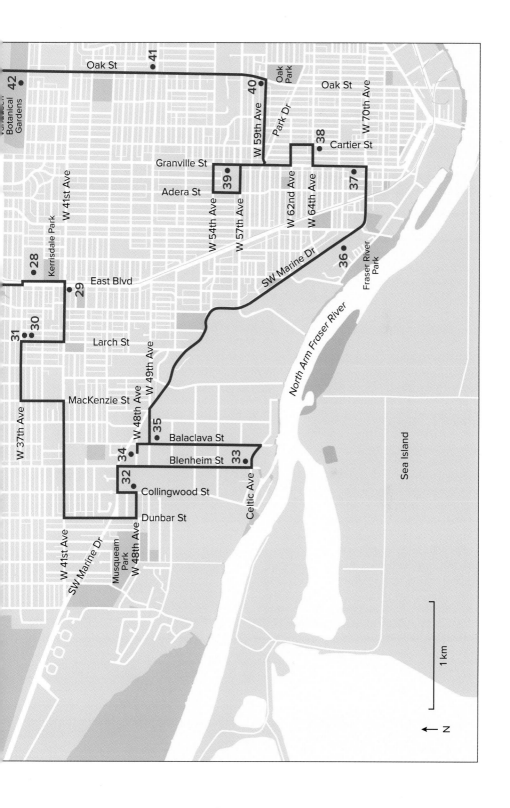

K1 Museum of Vancouver and H.R. MacMillan Space Centre
1100 Chestnut Street
Gerald Hamilton & Associates 1968; Hancock
Brückner Eng + Wright, Sears & Russell 2002

Covered by a landmark dome inspired by a Salish hat—some liken it to a flying saucer—the planetarium sits atop the exhibition galleries of the municipal museum. Delicate lacework of white precast concrete exemplifies the New Formalist architecture of the day, begetting the nickname "Taj Mahal on the Creek." Sculptor George Norris's stainless-steel *Crab* guards the entrance. A small educational wing was recently added at the rear. This and several other nearby institutions make a cultural enclave of Vanier Park, created in the 1960s at the tip of Kitsilano Point, on a former Indian reserve augmented by landfill. Three lie beyond the museum. Best is the semi-subterranean **City of Vancouver Archives** (1150 Chestnut Street, McCarter Nairne & Partners 1972), the first municipal archives in Canada, organized in the 1930s by the dedicated Major J.S. Matthews. The others are the **Vancouver Academy of Music** (1270 Chestnut Street, Vladimir Plavsic 1976) and the **Gordon MacMillan Southam Observatory** (Bain Burroughs Hanson 1979), operated by the space centre. Beyond them are the tents of the summer Shakespeare festival, Bard on

the Beach, as well as the Canadian Coast Guard heliport and a boat landing. The earliest museum on Kits Point is the Vancouver Maritime Museum (See next entry).

K2 Vancouver Maritime Museum †
ST. ROCH NATIONAL HISTORIC SITE
1905 Ogden Avenue
Raymond O. Harrison, C.B.K. Van Norman & Associates 1958–66

The 80-ton RCMP Arctic patrol boat *St. Roch*, built in North Vancouver (M7) in 1928 and the first vessel to conquer the Northwest Passage in both directions, rests inside a shingle-and-glass A-frame shelter. The early modernist maritime museum beside it celebrates the region's colourful and significant maritime past. The collection extends behind the museum, on the grounds and in the Heritage Harbour. The totem pole in front of the museum was carved in 1958 by Mungo Martin.

K3 Kitsilano Beach Restaurant & Lifeguard Facilities
1305 Arbutus Street
A.A. Robins Architect 2005

After divisive community debate, a private developer received permission from the Park Board to build an upstairs restaurant and bar with fabulous views in return for providing a public snack bar,

washrooms and lifeguard facilities at beach level. The execution is stylish, contemporary West Coast, with indoor–outdoor confines dissolved. Further west on popular Kitsilano Beach—packed with bodies on summer weekends—are the large heated saltwater **Kitsilano Pool** (1931; 1971) and the funky **Kitsilano Showboat** (1935), an amphitheatre for summer entertainment. The route up Arbutus Street crosses early brick pavers at 3rd Avenue.

κ4 **Arbutus Coffee ·**
2200 Arbutus Street
1908

This "boomtown-style" false-fronted veteran opened as the Eureka Grocery and remains a survivor of the once–ubiquitous corner store. It served what is now the oldest extant group of houses in Kitsilano. Development was stimulated by the inauguration in 1905 of the B.C. Electric Railway's interurban line to Steveston along the adjacent CPR tracks. The CPR abandoned the line in 2000, and the City went to the Supreme Court of Canada to be al-

lowed to expropriate the right-of-way for future rapid transit. The houses extending down the hill were built in the first decade of the twentieth century; the oldest is the **Murphy House** at 2078 West 6th Avenue, begun in 1901. All were acquired by the City in anticipation of demolishing them to extend Delamont Park. Two blocks away and passed on the route is **2322 Cypress Street** (c. 1900), a tiny, shingled "pioneer cottage," characterized by a square plan, pyramidal hipped roof and front porch. It represents a popular inexpensive house-type of the era.

K5 St. Augustine's Church
2028 West 7th Avenue
Twizell & Twizell 1931; Parish Centre,
DGBK Architects 1998

The parish was founded in 1911 to serve growing Kitsilano and placed in the care of the Missionary Oblates of Mary Immaculate. The brick Gothic Revival church was designed by Vancouver's leading ecclesiastical architects of the day. **Pandosy Place**, a residence for priests, is adjacent at 2015 West 8th Avenue. The addition of a respectful **Parish Centre** along 7th Avenue delivers a soothing architectural postmodern sermon, with matching brick and a courtyard garden. A single-storey cloister-like corridor connects, but visually separates, the new and old. The parish attained rezoning for the centre in return for heritage protection of the church. Around it is a cluster of three-storey apartment buildings, a building-type that nearly replaced old Kitsilano.

K6 Former Canadian Bank of Commerce
2199 West 4th Avenue
1910; Formwerks Architectural 2002

Streetcar service along 4th Avenue began in 1909, a year before Broadway, making it the "high street" of Kitsilano. The Canadian Bank of Commerce responded with this stalwart, brick-and-stone neo-classical branch. "Kits" and its businesses underwent changes over the years, first as the heart of 1960s hippie Vancouver and now as an upscale neighbourhood, reflected in the fashionista makeover of the former bank.

K7 Capers Building
2211–2285 West 4th Avenue
Hotson Bakker Architects 1994

This trendsetting block-long development, known by the original name of its grocery store, combines ground-floor retail with offices and 78 residential units above and 274 underground parking stalls. The cheerful modernist design is built flush to the sidewalk to respect the traditional streetwall, where funky "hubcapitals" recall the site's former car dealership. The building pioneered environmental awareness as Vancouver's first major application of geothermal heating (pipes bored below ground extract heat from the earth's core). High density is achieved in a medium-rise building, a planning objective for Kitsilano after a brief period (1960s–'70s) that permitted high-rises, seen scattered around the area. Just down the hill is the former **Kitsilano Presbyterian Sabbath School** (1855 Vine Street, 1910), now residences, whose dour sandstone façade and Corin-

thian columns must have looked quite out of place amidst a sea of frame houses. Nearby is **Seascapes** (2405 West 2nd Avenue, Hughes Baldwin 1990), a three-storey stucco apartment building whose curved balconies and floating roofs lift it high above the ordinary.

K8 Matthew Logan House
2530 Point Grey Road
Honeyman & Curtis 1910, Robert Lemon Architect 2011

Built for businessman Logan and later the home of brigadier-general, newspaper publisher and philanthropist Vic-

tor Odlum, son of Edward Odlum (E1), this elegant residence stands on a quiet and exclusive segment of Point Grey Road. Superb craftsmanship is seen throughout, as in the curved glass of the bow windows, the leaded panes and the balustrade. The stone wall distances it from the street. The many newer neighbours generally respect the scale and serenity of the area.

K9 Tatlow Court
1820 Bayswater Street
R.T. Perry 1928; Corner Group 1977

The courtyard apartment, with attached units around a landscaped court, came by way of California. This is Vancouver's best example, rendered in the cherished Tudor Revival—although an earlier scheme (by Frank Mountain) called for Hollywood Spanish (see K18). The 1977 renovations added a second storey within the roof, illuminated by large dormers. The apartments and the park behind it are named after founding Park Board commissioner and B.C. minister of finance R.G. Tatlow. The two-unit condominium next

door (**1870–1890 Bayswater Street**, Peter Wardle 1977), developed by the innovative Art Cowie (F5), achieves much the same in a more contemporary mode.

K10 **2100-block Macdonald Street**
Lockie & Miller builders 1911

Kitsilano developed with row after row of developer-built houses that lined the grid of streets, the skyline punctuated by gabled roofs. This group represents the dominant type just before WWI— often described as the Edwardian Builder style—with broader proportions than

the earlier, Victorian, Strathcona builder houses (C1, C5, C11) and wood brackets that anticipate the emerging California Bungalow (see next entry). Around the corner, the red-brick **General Gordon Elementary School** (2896 West 6th Avenue, Norman A. Leech 1912; F.A.A. Barrs 1925; 1957; 1961) was built to accommodate the rapid growth of the neighbourhood.

K11 **2900–3000-blocks West 5th Avenue**
Fred Melton, Cook & Hawkins builders 1919–21

The favourite middle- and working-class house after WWI was the California (or Craftsman) Bungalow, which spread from the western U.S. in builders' pattern books. The typical inexpensive bungalow has one storey (or a second floor tucked within the roof), a broad verandah, a gable or two facing the street, wood siding, abundant wood trim, and cobblestone, wood or brick posts. Sources include the English Arts and Crafts style, the early houses of Frank Lloyd Wright and a soupçon of Asian building. A larger version had a full second storey under the

slope of a steeper roof (see **3044–3066 Point Grey Road**, 1920). The bungalow and the Edwardian Builder house (see previous entry) are enjoying a popular revival. Kits sports countless new neo-traditional homes of similar appearance, encouraged by zoning that discourages innovation to maintain neighbourhood character (e.g., **3096 West 2nd Avenue**, EDG Homes 2011).

K12 **Shaw House**
3257 Point Grey Road
Patkau Architects 2000

A lap pool projects alongside a bedroom above the offset entrance of this spartan neo-modernist house. The weight of water and seismic safety required a re-inforced-concrete slab and heavy-duty frame, which is exposed inside. Watery light from the pool's glass bottom dapples the vestibule. High ceilings and un-adorned spaces visually expand the long narrow interior, which opens to the view of English Bay. The public's sight of this beachfront home is a fence and a garage.

Immediately west, Erickson/Massey's **Townhouses** (3267–3293 Point Grey Road, 1965), the area's first multi-unit development, similarly turn their backs to the street, like a Roman atrium house. Realtors call this waterfront strip the "golden mile." It feels miles away from Kits, although the neighbourhood's characteristic and inviting Craftsman homes and mature landscapes line the other side of the road.

K13 **Hastings Mill Store**
1575 Alma Street
c. 1868; 1932

The oldest building in Vancouver and the only one to survive the Great Fire of 1886, the structure was erected as the supply store for the Hastings Mill at the foot of Dunlevy Avenue (c19) and served as Gastown's first post office. The Native Daughters of B.C. saved it from demolition—Vancouver's first organized conservation effort—and barged it in 1932 to its present site in Pioneer Park, where it reopened as a delightfully quirky museum. Aside from some new windows and the shutters, it is unchanged from the original. Farther west are the **Royal Vancouver Yacht Club** (clubhouse built here 1927; expanded 1978, 1996) and the **Jericho Tennis Club** (1926; rebuilt 1960, 1998), two popular private sports facilities.

K14 **Brock House**
3875 Point Grey Road
Maclure & Fox 1913; John Keith-King 1976; Birmingham & Wood 1986

Architects Maclure & Fox exploited the Tudor Revival style with gracious homes for the social elite. This beachfront manor, resplendent in its gables, dormers and pseudo-half-timbered walls, was built for Philip Gilman, an English mining engineer, and is named after long-time owners Mildred and Reginald Brock. It is now a senior citizens' centre and public

restaurant. Visitors can admire the fine Arts and Crafts interior, with its lofty entrance hall, wood panelling and leaded windows. Just beyond is Jericho Beach.

K15 **Vancouver Jericho Beach Hostel**
1515 Discovery Street
Department of National Defence 1937

Jericho Park, a popular beach and bird sanctuary, gets its name from "Jerry's Cove," where pioneer logger Jeremiah Rogers produced fine spars for sailing ships. Set aside as a government reserve, it was developed in 1920 as the Jericho Beach Flying Boat Station, whose seaplanes defended the coast from rumrunners in the 1920s and a feared Japa-

nese invasion during WWII. The hostel served as barracks for the air station. Another survivor is the public **Jericho Sailing Centre** (1300 Discovery Street). The air station's wharf, which was used for Habitat Forum, the groundbreaking people's offshoot of the UN Habitat Conference on Human Settlements (1976), was demolished in 2011. Nearby is the **Jericho Arts Centre** (1675 Discovery Street, 1993), the 135-seat home of the United Players of Vancouver.

K16 **Ma House**
4608 Northwest Marine Drive
Daniel Evan White 1985; 2000

Dan White, who studied under Arthur Erickson, specialized in modernist residences designed with spatial and struc-

tural flair in response to site. This house on a sloping site overlooking Spanish Banks has a wood frame, with steel and glued-laminated (glulam) beams to support the many cantilevers that create multi-level decks. White's big, bold, sculptural forms (at a time when postmodernism seemed to be hijacking the profession) were moderated by precise detailing, seen here in the angled entry sequence, where steps and a waterfall (added during renovations) lead to a calm courtyard that draws light into the home.

K17 **J.F.J. Cashman House** †
4684 West 2nd Avenue
Perry & Fowler 1914

Cedar logs cut for telephone poles were towed from the Sunshine Coast and dragged by horses up the hill for this big, cozy Arts and Crafts home, built by lumberman (and supplier of the logs) Tom Murphy for American contractor Cashman. The verandah's stones were barged across English Bay from the Capilano River. The interior is well preserved. The garden, once known for its orchard, retains mature firs, cedars and wisteria.

K18 Kania Castle
4585 Bellevue Drive
1936

The Spanish Colonial Revival, with its red pantile roofs, stucco walls, arched openings and wrought-iron balconies, swept California in the 1920s and drifted north to B.C. This fantasy, built for broker Joseph Kania and perched high on a steep escarpment, displays the style at its showiest. The once-white walls have been painted salmon pink, with glorious historical inaccuracy.

K19 ROAR_one †
4387 West 10th Avenue
LWPAC Lang Wilson Project in Architecture Culture, Hotson Bakker Boniface Haden 2006

The upper end of 10th Avenue, the commercial hub of West Point Grey now promoted as "Point Grey Village," is undergoing a transformation to add density, the new Vancouver planning mantra. The former site of the Varsity Grill is now occupied by this mixed-use project, with two shops and ten loft-style residential units that adapt to individual preferences for living or live-work combos. The street and lane masses are separated by an east-west axial open-air courtyard. Primary materials (softened with wood decks and bamboo plantings) are metal, glass and concrete—light and relatively cheap. The styling is industrial chic, an approach that evokes the Bauhaus ideas of craftsmanship and objectification while also providing solar shading and passive energy control.

K20 **New Vancouver Special**
4360 West 11th Avenue
Stuart Howard 1985

Critical of the Vancouver Special (F13), the Vancouver League for Studies in Architecture and the Environment sponsored a competition for a better design. Winner Stuart Howard's prototype featured traditional materials, vertical massing, steep roofs and a semi-detached rear extension, providing the same density in a more attractive package. Howard's quest for better dwellings is also evident in his 16-foot "thin house" nearby at **4167 West 11th Avenue** (1987). Neither caught on.

K21 **Arthur Erickson House & Garden** †
4195 West 14th Avenue
1924; Arthur Erickson 1957

Celebrated architect Arthur Erickson bought this double-width lot, renovated the small pair of garages at the rear as his home and designed an enchanting garden, a place of delight and dreamy solitude. The unremarkable house opens to the garden's terrace and a concrete viewing platform that projects out to a pond. Reeds and water lilies, with a backdrop of bamboo, rhododendrons, pines and poplars, suffuse the miniature landscape with a Japanese tranquility, yet it is alive with the immediacy of an Impressionist painting. Soil excavated for the pond forms a berm that creates (with the wood fence) a sound baffle and privacy. "Architecturally, this house is terrible," Erickson said, "but it serves as a refuge, a kind of decompression chamber." Saved by "friends" after Erickson ran into financial troubles in 1992, the sanctuary is key to understanding his work and poetic spirit. It is managed by the Arthur Erickson House & Garden Foundation, which offers guided tours by appointment.

K22 Horace Barber House
3846 West 10th Avenue
Ross A. Lort 1936; Robert G. Lemon Architecture & Preservation 1990

The 1930s ushered in modernist tendencies that rejected period revival styles. Architect Lort, former partner of arch-traditionalist Samuel Maclure (J3), adopted the austere flat concrete walls—radical for the day—hard edges and abstract geometry of the moderne style. A compatible infill dwelling (3842 West 10th Avenue, Robert G. Lemon 1990) was built at the rear, providing the financial incentive to conserve and rehabilitate the house.

K23 3979 West Broadway
Ross Lort 1941; Bill Curtis & Associates Design, Donald Luxton & Associates 2009

A cozy Cotswold cottage was the model for this quaint home. The undulating shingle roof mimics thatching, and half-timbering, rubble stonework and stucco complete the fairy-tale imagery. Builder Brenton T. Lea built several speculative houses like this. Others are at 587 West King Edward Avenue and 885 Braeside Street in West Vancouver. As with the

previous house, revenue from a (retro) new infill home (3998 West 8th Avenue, Battersby Howat 2010) provided the money to enable conservation.

K24 CMHC Post-War Housing
2430–2456 West Broadway
c. 1950

Central (now Canada) Mortgage & Housing Corporation was created in 1946 to resolve the housing crisis created by returning war veterans. It assisted private developers with cheap financing and set up multi-government housing programs. This project, with sixteen two-storey suites and a much-used courtyard, is the last survivor of the clusters of affordable and livable two-storey housing that once dominated Broadway and 4th Avenue, between Arbutus and Alma. All became dispensable when the streets were up-zoned, and most have been replaced with four-storey buildings such as the **Larchway Gardens Apartments** across the street (2475 West Broadway, Bentall Developments c. 1992), which offers sixty-three

much smaller one- and two-bedroom units. Recent development has been even larger and denser; see, for example, the massive **2228–2288 West Broadway** (2008) just up the hill.

K25 **Arbutus Walk**
West 10th and 12th Avenues, between Arbutus and Vine Streets
IBI Group, master planners, various architects, begun 1996

After a controversial planning process, Concert Properties filled these four city blocks of former industrial land with mid-rise condos and sidewalk-hugging townhouses, attractively landscaped with a linear park. The land had been occupied by Canadian Brewing & Malting (later Carling O'Keefe), built in 1908 (additions to 1954) by immigrant Bavarian brewer Henry Reifel and serviced by the CPR's Arbutus line. After the brewery closed in the 1990s, city planners densified the area, a block south of the Broadway transit corridor. The resulting architectural styles and built forms were influenced by the new/old urbanism promoted by Jane Jacobs, overlaid with marketable "New York–style brownstones" and arty names such as Zydeco and Mozaik. **Tapestry at the O'Keefe** (2799 Yew Street, Downs/Archambault & Partners, Davidson Yuen Simpson 2002), an eight-storey seniors' residence promoted as retaining "the heritage and charm of the brewing precinct's golden years," is a bizarre replica of the brewery, which would not have been described so fondly by those who laboured there. A commemorative plaque recorded the history after the brewery's reusable cluster of structures had been bulldozed.

K26 **Ridge Theatre**
3131 Arbutus Street
Kaplan & Sprachman 1949–50

Despite belonging to an endangered species, namely the single-screen cinema, the eight-hundred-seat Ridge continues to attract audiences under the capable operation of Festival Cinemas, which also runs the single-screen **Park Theatre** (3440 Cambie Street, 1941). The moderne entry, capped by the name "Ridge" and sporting a billboard-sized stained-glass window, and the enormous rooftop bowling pin promoting the attached alley make this small (and early) strip mall a landmark on Arbutus Ridge. The oldest single-screen survivor is the Art Deco **Hollywood Theatre** (3123 West Broadway, Harold Cullerene 1935), owned since the

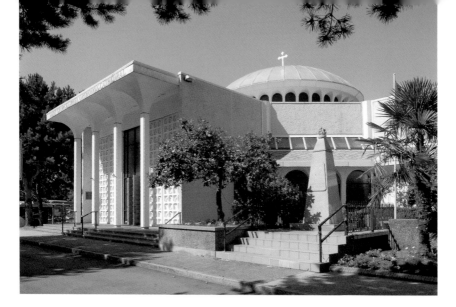

beginning by the Fairleigh family but sold in 2011, likely for redevelopment. Arbutus Street runs parallel to the CPR/interurban tracks (K4).

K27 St. George's Greek ✝ Orthodox Cathedral
4500 Arbutus Street
Hamilton Doyle & Associates 1971, 1977

Delicate arches and patterned screen walls of precast concrete are capped by a shallow dome, in an example of the architects' exercises in New Formalism (compare K1). The cathedral serves the city's large Greek-Canadian population, whose traditional commercial district is located along Broadway, west of Macdonald Street.

K28 Point Grey Secondary School
5350 East Boulevard
Townley & Matheson 1929; 1964

Standing between two eras, the building is structurally "modern" with its poured-in-place concrete walls, yet stylistically traditional with its Gothic Revival towers, arches, shields and quatrefoils that evoke the "dreaming spires" of Oxford. The

later gym and science block, designed by the Vancouver School Board's architects, are less distinguished.

K29 Bowser Block
5729 West Boulevard
1912

41st Avenue and West Boulevard was (and remains) the civic and commercial centre of Kerrisdale, named after Kerrydale, the Scottish family home of early resident Mrs. William MacKinnon. The B.C. Electric Railway's interurban line from Vancouver to Steveston (the present train tracks, which were laid by the CPR) stopped at 41st Avenue (formerly Wilson Road) from 1905, encouraging development. Streetcar service along 41st in 1912 further improved access. This was the

heart of the former Municipality of Point Grey. The genteel, Tudor Revival Point Grey Municipal Hall (1909) stood a block south, where the **Kerrisdale Community Centre & Library** (5851 West Boulevard) is today. The two-storey brick Bowser Block, which housed a bank at the corner, remains a modest landmark, perhaps best known for the vintage neon sign of the Avenue Grill (2114 West 41st Avenue).

K30 **Larchwood**
5300–5400-blocks Larch Street
Ramsay Worden Architects 1994

Here is contextual architecture at its best. Some forty-five "stacked" (that is, in two rows) courtyard townhouses have been squeezed into a block-long development, intended to achieve a higher density than Kerrisdale's dominant single-family housing while retaining its scale. Preserving one old house (5336 Larch Street, 1924) earned a density bonus. The neo-traditional gabled design fits into the neighbourhood while not attempting to look old.

K31 **St. Mary's Kerrisdale**
2490 West 37th Avenue
Sharp & Thompson 1913; Twizell & Twizell 1947; William Rhone 1989, 1994

Architects Sharp & Thompson evoked the spirit of an Anglican parish church in their native England, although with shingled and board-and-batten walls that exploit B.C. wood. Additions to either end in the 1940s, as well as recent upgrades to the church and parish hall, retain the character. The interior glows from the marvellous stained glass–and-brass lanterns. Sharp's own fine house (1912) is across the street at number 2427.

K32 **Don MacFarland House**
6290 Collingwood Street
Dalla-Lana/Griffin 1977

Fred Dalla-Lana, who trained with Arthur Erickson, was one of a group of talented architects who emerged in the 1970s and '80s. He updated the post-and-beam theme with more aggressive compositions that challenged the balance seen in earlier work. Here the stone

chimney and penthouse projections counter the horizontality of the lower floors in a masterly composition. Just around the corner is the **Barry V. Downs House** (6275 Dunbar Street, Barry Downs 1958), a discrete "townhouse" built for his family by architect Downs, which pays homage to Frank Lloyd Wright.

K33 Golden Oak Stables †
7376 Blenheim Street
Stuart Howard Architect 1990

Below Southwest Marine Drive the ground drops quickly to the Southlands, fertile land along the North Arm of the Fraser River, which was farmed from the 1860s by the McCleerys, Magees and Moles—before there was a Vancouver. The farms and market gardens have gone—replaced by nurseries—but the flats remain a semi-rural equestrian centre with agricultural zoning. Golden Oak is one of many commercial stables. Its houses, barn and outbuildings, designed by Maura Gatensby, evoke images of rural farm buildings. Two generations of new houses have replaced most of the modest cottages that once were dominant: first came some excellent early modern houses from the 1950s to '70s (K32, K34–K35) and now a number of enormous mansions.

K34 McLellan-Saddy House
3245 West 48th Avenue
Thompson, Berwick & Pratt 1958, 1974; D'Arcy Jones Design 2007

The office of Thompson, Berwick & Pratt led the way with West Coast modernism and was an incubator for many of Vancouver's most talented architects. This house began as a one-storey building designed by Ron Thom, Dick Mann and Bob Burniston; the second floor was added a decade and a half later. Architect Jones notes that his changes "undid previous renovations gone wrong," including minor additions, removing inappropriate recent interior finishes and inserting new floor-to-ceiling and clerestory windows in order to reinstate the close relationship between inside and out. The nearby **Saba House** (2870 West 47th Avenue, Sharp & Thompson, Berwick, Pratt 1947; Andre Rowland 1994) is an earlier example of the modernist manner, also with recent alterations.

K35 Kenneth Gardner House ↓
3152 West 49th Avenue
Kenneth Gardner 1958

Distinguished by being the first heritage-designated residential "recent landmark" in Vancouver, this minimalist house by South African architect Gardner features a crisp rectilinear block that floats above the recessed ground floor. Neither the house nor the architect had local roots. The International Style design contrasts with the West Coast version of modernism. It is uncompromising and structurally adventurous, formed with "lift slab" construction: the reinforced-concrete floor and roof slabs were framed, stacked and poured, then raised by hydraulic motors attached to eight steel posts. The horizontal, street-facing severity is softened by the colour and texture of the brick walls; the private, south elevation has two glazed recessed openings.

Gardner put the living area on the second floor as a precaution because the site is on the north fringe of the Fraser Delta floodplain.

K36 Casa Mia ↑
1920 Southwest Marine Drive
Ross A. Lort, 1932

George Reifel, who built this house, was the eldest son of Henry Reifel, the Bavarian-born beer maker who built the large Canadian Brewing & Malting plant at 11th and Yew (K25). George continued in the business. He built this Spanish

Colonial mansion on acreage that extended south to the Fraser River, where he moored his notorious speedboat used for rum-running during the American prohibition. He donated the George C. Reifel Bird Sanctuary in Delta to the Crown in 1972. His brother, Harry F. Reifel, raised cattle and built his own neo-Spanish fantasy, **Rio Vista**, just west of here (2170 Southwest Marine Drive, Bernard Palmer 1930). The brothers owned two downtown entertainment venues, the Vogue Theatre and Commodore Ballroom (H4).

K37 Safeway Store
8555 Granville Street
Frank Roy 1966; later alterations

Canada Safeway Limited built a number of supermarkets with this distinctive design—a sweeping double-curved roof defined by arched glulam beams and supported inside only by a few pipe columns. The glass façade was flanked by fieldstone walls; the stone has been removed. This is one of few stores that remain unchanged. Former rival SuperValu had its own distinctive arched form that avoided interior supports entirely (F9). This south end of Granville Street—originally called North Arm Road—is the commercial strip of Marpole (formerly Eburne), once a village that serviced the agricultural land on both sides of the North Arm of the Fraser River. The many retail signs in Chinese indicate the diversity of the neighbour-

hood. The area has a rich aboriginal heritage, including the Marpole Midden (also called the Eburne Mound or the Great Fraser Midden, near Granville and 75th), a rich deposit of Coast Salish materials from about 1,500 to 2,500 years ago.

K38 Joy Kogawa House
1450 West 64th Avenue
1912; subsequent alterations

Author Joy Kogawa resided here as a child from 1937 until 1942, when she and her family were interned along with all coastal B.C.'s Japanese Canadians (E19). The Land Conservancy of B.C. purchased the modest house in 2006, intending to restore it to its appearance when she lived here. TLC has also established a writer-in-residence program. The house is a lonely survivor of old residential Marpole, completely surrounded by newer residences.

K39 Shannon
7101-7201 Granville Street
Somervell & Putnam 1915–25;
Arthur Erickson 1973

The 10-acre Shannon estate, which features a grand brick-and-stone Georgian Revival mansion and the city's best

Italiante garden, was built for sugar king B.T. Rogers (C15, 111). Rogers died in 1918, leaving his widow to finish the work. Financier Austin Taylor purchased the property in 1935. The house, formal gardens, gatehouse, coach house (visible from West 54th Avenue and Churchill Street) and stone boundary wall all survive. They are supplemented by **Shannon Mews**, a bevy of exquisitely detailed and discreetly sited luxury, two-storey townhouse apartments designed by Arthur Erickson. A proposed redevelopment of the site has aroused considerable controversy.

K40 Fire Hall No. 22
1005 West 59th Avenue
Henriquez & Associates 1979

This large brick fire hall, which replaced a wooden structure now reused as **Marpole Place** (1305 West 70th Avenue), a community and seniors' centre, presents a utilitarian elevation to 59th Avenue and a distinctive detached false front "sign" to the public elevation on Oak Street. The two blocks are "hinged," allowing the atrium between them to be used as the hose tower. Richard Henriquez also designed the nearby **Temple Sholom**

(7190 Oak Street, Henriquez & Associates 1987), attended by the area's Reform Jews. Kitty-corner from the fire hall is **Marpole-Oakridge Community Centre** (1949), the first to be built in the city but likely soon to be replaced.

K41 Unitarian Church of Vancouver
949 West 49th Avenue
Wolfgang Gerson with Richard C. Hale 1964

This timeless building avoids the clichés of church design to express the Unitarian "non-dogmatic exploration of spiritual, intellectual and ethical growth" and distance it from mainstream Christianity. Three buildings are grouped around an open court: the tall, well-lit, serene sanctuary at the northeast, the Hewett Centre to the west and the administration block at the corner. The cubic

composition and overhanging roofs recall Frank Lloyd Wright's familiar Unity
Church near Chicago (1906) but without
Wright's eccentricity. **Unity of Vancouver**
(5840 Oak Street, W.D. Buttjes 1964), a
few blocks north, likewise breaks with
tradition in the soaring curve of its
arched roof. An early International Style
church whose austere design totally de-
nies history is the **Granville Chapel** (5901
Granville Street, Robert R. McKee 1950),
built for the Plymouth Brethren. Contrast
these with the conventional steep roofs
and spire of **St. Peter's Estonian Lutheran
Church** (6520 Oak Street, 1964) across
the street and the nearby **St. Matthias &
St. Luke Anglican Church** (680 West 49th
Avenue, Ross A. Lort 1960).

K42 **VanDusen Botanical Garden**
5251 Oak Street

W.C. Livingstone garden planner, Underwood,
McKinley, Wilson & Smith architects 1975;
Thompson, Berwick, Pratt & Partners 1976;
Perkins + Will Canada, Cornelia Hahn
Oberlander and Sharp & Diamond landscape
design 2011

A spectacular curved structure—a "living building" whose roof is inspired by a
native orchid and whose components all
adopt sustainable systems—is the showy
new Visitor Centre for Vancouver's botanical garden. The garden opened in
1975, fifteen years after the start of a
campaign to keep the CPR from developing this, the former site of the Shaughnessy Heights Golf Course. The land was
purchased with funds from the City, the
Province of B.C., the Vancouver Foundation and a large donation by Whitford J.
VanDusen. Bill Livingstone of the Vancouver Park Board supervised the development of the grounds, which feature a

variety of enchanting botanical experiences, from the tropics and the Himalayas to our own B.C. ecosystem. All occupy an undulating 55-acre site that includes three small lakes, whose concept Livingstone based on the English picturesque garden associated with Lancelot "Capability" Brown. The original wood post-and-beam structure was planned by the Park Board's architects. The former main building and Floral Hall have been retained, although the connecting breezeway was demolished. Architect Paul Merrick was the lead designer for MacMillan Bloedel Place in the northwest corner of the garden in 1976; today it serves as the Education Centre. The Bloedel Conservatory (F4) recently became a component of the VanDusen Garden.

K43 Children's & Women's Health Centre of B.C.

4480–4500 Oak Street
Mercer & Mercer 1940–45; Gardiner Thornton Partnership 1982; many later additions and alterations

B.C. Children's and Women's Hospitals share a campus with a long history. The concrete-and-steel-sided main building (1982) is the original Children's Hospital, now used by both institutions. The site was developed in 1919 for wounded soldiers as Shaughnessy Military Hospital. A WWII-era early-modern complex with Art Deco details survives on the east side, including the **Shaughnessy Building**

(1940) and **Jean Matheson Pavilion** (1945), the latter now the Mental Health Building (2007). Both are seen best from Heather Street. They are threatened with redevelopment, which began in 2011 with groundbreaking for the **Clinical Support Building** (CJP Architects) on 28th Avenue. Two distinctive recent additions are the cleanly contemporary **Translational Research Building** of the **Child & Family Research Institute** (950 West 28th Avenue, Musson Cattell Mackey Partnership 2008), which occupies the northwest corner of the site, and the exposed-concrete **Children's Ambulatory Care** building (IBI Group, Henriquez Partners Architects, Karlsberger Companies 2003) at the rear, north of the Shaughnessy Building.

Translational Research Building

The University of British Columbia

THE University of British Columbia was created by provincial legislation in 1908 and provided with a magnificent 260-acre site at the tip of Point Grey, away from the "city's nefarious influence." An international competition to design the new campus was held in 1912. The jury unanimously selected the partnership of G.L.T. Sharp and C.J. Thompson, two young architects recently arrived in Vancouver from England. They proposed a grandly scaled plan based on the planning principles taught by the École des Beaux-Arts, with grand boulevards, superb vistas and a hierarchical plan that placed the administration at the highest point on University Boulevard and assigned each faculty its own precinct—a distinction that is still largely maintained. The plan called for buildings to be designed in the "Modern Tudor" style—what we now call "Collegiate Gothic"—to "express and perpetuate the traditions of British scholastic life."

Two new buildings were begun in 1914 but delayed by WWI and insufficient funds. Students attended classes at Vancouver High School (D17) at Oak Street and West 12th Avenue. In 1922 students made the "Great Trek" to Point Grey and climbed on the concrete skeleton of the Science Building (L2). Their point was made—construction resumed, and the new campus opened for classes in September 1925.

Above: Museum of Anthropology (L7)

The next generation of buildings, including the Old Auditorium, was built more cheaply, with wood frames rendered in stucco, but retained allusions to the Gothic style. Sharp & Thompson and their successor partnerships (for many years Thompson, Berwick & Pratt) remained the campus architects until into the 1960s. The firm was a leader in introducing International Style modernism to Vancouver. This was reflected at UBC with their designs for the War Memorial Gymnasium (L1, designed in 1947) and the Buchanan Building (L13). Since the late 1960s, the university has commissioned a variety of firms to design individual buildings as the campus expanded. Some excellent architecture has appeared as a result.

The current building boom began in the 1980s. A comprehensive campus plan was produced in 1992 by Toronto planners du Toit Allsopp Hillier. They recognized the need to accommodate growth while respecting the grid, sightlines and values expressed by the Sharp & Thompson plan. The 1992 plan, in turn, was updated by the new campus plan of 2010. It makes sustainability a high priority, to help create a livable environment conducive to academic excellence. It does not refer directly to the century-old plan.

The architects of new buildings at UBC take sustainability principles to heart (the UBC Renew program—see L2—rehabilitates old buildings to sustainable standards). A stellar example is the Centre for Interactive Research on Sustainability (L6), designed to be one of the greenest buildings on the continent.

The largest capital initiative at present is branded UTown@UBC, a university town likened to Oxford and Cambridge. It is not a cohesive place, as is Simon Fraser University's UniverCity, since residential "neighbourhoods" are scattered across the campus. The intention is to change UBC's commuter culture by accommodating "members of the UBC community," though many residents have no relationship to the University. Eight new neighbourhoods are envisioned in all. One, Chancellor Place (L11), is included in the chapter.

The lands immediately east of campus are the University Endowment Lands, a green belt between the City of Vancouver and UBC. Much of the UEL have been developed residentially, including some fine early modern and recent homes, which are not visited. A large swath of the UEL was dedicated as Pacific Spirit Regional Park in 1989. A good part of it will become part of a land settlement negotiated with the Musqueam Band, whose people consider Point Grey their traditional land.

UBC has grown from a handful of buildings to an institution with forty thousand students and nine thousand faculty and staff. It runs programs in downtown Vancouver and operates a satellite campus in Kelowna. This chapter introduces the Point Grey campus. It starts and ends at the bus loop. Much of the campus is pedestrianized; automobile parking is available in the area.

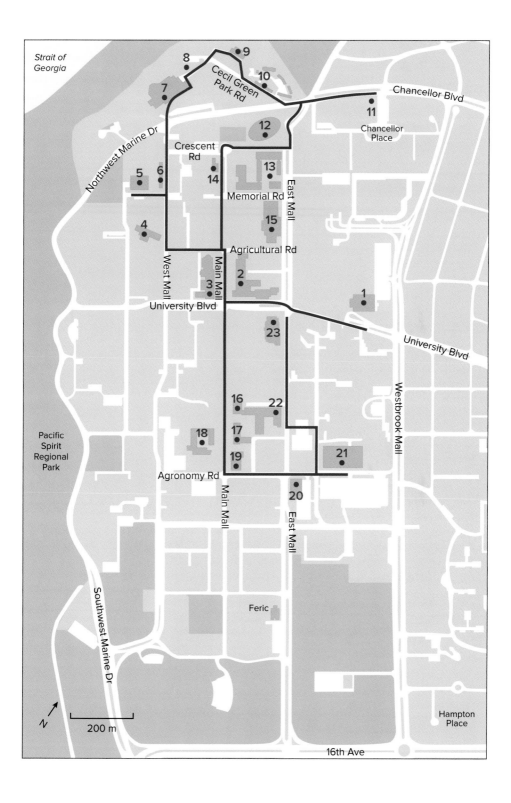

Strait of
Georgia

Chancellor Blvd

Cecil Green
Park Rd

8

9

7

10

11

Chancellor
Place

12

Northwest Marine Dr

Crescent
Rd

5 6

14

13

East Mall

Memorial Rd

15

4

West Mall

Agricultural Rd

Main Mall

3

2

University Blvd

University Blvd

1

23

Westbrook Mall

16

22

Pacific
Spirit
Regional
Park

18

17

21

19

Agronomy Rd

Main Mall

20

East Mall

Southwest Marine Dr

Feric

N

Hampton
Place

200 m

16th Ave

L1 War Memorial Gymnasium
6081 University Boulevard
Sharp & Thompson, Berwick, Pratt, Frederic
Lasserre, F.W. Urry 1947–51

This muscular, cubic gymnasium, UBC's first modern building, dominates the main gateway to the campus. Consulting architect and professor Frederic Lasserre and engineer F.W. Urry collaborated to design the massive structural roof truss that projects downward into the gym, avoiding the need for columns. Reinforced-concrete stairs cantilevered from the building are another instance of structural gymnastics. The adjacent open-air **Empire Pool**, by the same architects, was built for the 1954 Empire Games (E17). Across University Boulevard is the **David Strangway Building** (5950 University Boulevard, Hotson Bakker Boniface Haden 2006), used for medical teaching facilities, with rusticated granite pilasters that hearken back to the original Collegiate Gothic campus architecture, seen next.

L2 Chemistry Centre
2036 Main Mall
Sharp & Thompson 1914–25; Thompson,
Berwick & Pratt 1961; Henriquez Partners
Architects 2008

Architects Sharp & Thompson won an international competition to design the new campus of UBC, the province's first post-secondary school. Their Beaux-Arts master plan of 1912, with grand malls and vistas, called for buildings in the "Modern Tudor" style (we now call it "Collegiate Gothic") to "express and perpetuate the traditions of British scholastic life."

Originally the Science Building, this was the first structure on the new University of B.C. campus. Delays caused by war and underfunding left it a concrete skeleton, until students at the temporary university at Oak Street and 12th Avenue (D17) protested by parading out to Point Grey in the Great Trek of 1922. Only then was work resumed on this and the original portion of the main library (L15). Both buildings exhibit the Collegiate Gothic style that was deemed appropriate for academic architecture across Canada. New buildings continued to use the historicist mode until after WWII, although mainly in cheap, stuccoed-frame versions. In 2004 the UBC Renew program was introduced to preserve and upgrade the University's aging building stock, emphasizing sustainability. Rehabilitation has produced remarkable cost savings over demolition and new construction, leading UBC to

L

boast that "every third building is free." The Chemistry Centre was the first project undertaken. A complete renewal reconfigured spaces, upgraded (not replaced) existing systems, maximized passive ventilation and lighting to reduce energy consumption and met life safety standards, all while preserving the building's distinctive architectural features, including the stone elevations, the metal casement windows and an exceptional tiled corridor.

L3 Sauder School of Business
2053 Main Mall
Acton Ostry Architects 2010

This radical recycling of the **Henry Angus Building** (Thompson, Berwick & Pratt 1965; Reno C. Negrin & Associates 1976) stripped it back to its concrete frame and floor slabs and carved out an atrium that rises through the full height. A new curtain wall wraps the original structure, which has been clad with coloured panels to reflect the pattern language associated with business—a barcode. Seismic bracing is exposed on the main floor. The adjacent glazed tower was part of the **David Lam Management Research Centre** (CJP Architects 1992). The process continues the reuse approach seen with the UBC Renew program (L2). Phase two of the Sauder School is scheduled for completion in 2012.

L4 First Nations House of Learning
1985 West Mall
Larry McFarland 1992

Inspired by the longhouses of the Coast Salish, this impressive structure is a meeting place and support facility for First Nations students. The Great Hall features carved house posts supporting massive roof beams. Compare the modern replicas of longhouses behind the Museum of Anthropology (L7) and the museum itself, which was inspired by the same sources.

L5 Asian Centre
1871 West Mall
Donald Matsuba 1981

Like an oversized lid, a broad, pyramidal hipped metal roof covers this peaceful building, its steel beams reused from a pavilion at Expo 70 in Osaka. The centre contains part of the Department of Asian

Studies, its library, a gallery and an auditorium. A moat-like reflecting pool encircles it, and a traditional Japanese bell tower stands outside. Directly west is the serene **Nitobe Memorial Garden**, which prompted the visiting emperor of Japan to proclaim, "I am in Japan."

L6 C.K. Choi Institute for Asian Studies
1855 West Mall
Matsuzaki Wright Architects, Read Jones Christoffersen engineers 1997

"Conceived as a metaphor for change," as the architects put it, this unconventional building was at the forefront of sustainable design in North America. Douglas-fir trusses recycled from the nearby armoury (Sharp & Thompson 1941; demolished 1994) constitute 70 per cent of the structure; doors were salvaged from a downtown office renovation; the hundred-year-old bricks, originally ships' ballast from Europe, were salvaged from Yaletown streets; and most of the structural steelwork has recycled content. South-facing pagoda roofs were aligned for solar panels; this and double-glazing help reduce energy consumption to 50 per cent below municipal requirements. Rainwater is caught and recycled. The building was the first to be independent of the regional sewer system and the first institutional/commercial building on the continent with composting toilets. Ventilation is fresh air. The linear form

on a former parking lot spared adjacent trees; the alignment makes the most of natural light. The landscaping (Cornelia Hahn Oberlander) uses indigenous plants, is free of pesticides, is bio-fertilized and conserves water. UBC has since made sustainability a core element of its building and planning. The **Centre for Interactive Research on Sustainability** (2260 West Mall, Perkins + Will Canada 2011) adds a LEED Platinum-standard teaching and demonstration facility to the commitment.

L7 Museum of Anthropology
6396 Northwest Marine Drive
Arthur Erickson 1976, 1990; Arthur Erickson, Stantec Architecture 2010

Muscular concrete posts supporting broad beams, inspired by the cedar houses of coastal First Nations, frame this spectacular museum on a magnificent site above the Point Grey bluffs. The floor slopes down from the entrance, and the ceiling rises to create a dramatic and spacious setting for totem poles and house frames. The floor extends outside in a seamless transition—the essence of Erickson's West Coast style—to "the Haida country

of the Queen Charlotte Islands," as Cornelia Hahn Oberlander described her landscape, recently completed to include a "tidal pool." The museum expanded its scope and size with the Koerner Ceramics Gallery (1990) and more recently with the addition of the Centre for Cultural Research, the high-tech Multiversity Galleries and the refurbishment of many original spaces.

L8 Point Grey Battery
Service road between Museum of Anthropology and Cecil Green Park
Department of National Defence 1939

Defences were built along the B.C. coast during WWII to resist possible Japanese attack. The two concrete platforms (the eastern one restored in 1990) supported 6-inch artillery guns with an 8-mile range. A third platform is used as the base of Bill Reid's *The Raven and the First Men* (1980) inside the Museum of Anthropology (see previous entry). Ammunition was stored in the magazines beneath each platform. Enemy ships could be illuminated by searchlights along the shore below; the concrete searchlight towers survive as curiosities on Wreck Beach, Vancouver's nude beach.

L9 Cecil Green Park
6251 Cecil Green Park Road
Maclure & Fox 1912; B. Gordon Hlynsky Architects 1989

This exquisite Tudor Revival mansion, built for lawyer E.P. Davis, was bought in 1966 by UBC alumnus Dr. Cecil Green, who donated it to the university as a social and alumni facility. It is currently the home of Alumni Affairs. The grounds, which make the most of the marvellous view to Howe Sound, and the interior, with a galleried hall and splendid woodwork, complement the exterior.

L10 Green College
6201 Cecil Green Park Road
Birmingham & Wood, Paul Merrick Architects 1994

Cecil Green also funded Green College, which is a graduate residential college, an international society of scholars and a UBC community facility. The new residential buildings offer a contemporary rendition of the traditional Collegiate

Gothic quadrangle that "reflects West Coast values of openness and informality." Meeting spaces occupy the rehabilitated **Lefevre-Graham House** (Maclure & Fox 1915)—including the wood-vaulted Great Hall on the second floor—and its coach house.

L11 Chancellor Place/ Theological Neighbourhood
Chancellor Boulevard and Iona Drive
Ramsay Worden Architects 2007

The university is in the midst of an aggressive program of developing land adjacent to the academic campus for residential use. Called UTown@UBC, it envisions the creation of eight new neighbourhoods, of which this is one. The first was **Hampton Place** (Wesbrook Mall and West 16th Avenue; various ar-

chitects 1991–98), which built nearly a thousand units in eleven townhouse and medium-rise complexes on 28 acres, all with names and styles that provide a pastiche of Olde England. Chancellor Place, in contrast, benefitted from a ready-made identity. The iconic Vancouver School of Theology's **Iona Building** (Sharp & Thompson, west wing 1927, tower 1934; Thompson, Berwick & Pratt, east wing 1962; Rositch Hemphill & Associates 2004) lent a focus to the new development. The view from Chancellor Boulevard up to the Iona Building's tower is now framed by duplex townhouses and apartments. The style is eclectic, vaguely West Coast with overlays of granite that reflect the Iona Building's cladding and aspects of its traditional UBC style.

L12 Chan Centre for the Performing Arts †
6265 Crescent Road
Bing Thom Architects 1997

The entrance to this curvilinear, zinc-panelled gem flows from a landscaped plaza (Cornelia Hahn Oberlander, Elizabeth Watts) into a crescent-shaped glazed lobby like the overture to a pastoral sym-

phony. The elegantly refined ovoid interior of the 1,365-seat Chan Shun Concert Hall is finished in exposed concrete and wood panels and enlivened by visible metal structural components. The superb, adjustable acoustics (Artec Consultants) make this Vancouver's best performance space for recitals and for small and medium-sized ensembles. Adjoining halls with 275 and 160 seats complete the performance.

L13 Buchanan Building †
1866 Main Mall
Thompson, Berwick & Pratt 1956–60;
Toby Russell Buckwell & Associates 1972;
Busby, Perkins + Will 2010

UBC and its campus architects, Thompson, Berwick & Pratt, introduced the modernist International Style to the campus around 1950 (L1). The four low blocks of the Faculty of Arts' Buchanan Building, with their precise, rectilinear walls of grey glazed brick, painted concrete, enamel panels and glass, typify the style. The 1972 tower offers a later, more brutalist touch. The Buchanan complex was rehabilitated as part of the UBC Renew program (L2). Work in-

cluded internal reconfiguration, seismic and mechanical upgrades, and new double-glazed windows, while retaining the features of the early modern exterior, and it also involved landscape renewal (Phillips Farevaag Smallenberg) in the courtyards. In contrast to the unadorned Buchanan Building, **Brock Hall Annex** (1874 East Mall, Thompson, Berwick & Pratt 1957) intrigues the visitor with the mosaic *Symbols for Education* (Lionel A.J. Thomas & Patricia Thomas 1960).

L14 Morris & Helen Belkin Art Gallery
1825 Main Mall
Peter Cardew Architects, C.Y. Loh Associates engineers 1995

The modestly scaled Belkin Gallery is enlivened by a tall, partly two-storey, luminous interior whose metal roof is supported by elegantly arched steel members. The urbane and rectilinear white brick exterior respects its early modernist older neighbours: the **Frederic Lasserre Building** (Thompson, Berwick & Pratt 1962), which honours Swiss-born modernist Frederic Lasserre, first director of the School of Architecture; the **Frederic Wood Theatre** (Thompson,

Berwick & Pratt 1963); and the **Music Building** (Gardiner Thornton Davidson Garrett Masson & Associates 1968). Those three softened the austere orthodoxy of the International Style; contrast the Buchanan Building (see previous entry). The expressive Belkin Gallery extends that idiosyncratic regional tradition and, with the Chan Centre (L12), completes the 1950s vision of an arts centre, while its glazed brick elevations engage with the legacy. UBC's Fine Arts Gallery had spent a half-century (from 1948) in the basement of the main library (L15), sharing inadequate space with the Museum

of Anthropology before acquiring this proper home. The first gallery was curated for many years by Alvin Balkind. He and architect Abraham Rogatnick (later a professor of architecture) arrived in Vancouver in 1955 and opened the New Design Gallery, the city's first contemporary art gallery.

L15 Irving K. Barber Learning Centre ✝
1961 East Mall
Sharp & Thompson 1925, 1948, 1960;
Pfeiffer Partners Architects, DA Architects + Planners 2008

The Irving K. Barber complex supersedes the former Main Library, whose Collegiate Gothic centrepiece—retained and partly reconstructed as a learning commons, and memory to inform a large, new library complex—was one of the two original buildings at UBC (see L2). Three old wings were replaced in a contrasting modern style, an old–new distinction that is also clear inside. The spatial reorganization focuses on a full-height atrium, entered from a corridor through the old building or from East

Mall through a wall of glass. The atrium's chandelier, *It's a Mystery* (John Nutter 2008), inspired by manuscripts from global cultures, reflects the centre's philosophy. Off this generous space are study, lecture and meeting areas, and stacks serviced by the "library robot," an automated storage and retrieval system linked to the online catalogue. Above the entrance to the old Main Library are two tablets—the *Monkey & the Bearded Man* (1925)—by sculptor Charles Marega. They allude to the Scopes Monkey Trial held in the U.S. that year, which contested Darwin's theory of evolution. The sculpture provides a poignant symbol of free inquiry and enlightenment.

Alongside Main Mall, a hollow reveals the below-grade **Sedgewick Undergraduate Library** (Rhone & Iredale 1972). It was subsumed by the wide but shallow **Walter C. Koerner Library** west of Main Mall (1958 Main Mall, Architectura with Arthur Erickson 1996). Expansion of the Koerner Library was stymied when the Barber Learning Centre was conceived. The **Ladner Clock Tower** (Thompson, Berwick & Pratt 1968) north of the library honours

a pioneer B.C. family. At the southeast corner of Main Mall and Memorial Road is the *Millennial Time Machine* pavilion (superkül architecture 2003), part of the outdoor art program of the Belkin Art Gallery (L14).

L16 Biodiversity Research Centre & Beaty Biodiversity Museum ↑
2212 Main Mall
Patkau Architects 2009

The most prominent object here is not the building but the whale—a 25-metre-long blue whale skeleton exhibited as a symbol of life's mysteries and complexity. The display pavilion, parallel to Main Mall, is a see-through box, a perfect commission for architects known for creative restraint. The whale is suspended over ramped access to displays, as if raised from a pit, also symbolic because the bones were excavated from a beach on Prince Edward Island. The research centre floats off behind, perpendicular to Main Mall, shielded by a shimmering sunscreen. It completes a quadrangle begun by the **Aquatic Ecosystems Research Laboratory** (2202 Main Mall,

Patkau Architects 2006). The façade windows are shaded by steel mesh *brises-soleils*; an atrium orients users to all floors and allows air to circulate by "thermal stack effect" with no need for conditioning; lighting is monitored automatically. The landscaped quadrangle (Perry + Associates) is a pleasure, the sustainable plantings minimalist, mostly grasses. The entrance to the quad is a contextual gesture to that of the MacMillan Building (L18) across the mall.

L17 Fred Kaiser Building ↑
2332 Main Mall
Omicron, architectsAlliance 2005

Shadows from trees along Main Mall dapple this building with nature's approval because of the spectrum of green features: a perforated steel canopy shades offices on the top floor loggia; concrete floor slabs act as heat exchangers; cool air enters through windows, not a mechanical system; motion sensors turn off lights in unoccupied rooms; sunlight is reflected from solar-protectant, ceramic-layered window glass, patterned

like a forest. Built for the Faculty of Applied Science, Electrical & Computer Engineering—partly above a deconstructed 1970s building—the overlay's modernist aesthetics are softened by the ceramic coating and in the wood-panelled atrium, where visible photovoltaics make the green agenda clear.

L18 MacMillan Learning Commons
2357 Main Mall
McCarter Nairne & Partners 1967

The Faculty of Land & Food Systems (formerly Agriculture) occupies a superb reinterpretation of Collegiate Gothic, enlivened with a soupçon of Frank Lloyd

Wright and Ron Thom. A post-and-beam gateway frames a landscaped quadrangle leading to the entrance. The red-brick building, with pale concrete bands, is syncopated with buttress-like piers. The nearby **Frank A. Forward Building**, designed by the same architects (6350 Stores Road, 1968), continues the theme.

L19 Institute for Computing, Information & Cognitive Systems ↓
2366 Main Mall
Hotson Bakker Boniface Haden, Bregman + Hamann Architects 2005

Glazed stair towers reminiscent of the Bauhaus bookend the exterior of this smooth-surfaced structure. Designed for interdisciplinary research, it stands poised for use like a scaled-up computer hard drive, linked by a skywalk to its predecessor (Chernoff Thompson 1993), which fronts Main Mall somewhat awkwardly.

L20 Technology Enterprise Facility III
6190 Agronomy Road
Chernoff Thompson Architects 2003

Three terracotta nurses in WWI uniforms, mounted at corners of brick-faced elevations, were salvaged from the Art Deco Georgia Medical Dental Building (McCarter & Nairne 1929) when that building was demolished for Cathedral Place (H53). Technology facilitator Discovery Parks bought them, providing funds for the Vancouver Heritage Foundation, and fitted them to this energy-efficient wet-lab research centre, which is all contemporary behind the retro brickwork. Further south, past the new **Hawthorn Place** neighbourhood, is the **Forest Engineering Research Institute of Canada** (2601 East Mall, Henry Hawthorn 1990), whose character and purpose are defined by wood and an almost Arts and Crafts sensibility.

L21 Life Sciences Centre
2350 Health Sciences Mall
Bunting Coady Architects, Diamond + Schmitt Architects 2005

Home to UBC's renowned medical school, the Life Sciences Centre attained LEED Gold certification for sustainability, the largest building in Canada to do so. Twin atria spanned with steel trusses are a surprise behind the south-facing glazed bays

on Agronomy Road, which visually divide the complex's three blocks—clad in brick on the main elevation, zinc at the sides, and brick again at the rear, where two low-rise lecture theatres are located. The flush-to-the-sidewalk urbanism illustrates UBC's densification in a manner that is somewhat unsympathetic to the landscaped boulevard plan and collegiate personality of the original campus master plan. Just north is **UBC Hospital** (2211 Wesbrook Mall), affiliated with Vancouver General Hospital (D17) as well as UBC and operated by Vancouver Coastal Health.

L22 Earthquake Engineering Research Facility
2235 East Mall
Ramsay Worden Architects 2003

Seismic bracing and structural fastenings are exposed to express the activity inside this big shed, which tests structural and soil performance under strain from simulated earthquakes. The 10-metre height

accommodates large models and full-size components. A window gives passersby a view of one of three shake tables, whose foundations are separate from those of the building. The analyzed data can be swiftly shared online with similar facilities on the Pacific Rim (the source of 90 per cent of the planet's earthquakes) and around the world.

L23 Michael Smith Laboratories
2185 East Mall
Henriquez Partners Architects 2005

The Advanced Molecular Biology Laboratory is named for founding director Michael Smith, whose research on DNA won him a Nobel Prize. The building's DNA is architect Richard Henriquez, master of the visual metaphor (D19). The symbolism here is a two-storey mural, printed on glass, which runs like a ribbon along the east elevation. The graphic illustrates the double-helix molecular structure of DNA. The motif reappears in the atrium, in a sequence of glued-laminated (glulam) hoops. The building's concrete frame is emphatic on the sidewalk colonnade, where solar-shade frames are hung from the elevations. Part of the structure steps over the **UBC Bookstore** (6200 University Boulevard, Zoltan S. Kiss 1983).

North Vancouver and West Vancouver

FORESTS of Douglas-fir attracted loggers and settlers to the North Shore in the nineteenth century. The first sawmill on Burrard Inlet was built c. 1860 at the mouth of Lynn Creek. A logging community, Moodyville, named for entrepreneur Sewell Prescott Moody, "a Yankee trader," who bought the mill in 1865, once stood east of Lonsdale Quay, near the Saskatchewan Wheat Pool grain elevators. Moodyville was the first European settlement on the inlet, which had native villages on its shores. It boasted the first electric lights on the West Coast north of San Francisco in 1882. With electric light allowing the loading of sailing ships day and night, the mill was the biggest export earner in the province until a depression in the 1890s and its closure in 1901. Moody was a temperance man (Moodyville was dry) who inadvertently lubricated Gassy Jack's saloon (A1). He drowned in a shipwreck off Cape Flattery, en route to San Francisco in 1875. The Royal Navy and merchant marine had been key buyers of Douglas-fir ships' spars, before steam superseded sail. Moody's mill was taken over by B.C. Mills, Timber & Trading Company (C19, E4).

Development shifted to today's Lower Lonsdale (named for an English investor in Moody's mill) when a ferry service to Vancouver was launched c. 1900. The B.C. Electric Railway (BCER) began a streetcar service up Lonsdale Avenue in 1906, the year Alfred

Above: Harbour House (M38)

Wallace relocated his shipyard from False Creek for more space at the foot of the avenue. The Edwardian boom saw the construction of several impressive buildings (M8). The increasingly populous area was incorporated as the City of North Vancouver in 1907, divorcing the District of North Vancouver (which had been incorporated in 1891 and covered the North Shore from Deep Cove to Horseshoe Bay). Moodyville was absorbed by the City in 1915. The district appeared merely rustic after the booming city separated from it.

Both the City and District, mainly working class, defaulted on bond payments during the Depression (West Vancouver remained solvent and "respectable"; Burnaby also defaulted). They were pulled out of trouble by port activity, resource industries and shipbuilding during WWII. Postwar growth expanded the street grid (imposed methodically on the topography) with new homes. Upper Lonsdale developed but remains low density. Lynn Valley Town Centre (M17) is being promoted as a new urban hub.

Lower Lonsdale slumped after its ferry service stopped in 1958. SeaBus, initiated in 1977 as an integral ferry link in the metro region's transit system, attracted new commercial development (M4), but shipbuilding foundered in the 1990s. The huge Wallace Shipyards site, once "the Clydeside of Canada," was taken over by Versatile Pacific and closed in 1992 after failing to get a federal ice-breaker contract. After a decade of dereliction and debate about how it might be revitalized, the site has been "master planned" for redevelopment. A Shipyards Historic Precinct (M7) is its heritage attraction; there is a waterfront promenade. Mixed-use, mainly residential construction, with some high-rises, seeks the success of False Creek's template (G11, G19) in Vancouver.

The District of West Vancouver separated from the District of North Vancouver in 1912. It had failed to attract industry—not that its seaside-cottage owners wanted it—other than logging, which ran out of accessible trees. The city fathers declared the district exclusively residential in 1925 and banned industry. Exclusive is the word, because the first enterprise, some ten years later, was the British Pacific Properties, a mountainside "garden city" with fabulous views from its lawns and streets, winding up to 1,200 feet, a restriction that still applies. These Irish Guinness brewer-backed "Properties" were not developed until 1938, when Lions Gate Bridge (M1) opened to serve them.

The first significant postwar development was Park Royal Shopping Centre (M21), built to serve the Properties. In the 1960s,

M

high-rise apartment buildings began to densify the waterfront west of Lions Gate (M31). The Upper Levels Highway, begun in 1958 to Horseshoe Bay, drew traffic, new homes and strip malls (B.C. Ferries' Horseshoe Bay ferry terminal serves the Gulf Islands, Bowen Island and Vancouver Island). Despite recent development, the character of "West Van" remains a largely wooded coastal suburb on steep ground all the way to Horseshoe Bay. The only stands of old-growth trees remaining are Douglas-firs in Lighthouse Park (M36).

Half a century ago, West Van earned a reputation for avant-garde architecture, with clients willing to commission modernist house designs that collectively became known as the West Coast style. This was noted nationally for its open-plan living, glazed to dissolve conventional indoor-outdoor barriers, arranged and constructed mainly with natural materials to be sympathetic to the landscape. These unadorned, mainly rectilinear buildings have become West Vancouver's most valuable heritage resource: valuable culturally but also for the land they occupy. Preservation is a challenge, requiring owners' consent. Many buyers prefer bigger houses and gaudy eclecticism that knows nothing of the past. But the West Coast style remains a strong influence, absorbed as a "civic" symbol, as recent projects show (M30, M39).

Only one West Coast-style home (M33)—one of the very first and finest—is at present open to the public. Some others feature on West Vancouver Museum's annual West Coast Modern Home & Garden Tour. Few are visible from the street, a restriction that has influenced the selection here.

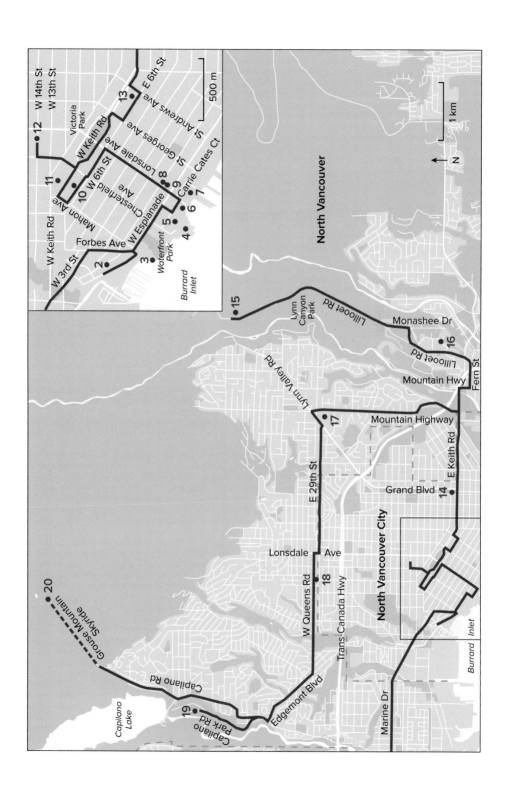

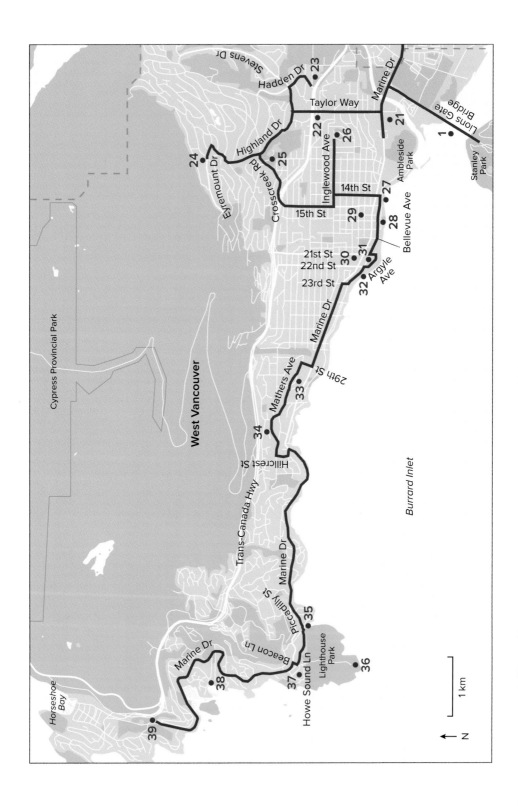

NORTH VANCOUVER

M1 Lions Gate Bridge

Monsarrat & Pratley, Robinson & Steinway,
W.G. Swan engineers, John Wilson Wood
architect 1938; 2002

It took two referenda and approval from Ottawa before the British Pacific Building Company's A.J.T. Taylor got a green light to span the First Narrows in 1936 with the "largest suspension bridge in the British Empire." Taylor had enticed the Guinness brewing family to invest in the enterprise, open up West Vancouver and develop the Guinness-owned British Properties. The bridge was named after the iconic pair of mountain peaks on the North Shore. Two concrete lions (Charles

Marega 1939) guard the moderne portal in Stanley Park. Some of the park's remaining old-growth trees were logged to make way for construction. The Dominion Bridge Company, which had made the steel frame for the Marine Building (H34), supplied steelwork, some fabricated on False Creek where The Village on False Creek (G11) now stands. The bridge featured in the first royal visit to Canada in 1939, when King George VI and Queen Elizabeth were driven across it.

Originally there were two vehicle lanes, wide enough for a third to be added in 1952. The deck rusted and took more traffic than it was designed for. The need to upgrade (or replace) Lions Gate Bridge revived a debate, begun in the 1960s, about car and transit options, a new bridge or tunnels, the sanctity of the park and heritage. In 2002, the bridge was given a structural upgrade, including replacement of the fifty-one-section main deck. Sidewalks and cycle lanes were slung outside the deck and the traffic lanes widened. In 2005, it was designated a National Historic Site.

M2 St. Paul's Church

424 West Esplanade

1910; Harrison Carlson Pearce Architects 1983

The French Oblate missionaries came to B.C. in the 1850s and erected a chapel in 1868 in partnership with the Squamish people whose village of Ustlawn was sited here. The chapel was replaced by a frame church in 1884 and rebuilt in 1910 with Gothic Revival corner towers, a rose window and transepts. The towers overlooked tidal flats, now filled, and were the official landmark for ships entering Vancouver Harbour. The vertical proportions, culminating in twin steeples, evoke the churches of French Canada and France, although the wood siding and carpenter Gothic detailing

are more characteristic of the West Coast. The building, the oldest extant mission church in the Vancouver area, was restored after a campaign in the 1980s.

M3 British Columbia Institute of Technology Marine Campus
265 West Esplanade
Waisman Dewar Grout 1981

A gleaming white metal superstructure and semicircular and rectilinear massing make this facility look like a beached ocean liner; portholes, metal guardrails and stairways, and a cluster of flag-flying masts add to the illusion. The building hosts BCIT's courses in navigation, ma-

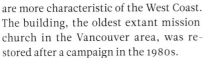

rine engineering, safety and seamanship. There are simulators, a machine shop, an indoor training tank and library and computer labs. A pier allows students to access Vancouver Harbour. A plaza, **Sailors' Point**, inaugurated in 1986, commemorates aspects of maritime history from 1792, when Captain George Vancouver surveyed and named Burrard Inlet. Sharing this space is the **Trans Canada Trail Pavilion**, with two Squamish Nation greeting figures (Darren Yelton 2003).

M4 Lonsdale Quay Market ✝
123 Carrie Cates Court
Hotson Bakker 1986; 2004

SeaBus, initiated in 1977 as an integral ferry link in the region's transit system, helped revive lower Lonsdale as a transit hub where North Shore bus riders transfer. Transit attracted new development focused at Lonsdale Quay, opened for Expo 86 as a multi-level marketplace and hotel. The market responded to the success of Granville Island (G6) and retained the same architects. The glazed and galleried interior recalls nineteenth-century iron-and-glass arcades and Wallace Shipyards' fabrication sheds, which once dominated the waterfront to the east (M7). The exterior and plaza have nautical references; a stair pylon is topped with a giant letter "Q"—like a semaphore response to the famous Woodward's "W" (A25) seen across Burrard Inlet.

M5 Insurance Corporation of British Columbia
151 West Esplanade
McCarter Nairne & Partners, John Bryson & Partners engineers 1984

A steel framework expressed externally in high-tech style was designed to support this massive corporate headquarters above a bus depot at grade inside the structure. The building—the horizontal equivalent of a multi-storey tower—sliced into the Lonsdale Quay development site, preventing easy integration of the eastern and western sections. These are connected by Carrie Cates Court beneath the building and a pedestrian passage between the Quay's plaza and the SeaBus dock and bus depot. An escalator link to ICBC was included to make transit use convenient for employees. The corporation is a significant economic factor, auto insurance being a provincial responsibility in B.C.

M6 Pacific Great Eastern Railway Station Museum
107 Carrie Cates Court
1913

The builders of the PGE began the line from North Vancouver to Prince George in 1913, not knowing it would take more than forty years to complete and connect its several sections. The railway was taken over by the provincial government in 1918 after financial problems and only became profitable in 1980, by which time it was known as B.C. Rail. "Prince George Eventually" was one of several scathing soubriquets it acquired, until the final section was completed along Howe Sound in 1956. That did not please some residents in West Vancouver, who had encroached on the original section from North Vancouver to Horseshoe Bay after passenger service was suspended in 1928.

This Craftsman-style original station stood at the foot of Lonsdale until that year. Tugboat operator Cates Towing (founded in 1913), whose slip is adjacent to Lonsdale Quay, converted it to an office. The City bought the station in 1971 and relocated it to Mahon Park, where it became a part of North Vancouver's museum and archives network. It was returned to its old site in 1997 and rehabilitated as a museum. The railway tracks, now operated by Canadian National (which bought B.C. Rail in 2004), are in a tunnel below Esplanade.

M7 Shipyards Historic Precinct
East of the Foot of Lonsdale Avenue
Begun 1906; Durante Kreuk, Pechet & Robb
landscape design, Bingham + Hill Architects
2010

Wallace Shipyards (subsequently Burrard Dry Dock and finally Versatile Pacific Shipyards) was once the largest shipbuilding and marine repair centre in B.C. Between 1906 and 1992, 379 vessels were built and launched here. Production peaked during WWII, when 109 Victory Ships were produced, employing up to 13,000 men and women. After several years of decline, Versatile Pacific went into receivership in 1992. Following a site auction, the heritage of cranes, sheds, piers and slipways was abandoned, the post-industrial wreckage a location for film crews in "Hollywood North."

The site is bounded by Lonsdale and St. George's Avenues, Esplanade and the shoreline. A Land Use Study was endorsed in 1997 and rezoning adopted in 2001, setting the stage for revitalization, launched as the **Pier Development**. This is a mixed-use project: significantly residential (partly high-rise) but with retail and the **Pinnacle Hotel at the Pier** (138 Victory Ship Way, IBI/HB Architects 2010). Its heritage component—the Shipyards Historic Precinct—was secured, with public waterfront access, through the rezoning. The precinct, which opened in phases in 2005 and 2010, includes the St. Roch (floating) Dock (1909) and the 650-foot-long Burrard Dry Dock Pier (1925). They were refurbished in 2005 for visiting vessels and leisure craft and extend the public walkway. Two WWII buildings have been rehabilitated (a third—the Machine Shop—was dismantled for overhaul); a crane has been preserved; a gantry structure was replicated. The ensemble is the backdrop for **Shipbuilder's Square**, the precinct's outdoor public venue. Paving, benches, lights, boardwalks and interpretive signage throughout are exceptionally well designed and detailed, to evoke the shipbuilding history. The City had previously developed a proposal to the federal and provincial governments for a National Maritime Centre here, but it foundered in 2010.

M8 Bank of Hamilton Chambers
92 Lonsdale Avenue
Mills & Hutton 1911

The Ontario-based architects anchored this building to its steep sloping site with an entrance angled at forty-five degrees to the elevations, which are distinguished by Ionic pilasters below an as-

sertive cornice. A curved pediment and cast-iron sconces at the entrance turn the corner of Lonsdale and 1st Street with a flourish. The original elevator, the first to be installed on the North Shore, remains in situ. The bank and the abutting Aberdeen Block (see next entry) form a pleasing period streetscape, a relic of a brief commercial building boom that never went much farther up the hill but did establish Lonsdale as the "high street" of North Vancouver.

M9 Aberdeen Block

88 Lonsdale Avenue
Mills & Hutton 1911; Daniel J. Epp Architect 2005

This was home to one of lower Lonsdale's first retailers, Paine Hardware, a time capsule destroyed by fire in 1998. The B.C. Electric Railway, which inaugurated a streetcar service from the ferry dock at the foot of Lonsdale in 1906, had an office in the building. The BCER supplied power to North Vancouver from its hydroelectric plant at Buntzen Lake; the office was where consumers came to pay their utility bills. The company also supplied power for street lights, along with the streetcar

line—a business initiative proposed to the City by Johannes Buntzen, the Danish-born managing director of the electric company. The streetcar system extended to Capilano, Upper Lonsdale and Lynn Valley. Services ceased in 1947.

The Aberdeen Block has since been filled with condos, with two added floors set back to respect the façades, which were restored, and ground floor retail was retained. The letter "K" on the stone shield above the entrance refers to James Cooper Keith, banker, developer and community leader after whom Keith Road was named. An earlier **Keith Block** (93 Lonsdale Avenue, attributed to Honeyman & Curtis 1908) is across the street.

M10 Stephens House
234 West 6th Street
Mackay & Mackay 1911

Precast concrete blocks imitate stone on this Edwardian home owned by Thomas Stephens, who worked for Leckie Shoes in Gastown (A10). It overlooks Ottawa Gardens, planned by the North Vancouver Land & Improvement Company in 1906 as an exclusive residential district, like the later Grand Boulevard (M14)—both attempted to market North Vancouver as a high-end residential area. Several old homes face the grassy median, including an **Italianate villa** (1907) at 214 West 6th Street, thought to have been the show home for the development. **St. Edmund's Roman Catholic Church** (545 Mahon Avenue, 1910), in frontier Gothic garb, accentuates the gardens' formal perspective.

M11 Queen Mary Elementary School
230 West Keith Road
William Charles Frederick Gillam 1914; DA Architects + Planners 2012

The size of this school and its stately architecture show the effects of population growth and civic aspiration during the Edwardian boom years, from 1905 to 1914 in North Vancouver. The elevation is Palladian, with a neoclassical pedimented centrepiece and symmetri-

cal wings. The "broken pediments" at the doors are baroque, a style the English-born and -trained architect used for Ridgeway Elementary School (420 East 8th Street, 1912). Ridgeway School's front and side elevations and cupola were retained as part of a complete rebuild and expansion to seismic code (DA Architects + Planners 2011). A similar upgrade was undertaken at Queen Mary School, including an atrium behind the central pediment.

M12 City of North Vancouver Library
120 West 14th Street
Diamond + Schmitt Architects,
CEI Architecture 2008

This sleek building successfully resolves three distinct but interconnected aims. It functions as a médiathèque (a library

for mixed media), where conventional hierarchies dissolve, attracting citizens with varied interests to use its light-filled floors and roof terrace; sustainable features were a core requirement, part of the City's take-up of the LEED green building rating system; the project's plaza expanded and enhanced the public realm. Quotations set in the paving echo these aims. One from Cicero sums up the spirit of the project: "If you have a garden and a library, you have everything you need," to which might be added "a café"; there is one, which encourages plaza and library users to interact.

The plaza is a graceful and intelligent piece of urban design that connects to the **City of North Vancouver Civic Centre** (141 West 14th Street, Downs/Archambault 1974). In this municipal hall and former library, designer Barry Downs translated the West Coast residential style (M37) into a pair of separate, but integrated, public buildings. The two reinforced-concrete structures partly clad in cedar nestled in the hillside, as if they had grown out of it. Most of the site was given over to park space, leaving the buildings understated, so well integrated into the landscape that they lacked civic presence—an example of the light imprint of the West Coast style at its most sensitive and a reflection of the architect's modesty. City Hall gained an addition (mcfarlane green biggar 2011) during a civic centre revitalization that has replaced the old library, on whose concrete slab the attachment was constructed, styled and oriented to dramatically improve City Hall's public profile.

M13 McNair House
256 East 6th Street
1907; Graham Crockart Architect 1995

James Archibald McNair moved from Strathcona (C5) in 1905 and built this lavish family home on nine lots from where he could oversee his empire, which included Lynn Valley logging operations and mills in Washington State and

M

Vancouver. The *News-Advertiser* called the house "one of the finest residences on the Coast . . . finished in elaborate style." Following use as a seniors' lodge, it was rehabilitated as the focus and inspiration for an apartment and townhouse complex that borrows its architectural style. Rezoning included a leafy public amenity—McNair Park (Forma Design 1995), between 6th Street and Keith Road.

M14 Doney House
745 Grand Boulevard
1909

Promoted as the finest residential avenue in Canada when it was conceived in 1906 by the North Vancouver Land & Im-

provement Company (M10), Grand Boulevard never quite lived up to its name. The ambition—inspired by the Garden City movement—was to develop a sort of Shaughnessy with a Champs-Élysées, lined with massive mansions. Only a handful of large homes were built before the Edwardian boom died, as the subsequent mix of house styles shows. This Swiss chalet-style home, with Craftsman influences, fitted the original vision of a development for high-ranking, wealthy citizens. It was originally owned by L.W. Doney, a silver and gold bullion broker and North Vancouver police magistrate. The BCER's Lynn Valley streetcar line, completed in 1910, ran on the wide median.

M15 Seymour Capilano Filtration Plant
4400 Lillooet Road
Stantec Architecture 2010

In 1889, the Vancouver Waterworks Company laid a pipe from the Capilano River (first dammed the year before) under the First Narrows to provide Vancouver with fresh water. The City of Vancouver acquired the company in 1891. The infrastructure was expanded when the Cleveland Dam (M19) created Lake Capilano in the 1950s; the Seymour River to the east was also dammed in phases. These two watersheds supply up to 70 per cent of the Lower Mainland's drinking water.

This new water supply and treatment facility—the largest of its kind in Canada—built by Metro Vancouver, which is responsible for regional water supply, improves the quality of drinking water from both sources. It is situated in a conservation area—one of the few undeveloped flat sites on the mountainous North Shore. The plant is designed to treat and distribute Seymour water—and import

and return Lake Capilano reservoir water, through twin tunnels—for distribution in existing mains. Energy is recovered from piped water flow to generate electricity; eco-smart concrete was used; remedial planting of native species repairs construction damage. The project conforms to Metro Vancouver's Sustainable Region Initiative. The LEED Gold-certified Operations & Maintenance Centre looks suitably technological, with West Coast timber touches.

M16 Capilano University

2055 Purcell Way
Henriquez Partners Architects 1993,
1996; Cannon Design, PWL Partnership
landscape design 2011

Capilano College opened in 1968 in a temporary space at West Vancouver Secondary School. The present campus opened in 1973, but it took twenty years to acquire architecture worthy of its emerging status (it became a university in 2008). The library and separate, later Birch Building, which has a performance theatre, created an environment for study and cultural recreation that is spacious, informal and idiosyncratic. The plan is irregular, anchored in the **Birch Building** by a bright atrium with a butterfly roof that bisects the theatre's concrete drum, extending to a bookstore and plaza. To symbolize enlightenment, the library's rotunda (facing a second, slightly hidden plaza) is topped with a feature reminiscent of Tatlin's Tower, an unbuilt Russian constructivist symbol of social and cultural progress. The horizontal, steel-trussed **Bosa Centre for Film & Animation**, western Canada's largest film school, suggests a production line of eager students—a "machine for film," as the architects' oblique reference to Le Corbusier claims.

M17 Lynn Valley Town Centre & Library
Lynn Valley Road and Mountain Highway
Henriquez Partners Architects 2007

Lynn Valley is becoming an alternative town centre for North Vancouver, thanks to this civic square, which follows Metro Vancouver's 1996 Livable Region Strategic Plan. The plan encouraged the development of pedestrian-oriented "town centres" to counter and compress the effects of suburban sprawl. The project's modernism mixed with timber posts inspired by North Vancouver's logging industry heritage creates a dramatic tension between the present and the past.

The nearby **Fromme Block** (1303–1305 Lynn Valley Road, 1912), built by Julius Martin Fromme, established the intersection of Lynn Valley Road and Mountain Highway as the area's commercial centre, near the skid roads that took logs to Burrard Inlet and mills. Fromme, who formed the Lynn Valley Lumber Company after working for the McNairs (M13), lived at 1466 Ross Road, where his family house still stands. The celebration of the past can also be seen at the North Vancouver Museum & Archives **Community History Centre** (3203 Institute Road, Blackadder & Mackay 1920; Boni Maddison Architects,

Commonwealth Historic Resource Management 2006) an adaptive reuse of the old Lynn Valley Elementary School.

M18 District of North Vancouver Municipal Hall
355 West Queens Road
Busby Bridger Architects 1996

The District of North Vancouver opens out from the City of North Vancouver like a fan on the forested uplands of the North Shore. Municipal Hall is located at its geographical centre, suburban rather than urban. The high-tech-style building replaced an inefficient and tired 1950s

structure and reorganized Council's relationship with the citizens it serves. The luminous atrium symbolized a new openness, and the materials chosen for construction and finishes—concrete, aluminum, glass and steel, softened with beech wood—created a sense of modernity and accessibility for this public service. Architect Peter Busby had worked with Foster + Partners on their Hongkong and Shanghai Bank Building (1986) and became a leading proponent in Vancouver of high-tech design as a means to sustainable architecture.

M19 Capilano Salmon Hatchery
4500 Capilano Park Road
Underwood, McKinley & Wilson 1971

This wood-and-concrete building flows unobtrusively across the rocky riverbank in the Capilano River gorge. Indoor and outdoor circulation in the public areas allows study of display tanks and the river as one. The building's clerestory-lit horizontals owe much to the modernist residential work of Fred Hollingsworth in the nearby Capilano Highlands subdivision. Upstream, the deep gorge is spanned by the dizzying **Capilano Suspension Bridge** (3735 Capilano Road) first built by pioneer George Grant Mackay. The bridge (originally rope; later wire cable) opened in 1889 and is said to be Vancouver's oldest tourist attraction—fans of Stanley Park's Hollow Tree (133) might disagree.

At the top of the gorge is the **Cleveland Dam** (J.T. Savage engineer 1954), its rugged engineering as dramatic as the setting. It created Capilano Lake, a vast, picturesque reservoir backdropped by the Lions' twin peaks.

M20 Eye of the Wind
Grouse Mountain
6400 Nancy Greene Way (Skyride)

Dominating the North Shore—and Vancouver generally—is Grouse Mountain. The first recorded ascent was made by hikers, who named the 1,250-metre (4,100-foot) peak for the blue grouse they spotted as they climbed in 1894. Developed as a ski hill in the 1920s, it was accessed by a rudimentary service road (now inaccessible to the public) and by a chairlift in 1949. The Skyride, opened in 1966, was augmented with North America's largest aerial tramway (the present Skyride) in 1976. Facilities were upgraded for the 2010 Winter Olympic Games. That year saw the opening of the Eye of the Wind (Leitwind AG), a giant wind turbine as high as a twenty-storey tower. This prominent commitment to alternative energy was designed, fabricated and installed by international effort—from nine countries on four continents. It is the world's first wind turbine to have an elevator-accessed public observation pod, from which a fantastic 360-degree view is gained.

M

WEST VANCOUVER

M21 Park Royal Shopping Centre
Marine Drive and Taylor Way
C.B.K. Van Norman, J.C. Page 1950;
many later additions and alterations

Built with Guinness money partly on land acquired from the Squamish band at the Capilano reserve, this was planned as the commercial centre for the British Properties, named for the company that developed the area after Lions Gate Bridge was opened in 1938. It was the second shopping centre in Canada; the country's original shopping centre was Norgate strip mall in Ville St-Laurent, near Montreal (Maxwell M. Kalman 1949).

Shopping centres oriented for the convenience of car-driving consumers were big enough for at least one "anchor" tenant, typically a department store or supermarket. Park Royal's first anchor was Woodward's (A25). The original structure—a gleaming, modernist horizontal slab on the north side of Marine Drive—is much altered. It was given a postmodern makeover in the 1990s, as was Park Royal South (John Graham Jr. 1962). A recent addition is **The Village at Park Royal** (F+A Architects, Musson Cattell Mackey Partnership 2004). Its walkability, stores disguised externally as sidewalk-oriented shops and pseudo-vernacular architectural packaging respond to baby boomer nostalgia for "Main Street."

M22 Har-El Synagogue & Community Centre
1305 Taylor Way
Acton Johnson Ostry Architects 1998

"Har-El" means "Mountain of God," and it was the landscape as much as the building program that influenced this house of worship on a difficult site at the intersection of two busy highways. The name is inscribed on a rugged slice of Jerusalem limestone; the sanctuary faces east towards the Holy City. The ancient Temple of Jerusalem was a reference point, but the architectural response was also West Coast. Materials are concrete and timber. A protected salmon creek that divides the site diagonally required a pedestrian bridge, integrated into an L-shaped plan that turns inward to face a courtyard, insulated from traffic noise. The bridge's concrete piles and deck ease the transition from the stony creek to the synagogue, reached by a covered walkway—a protective screen from rain and snow that often fall at this upper level. The mountains to the north loom above, magnifying the impression of a remote sanctuary built for contemplation.

M23 West Vancouver Baptist Church
450 Mathers Avenue
Arthur John Mudry 1967

In this "late modernist" alternative to the austere International Style, an expressive roof in four sections, each slightly concave outside, wood panelled inside, springs from stout stone piers to cover the church's square sanctuary. The ridges are split, filled with narrow strips of glass that form a skylit cross above worshipers. The roof's four gables are glass, an inspired installation that opens the sanctuary to a blaze of natural light and the forest outside. The space is at once contemplative and liberating. The landscape, its spirit and the building seem as one— the essence of the West Coast style.

M24 Forrest House
1143 Eyremount Drive
Thompson, Berwick & Pratt 1964

The talented Ron Thom trained as an artist at the Vancouver School of Art, where B.C. Binning (M33) taught. Under Binning's influence, Thom shifted to architecture, an art for which he proved to be exceptionally gifted. This magical house in the British Properties lands lightly on its sloping site like a paper airplane. That is how it appears—with flat roof planes, some angled to match the slope, hovering above the glazed living spaces—but the ethereal effect is achieved by engineering. The base is a concrete slab; interior walls are cedar, concealing tubular steel posts; the wing-like roof is cantilevered on steel beams. The complexity of the overlapping roof forms is repeated inside where four levels, bathed in white light from the roof undersides, step down to a panoramic view of Vancouver. Thom and many of his Vancouver colleagues were influenced by the work of Frank Lloyd Wright, who whispers here.

M25 LeBlanc House
1175 Sutton Place
1964; Peter Cardew Architects 2006

This unlikely exercise in sustainability rehabilitated a banal 1960s split-level house in the British Properties. The notion that, as Peter Cardew put it, only "that which is very old or very new" is desirable was contested. Housing stock from the 1960s and '70s is generally ignored or derided, but this open-plan makeover shows how it can be reconfigured and updated. At the rear, floor-to-ceiling glass fills the interior with garden light; panels slide open to extend the kitchen and dining area onto a terrace; floors are polished concrete. The street elevation says very little has happened. It was repainted and slightly modernized but remains unpretentious, an implicit rejection of the "McMansions" that are the scourge of West Vancouver.

M26 Gerson House
1040 Aubeneau Crescent
Wolfgang Gerson 1958; Gersonae Architecture 1995; Elizabeth Mackenzie 2006

Built on a steeply sloping treed lot on the west side of Sentinel Hill, this West Coast modern residence was oriented to take advantage of stunning views. The plan was innovative: three elliptical-vaulted "pavilions" divide the house into zones; walls were white, stressed-skin; interiors are open-plan for flexible living. The German-born architect (K41)—one of many European design professionals who immigrated to Vancouver after WWII—helped introduce modern design theory to Western Canada through his position at the University of British Columbia (his house was an informal meeting place for the local artistic community). Architects Kate and Erika Gerson, Wolfgang Gerson's daughters, rehabilitated the house in the 1990s.

M27 Ferry Building Gallery
1414 Argyle Avenue
Thompson & Campbell 1913; Howard/Yano Architects 1988

Pioneer John Lawson, the "father" of West Vancouver, its first postmaster and second reeve, founded the West Vancouver ferry service in 1909. When West Vancouver separated from the District of North Vancouver in 1912, the new municipality took

over the service and built this Arts and Crafts clapboard structure as the ferry terminal and office. Lions Gate Bridge challenged the ferries' viability, and service was discontinued in 1947. The pier was rebuilt and the shoreline landscaped with a water sculpture (Don Vaughan 1989). The Ferry Building was used by buses until 1986 and then rehabilitated as a charming community art gallery, with varied programs and events. It is complemented by the **Silk Purse Arts Centre** (1570 Argyle Avenue, 1925), home of the West Vancouver Community Arts Council, typical of the seaside cottages built on Ambleside Beach in the early twentieth century.

M28 Navvy Jack Thomas House
1768 Argyle Avenue
c. 1873; c. 1921

This is considered to be the Lower Mainland's oldest continually occupied house, if much altered. Welsh-born John Thomas joined the Fraser River gold rush in 1858, ran an unscheduled ferry service on Burrard Inlet and married a Squamish Nation woman in the early 1870s. He hauled gravel from the mouth of the Capilano River for construction (men who laboured at excavations were called "navvies," a British term from the Industrial Revolution). J.C. Keith (M9) owned it briefly, followed by ferry operator John Lawson, who bought it in 1907.

The house, now owned by the municipality, was moved slightly west and south of its original site (c. 1921) to allow for the opening of Argyle Avenue. The gable roof with the ridge parallel to the sea is the most visible original feature; old structural timbers survive inside.

M29 West Vancouver Museum & Archives
680 17th Street
1940; Gertrude Lawson 1994

Gertrude Lawson, the daughter of John Lawson but important in her own right to gender equality and the arts, built this house, reputedly with the first mortgage granted to a woman in B.C. A teacher for many years at Pauline Johnson and Hollyburn Schools, she bought the land in 1929, designed the house as her retirement home and supervised its construction. The structure is sheathed in stone that includes blocks originally from New Zealand used as ship's ballast and Capilano River rock (John Lawson saved the stone for years to build such a house). A trip she made to Scotland inspired its Highland hunting lodge appearance. A piper's podium for Scottish country dancing was on the main floor, now West Vancouver Museum & Archives' exhibit area. The building is also home to the West Vancouver Historical Society.

M30 West Vancouver Community Centre
2121 Marine Drive
Hughes Condon Marler Architects, Phillips Farevaag Smallenberg landscape design 2008

Glass, concrete and timber update West Coast modernist materials and transparency in this eco-friendly centre, which employs geothermal technology and reused every piece of cedar roof decking from the building it replaced. The centre's hub is the glazed atrium, a lofty space partly clerestory lit, from which a long, three-storey spinal corridor (also clerestory lit) links up various facilities and two gymnasiums. The atrium connects the community centre to the **West Vancouver Aquatic Centre** (also by Hughes Condon Marler 2008), a rebuild rather than a replacement but one that looks as new as its neighbour. Both buildings are oriented on open ground as artifacts in a landscape, with a backdrop of mountains. A south-facing plaza is an informal, unobtrusively landscaped gathering place.

M31 Crescent Apartments
2135 Argyle Avenue
Kenneth Gardner, Warnett Kennedy 1961

The first high-rise in West Vancouver, this was designed to offer both privacy and panoramic views from its sweeping, curved balconies. The latter are low tech, with parapets formed with cylindrical terracotta "pots" to save weight and add texture. Warnett Kennedy, an immigrant Scots architect who arrived in Vancouver in 1952, became a Vancouver alderman; he was also an urbanist who predicted and championed many of the innovations and policies (including downtown living and density bonuses to provide civic amenities) that have since become orthodox. Gardner, also an immigrant, from South Africa, was an innovative modernist whose house, which he designed (K35), is a classic of the International Style.

M32 Les Terraces
2250 Bellevue Avenue
Matsuzaki Wright Architects 1991

Residual concrete brutalism (a legacy of Arthur Erickson, with whom Eva Matsuzaki worked) is softened here by applied brickwork, attention to detail and the poise with which the tower rises from *pilotis*. These provide a porte cochère and prevent the building from completely blocking the view of the sea from the street. The slab-like bulk is fragmented, almost deconstructed. Visible step-backs

from the entrance, is lit by a south-facing clerestory—an inspired touch. The flat roof and glazed southern exposure were radical at the time.

Binning taught at the Vancouver School of Art and founded UBC's Department of Fine Arts. He had studied in New York and London in the 1930s, and his outlook was international. Among his contacts was Richard Neutra, the California-based Viennese modernist architect, a pioneer of the West Coast International Style, who visited Vancouver at Binning's invitation. Modernism flowed to B.C. from California and was incubated from other sources: the Bauhaus and Frank Lloyd Wright, the Arts and Crafts movement, and Japanese and West Coast native architecture. Binning's genius was to understand these connections and to help them flourish and coalesce as a distinctive West Coast style. Arthur Erickson met future partner Geoffrey Massey here for the first time. Binning's widow Jessie requested that the house be designated by the municipality. It became a National Historic Site in 2001. It is now owned by The Land Conservancy of British Columbia, which conducts tours.

are handled in the Erickson manner, reminiscent of the Provincial Law Courts (H50) at Robson Square. In complete contrast is **Villa Maris** (2222 Bellevue Avenue, 1965), known as "The Pink Palace," a flamboyant apartment tower from the previous generation rendered in the American resort style of the time.

M33 Binning House
2968 Mathers Crescent
B.C. Binning with R.A.D. Berwick,
Charles E. Pratt consulting architects 1941

Bertram Charles Binning, artist, tutor and sage of West Coast modernism and mentor to many of its practitioners, conceived this modest but resonant dwelling, one of the earliest examples of the International Style in Vancouver. The design seems an essay in simplicity but is a subtle and sophisticated division of space, decorated with two murals by Binning. The modular arrangement is illusory: the plan is trapezoid, the spaces irregular. The spinal hall, which splays slightly

M34 McNab House
3290 Westmount Road
Duncan McNab 1956; later additions

A coterie of Vancouver architects developed the West Coast style in the years after WWII. The principal elements were low-pitched or flat roofs, wood post-and-beam construction, cedar siding, open planning and large areas of glass opening onto the landscape integrated with the structure. All are evident in architect McNab's family home, with a tree now mature in the porch. At the entrance, a stair is cantilevered to the living area; a two-sided fireplace serves the sitting room and master bedroom; existing rocks were incorporated into the ground-level recreation room. Later additions (also by McNab) included a pool and decks.

McNab studied architecture at McGill University in Montreal in the late 1930s, at a time when Canadian architecture largely relied on the traditions of the Beaux-Arts. He started his own practice in 1952, after having moved West and joining Sharp & Thompson, Berwick, Pratt, the large firm that took a leading role in the local modernist movement. The West Coast trend filtered down to general contractors, notably Lewis

Construction, which simplified the style and spaces for the average home buyer on the North Shore.

M35 St. Francis-in-the-Wood Anglican Church ✝
4773 South Piccadilly
Harry A. Stone 1927; Underwood,
McKinley & Cameron 1957

This charming church with a lych-gate overlooks an English-style "village green" at Caulfeild, the picturesque subdivision planned by English university professor and developer Francis Caulfeild who settled here in 1889. His leafy, curving lanes, enhanced with traditional architectural design that emphasized stone and timber, followed the contours of the natural terrain. His benign vision in-

cluded a public park, set around the cove that bears his name. The church illustrates West Vancouver's transition from sparsely populated weekend and summer resort community to year-round dormitory suburb. To serve that, the church was expanded in 1957. The original small sanctuary, illuminated by stained-glass windows by Morris & Company of London, was enclosed by an A-frame roof, at which time the granite and cedar parish hall was erected.

M36 Point Atkinson Lighthouse ↑
Lighthouse Park
Colonel William P. Anderson 1912

Point Atkinson was named by Captain George Vancouver in 1792. The park was set aside in 1881 to provide dark background for a wooden lighthouse built in 1874 to guard the outer entrance to Burrard Inlet and Vancouver Harbour. Colonel Anderson, Chief Engineer at the Department of Marine & Fisheries in Ottawa, was a prolific designer of lighthouses on the Great Lakes and the east

and west coasts (132). He advocated concrete construction, expressed here as a hexagonal reinforced-concrete tower with six buttresses. Its two-tone fog horn was familiar to the many residents within its range. The clapboard ancillary buildings are a reminder that it was staffed by a keeper and his family. The last keeper, Don Graham, wrote books that raised public awareness of B.C.'s coastal beacons. Most are now automated. This one was in 1996, two years after it was designated a National Historic Site.

M37 Smith House
5030 The Byway
Erickson/Massey 1965

Designed as a home and artists' studio for Gordon and Marion Smith (the adjacent studio was constructed later; Russell Hollingsworth 1990), this is the epitome of West Coast style. It was awarded the Royal Architectural Institute of Canada's Prix du xxe siècle in 2007 for its "enduring excellence and national significance." The design fuses the "organic" dwellings

M

of Frank Lloyd Wright, the minimalist glass boxes of the International Style and the spatial elegance, clarity and austerity of Japanese design that Erickson had seen on his first visit to that country in 1961.

The horizontal, rectilinear dwelling is set in a rocky clearing in the forest. Cedar posts, projecting beams and expansive glazing define four wings that spread around an inner courtyard that steps under one wing to a south-facing garden terrace. The equilibrium is delicate yet powerfully composed, as if the architect himself had hauled the posts and beams into place on the rocks, such is the respect for the landscape he contemplated. He stated, "I wanted the Smith house to reveal the site in the same way that I had found it revealed to me when I first walked onto it."

M38 Harbour House →
5717 Eagle Harbour Road
Helliwell + Smith: Blue Sky Architecture 2008

Classic West Coast–style homes are inspired by their settings: architect Barry Downs built a "Sky House" (6664 Marine Drive, 1979) perched high on a cliff; Paul Merrick fabricated a treehouse (5762 Lar-

son Place, 1974) deep in the forest. The form of Harbour House was determined by its location, overlooking picturesque Eagle Harbour. It also has the virtue that it can be seen easily by the passerby.

The site is a steep rocky contour that curves above the road. The home's elevation is stretched organically to fit the curve and the interior spaces are oriented accordingly, set back from a sweeping deck, shaded by wide eaves on projecting beams. The evident delight in the use of wood and the attention to the details of its assembly and finish recall the Arts and Crafts movement, an influence on West

Coast residential design since the days of Samuel Maclure. Architects Bo Helliwell and Kim Smith are based in West Vancouver but known for their work on the Gulf Islands; this is a rare mainland example of their style, which acknowledges West Coast tradition but adapts and advances it.

M39 Gleneagles Community Centre
6262 Marine Drive
Patkau Architects 2003

This visually striking and tectonically showy civic symbol in a suburban setting is generous with outdoor spaces—a linear plaza where the building is entered on Marine Drive and a courtyard and walkway shaded by trees on the edge of Gleneagles Golf Course. The building is organized on three levels, the main one at the Marine Drive grade (with a fitness level above), the lower at the rear, facing the golf course. Open planning encourages human interaction. The building program included multi-purpose rooms, studios, child care and administrative facilities. The gymnasium is the centrepiece—a spectacular full-height space rising from the rear, low level, re-

vealed dramatically from the entrance circulation and café space. The building is wrapped by a graceful curving roof ribbed with glued-laminated (glulam) beams and visibly supported on struts. Concrete, glass, steel and timber exhibit the building's structural clarity, which adheres to the modernist "form follows function" philosophy, but the architects' response to site—and the centre's numerous eco-smart features—are pure West Coast.

Richmond, New Westminster and Burnaby

METRO Vancouver (formally the Greater Vancouver Regional District) is made up of twenty-four independent jurisdictions, the largest of which is the City of Vancouver. Richmond, New Westminster and Burnaby are all substantial cities and are the closest to Vancouver's east and south flanks.

RICHMOND, located on islands on the Fraser River floodplain, had established agriculture and the fishery as the mainstays of its economy when it was incorporated in 1879. Lulu Island, the largest (Sea Island is the second largest), was reportedly named in 1863 by Colonel Richard Moody, commander of the Royal Engineers, for Lulu Sweet, a San Francisco dancer who performed in nearby New Westminster. The Royal Engineers surveyed Lulu Island around 1860 with 160-acre lots (quarter-sections, one-quarter square mile each) for new settlers. Dikes were built and the land drained and cultivated, mainly for dairy farming and berry growing. By 1887 the key north–south roads had been constructed; they retain the surveyors' prosaic names: No. 1 Road, No. 2 Road, etc. In 1905, the B.C. Electric Railway built its interurban line to Steveston, whose salmon canneries were the dominant industry.

Richmond's resource industries continued to be important through much of the twentieth century. After wwii it also

Above: Brentwood Town Centre SkyTrain Station (N35)

became a bedroom suburb of Vancouver. It was best known to Vancouverites for its fish docks, farm markets, affordable housing, malls along No. 3 Road and the airport.

The community began to take itself seriously in the last quarter of the century, by enforcing smart planning regulations, attracting a diversity of new land uses (such as offices, hotels and light industry), designating a Town Centre at No. 3 Road near Granville Avenue, and finally, in 1990, declaring itself the City of Richmond. The municipal government began to commission good architecture (N8), and many private and institutional developers followed the lead.

Richmond's older architectural heritage reflects the fishery and agricultural origins, and some residential areas contain interesting pockets of postwar housing projects. Vancouver International Airport on Sea Island (N1) continues to be an economic stimulus. A series of bridges and tunnels built after WWII integrate the island community with Metro Vancouver's growing transit infrastructure and has been a further catalyst for urbanization. The construction of the Arthur Laing (1975) and Knight Street (1974) Bridges provided road links to Vancouver, supplementing the Oak Street Bridge (1957); the Massey Tunnel (1958), which replaced a ferry to cross the broad South Arm of the Fraser, is the main road to the U.S. border. The Alex Fraser Bridge (1986; the world's longest fixed-stay bridge when built) provides a second automobile route south. The Canada Line rapid transit to the airport and Richmond town centre (2009) crosses the North Arm of the Fraser River on its own, and quite wonderful, bridge.

NEW WESTMINSTER, situated on the north shore of the Fraser upriver from Richmond, was founded in 1859 by a detachment of Royal Engineers, which had been sent from Britain to provide law enforcement, survey work and road construction that were required because of the Fraser River gold rush of 1858. Queen Victoria named it as the capital of the mainland Colony of British Columbia. Colonel Moody planned the townsite, with a street grid carved out of the forest rising from the Fraser River. British imperial rule and justice, administered by Governor and former Hudson's Bay Company Chief Factor James Douglas in Victoria and by Colonel Moody, who became lieutenant governor and land commissioner in New Westminster, was the foundation of civic society in "The Royal City."

The local detachment of Royal Engineers, based in Sapperton (the engineers were called "sappers") just upriver from New

Westminster (N31), was disbanded in 1863. Moody returned to England, but most of his men, some with families, stayed on. Their expertise was a vital part of the development of "New West" as an administrative centre and the industrial, banking and commercial hub for the Fraser Valley. Their legacy is a collection of Victorian architecture of exceptional variety and quality.

New Westminster's crown was removed when Victoria became the colonial, then provincial, capital in 1866 when the mainland colony merged with the Colony of Vancouver Island. The "Royal City" moniker remained and is still used today. Colonel Moody had dreamed that the Royal City be a major Pacific port, "Queen-like and shining in the midday sun," but that was never realized. The CPR chose Vancouver as its terminus. New Westminster had docks and got a spur line to serve them in 1886, as well as a station and freight yard, which were destroyed in the 1898 Great Fire that reduced downtown to rubble. Rebuilding was quick, financed by the boom in trade and industry during the Edwardian era. Columbia Street, the city's main drag, thrived and was the local terminus of the BCER interurban railway to Chilliwack, opened in 1910. Queen's Park grew as an exclusive residential district, where numerous heritage homes survive thanks to owners' care and the City's progressive heritage management.

The Royal City experienced the same economic setbacks and revivals as the rest of Metro Vancouver, through the Depression, WWII and the 1950s. Postwar suburban development and a relocation of City Hall drained downtown of much vitality. Optimism overflowing from Vancouver's Expo 86 and the arrival of the Sky-Train line—its cable-stayed "Skybridge" (1989) across the Fraser is an engineering marvel—encouraged attempts to revive the old centre and its waterfront, which continue today.

BURNABY was incorporated in 1892 and achieved city status a century later. Its pattern of incoming settlement, like Richmond but over more varied topography, was agricultural, then suburban, and is increasingly urban. Because South Burnaby was the original population and economic centre of the district, the first municipal hall was built in that neighbourhood, at Kingsway and Edmonds, in 1899. By the time the building was outgrown, North Burnaby had become a force to reckon with, developed in the pre-WWI real estate boom, particularly after it acquired streetcar service to Vancouver in 1913. Since neither neighborhood would agree to a new municipal hall on the other's turf, a compromise saw the new facility located in the geographical centre near freshwater Deer Lake in 1956 (N38). That decision encouraged a civic and cultural enclave that celebrates traditions and more recent cultural diversity.

Transportation corridors—from the CPR and BCER to Highway 1 and SkyTrain—influenced Burnaby's development, particularly when the land along the BCER line between Vancouver and New Westminster was subdivided for sale in 1891. The old BCER route was used when the SkyTrain Expo Line was constructed in the 1980s, resulting in high-rise urbanization around Metrotown SkyTrain station in South Burnaby; the Millennium Line's arrival at Brentwood Town Centre (N35) in north Burnaby in 2002 has had a similar effect. These are outcomes of Metro Vancouver's Regional Growth Strategy, which supports transit and density in regional town centres. These are easier to develop in Burnaby (and Richmond) than in New Westminster, with its streets of heritage architecture.

Burnaby boasts two major post-secondary educational institutions: Simon Fraser University (N32) and the British Columbia Institute of Technology. Space precluded the latter's Burnaby campus's being featured in this chapter (two BCIT buildings appear in this book, one in Richmond, N3). SFU demands attention for its legacy of Erickson/Massey, the educational acropolis on Burnaby Mountain that expressed the enlightened, optimistic cultural patronage that existed in Canada in the 1960s. Now, the optimism of "sustainability" is evident on the mountain, where UniverCity is emerging as a model community for the future.

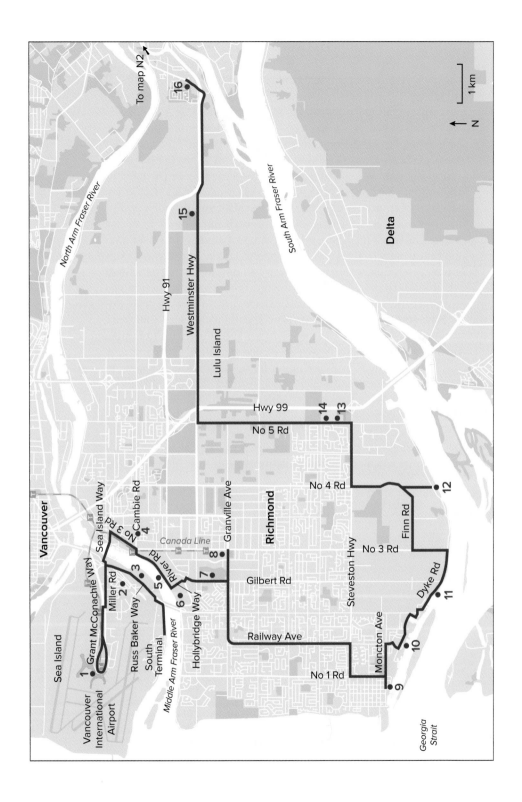

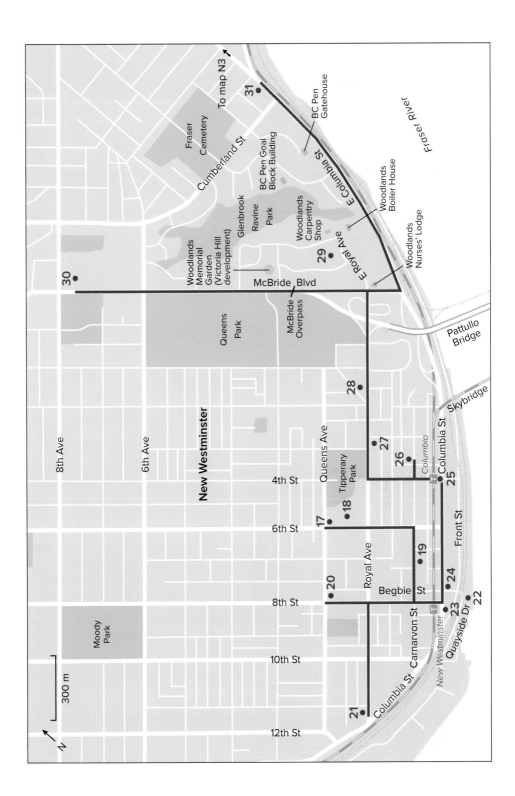

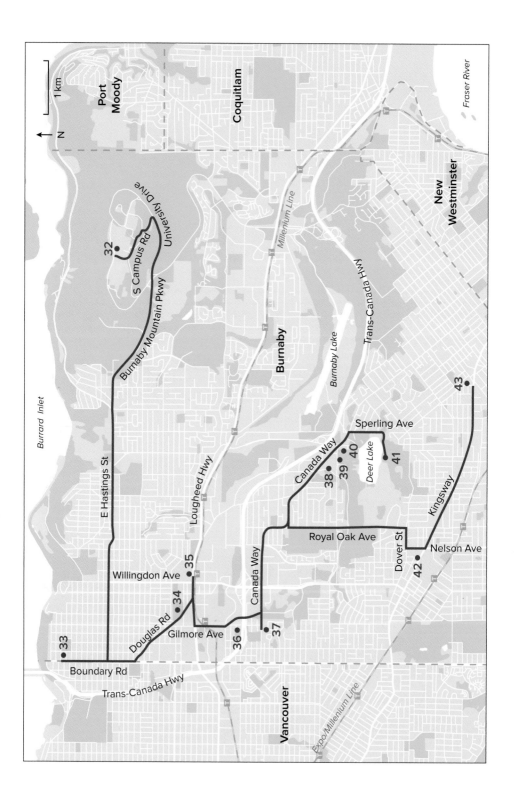

RICHMOND

N1 YVR Vancouver International Airport
3211 Grant McConachie Way

DOMESTIC TERMINAL
Thompson, Berwick & Pratt 1968; Kasian Architecture, Read Jones Christoffersen engineers 2002

INTERNATIONAL TERMINAL
Architectura, Bush, Bohlman & Partners engineers 1996, 2000; Stantec Architecture, Bush, Bohlman & Partners 2007

LINK BUILDING
Kasian Architecture, Read Jones Christoffersen 2007, 2009

YVR-AIRPORT STATION
Kasian Architecture, Sharp & Diamond landscape design 2009

Vancouver International Airport—the "gateway to the Orient," as *The Province* called it when it opened in 1931—started with a single runway, a wood-frame administration building, two vaulted-roof hangars (N2) and a floatplane dock. Fewer than six hundred passengers arrived in its first year. The airport expanded during WWII and into the jet age. The domestic terminal was Flash Gordon sci-fi with a clear-span check-in hall and weird curved features that included a stone-clad ramp, flanked by two sculpted air vents, leading to the departures level. The ramp and vents survived a seismic retrofit and makeover, part of the enlargement of YVR since 1992 when Transport Canada transferred operations (but not ownership) to the Vancouver Airport Authority. A colossal air-traffic **control tower** (CWMM engineers 1996) was constructed with the international terminal. The terminal's structural system is a forest of steel pillars, struts, beams and trusses, hardly symbolic of flight but easy to fabricate and functional—essentially the same system used at the CPR roundhouse in 1888 (G20)

INTERNATIONAL TERMINAL

YVR—AIRPORT STATION

but with modern structural steelwork's seismic performance. Structural novelty is seen in the departure level's rotunda where eight canoe trusses provide a clear span; curtain-wall glazing introduces natural light and allows scenic views.

A "land, sea and sky" decorative theme has been rolled out throughout the airport complex, with First Nations artwork prominent, irony unintended (colonialism in the nineteenth century almost erased B.C.'s native culture). Examples include *The Spirit of Haida Gwaii: The Jade Canoe* (Bill Reid 1996) in the international terminal's main hall, *Flight Spindle Whorl* (Susan Point 1996) in the customs hall and a Haida totem pole (Don Yeomans 2009) in the oval atrium of the Link Building.

The steel-and-glass "link" visually and physically connects the two terminals and permits access to the Canada Line's elevated YVR-Airport Station, where a glazed aerofoil-like canopy shelters the platform above a living wall, the largest on the continent when installed. The YVR Master Plan (2007-27) anticipates over 26 million passengers annually (the number was 16.8 million in 2010) and more expansion, including a third runway.

N2 Burkeville ↓
Hudson Avenue at Russ Baker Way
1941

Part of the Ottawa's Wartime Housing Plan, this apparently incongruous community of bungalows—a miniature garden city in the shadow of YVR—accommodated workers at the Boeing Aircraft of Canada plant constructed in 1941. Burkeville took its name from Stanley Burke, president of Boeing; the streets were given aircraft names. The plant—which produced PBY Canso flying boats for the Royal Canadian Air Force and B-29 Superfortress fuselage sections for the U.S. Air Force—is now the site of YVR's South Terminal (regional and general aviation), where the airport's two original hangars, **Hangar No. 1**, 5160 Airport Road, and **Hangar No. 2**, 4680 Cowley Crescent, (both by Arthur Julius Bird 1931) survive. They are wood with concrete buttresses and remarkable wood vaulted roofs using "lamella" criss-cross framing. Nearby is

the elegant, concrete-arched former **Canadian Pacific Air Lines** (later the BCIT) **hangar** (Otto Safir engineer 1957).

N3 **BCIT Aerospace Technology Campus** †
3800 Cessna Drive
Kasian Architecture, Perry + Associates landscape design 2007

A triangular site under the flight path of YVR's south runway by the Fraser River's Middle Arm influenced the orientation and composition of the campus architecture. The wedge-shaped "partnership" building flows in a sinuous line parallel to the river, which its classrooms and offices overlook; it also slopes from five to two storeys to fit flight-path restrictions. Acoustic roof tiles and glass minimize overhead aircraft noise. A hangar complex with a long-span, steel-truss structure—a space big enough for a Boeing 737—houses workshops and training aircraft. The hangar's concrete floor slab is a source of radiant heat for the whole complex, which uses geothermal heating and cooling. The built forms are linked to a hub as in an airport terminal. The river's edge provides pleasant footpaths in a protected natural habitat.

N4 **Aberdeen Centre**
4151 Hazelbridge Way
1989; Bing Thom Architects 2004, 2008

The Aberdeen Centre (named after Aberdeen Harbour in Hong Kong) opened to cater to Richmond's increasing Chinese population. A decade later it had become obsolete. After its demolition, Hazelbridge Way was realigned. The new mall follows the street's curve with a glass elevation conceived as public art (*Pixel*, Bing Thom, Chris Doray & Stephanie Forsythe 2003), a three-storey wrap of coloured panels that glow at night like a lantern. Sidewalk entrances and courtyards connect the mall to the street rather than the usual surface parking lot.

Inside, the spatial interplay is also unconventional. The central court is a clerestory-lit atrium covered by a "floating" leaf-shaped roof that spreads over the sidewalk above the main entrance (expressive roofscapes have since become a Bing Thom signature). Oval skylights bring daylight to walkways that branch off on three levels from the atrium and lead to a parkade where most shoppers arrive. Richmond's sidewalks are not overused by pedestrians, but that should change as the city densifies, which Aberdeen Centre's street edge anticipates. The expanding centre includes an eight-storey condominium (8080 Cambie Road, Bing Thom Architects). The adjacent **Canada Line Aberdeen Station** (No. 3 Road, Busby Perkins + Will 2009) adds to Aberdeen Centre's pedestrian friendliness.

N5 John M.S. Lecky UBC Boathouse
7277 River Road
Larry McFarland Architects, Fast + Epp structural engineers 2007

Named in honour of a UBC Olympian who won a silver medal at the 1960 Rome Olympics and a great benefactor of Canada's national rowing team and development programs at the high school and university levels, the boathouse has two timber-frame structures on concrete floats moored to steel pipes anchored in the riverbed, eliminating costly seismic work. The facility has storage for sculls, dragon boats and equipment on float level

and offices, showers and changing rooms above. The exteriors are metallic, with lightweight interlocking, glazed panels. Each structure's upper deck has horizontal cedar slats fixed to steel frames for partial shade, without blocking users' views. The slatted arrangement curves like a boat hull, as does the timber roof in the event hall in the upstream unit. The architecture is sleek, efficient, like the rowing sculls launched here.

Downstream from the boathouse, a plaque on the Middle Arm Waterfront Greenway (part of the Middle Arm Open Space Master Plan, Phillips Farevaag Smallenberg 2004) marks a grove of trees, the site of Vancouver and Richmond pioneer Sam Brighouse's homestead in 1864.

N6 Richmond Olympic Oval
6111 River Road
Cannon Design, Fast + Epp engineers, Phillips Farevaag Smallenberg landscape design 2008

The 100-metre-wide oval with seating for eight thousand spectators was built as the long-track speed skating stadium for the 2010 Winter Olympic Games. It is a major legacy building from the Games and has been reconfigured as a multi-sport venue. The structure sits on a raised concrete slab and parkade (Glotman Simpson engineers) on a raft-and-pile foundation required because of the Fraser River delta's soft soil. It has won multiple awards for the novelty and clarity of its engineering and sustainability, especially the use of wood, which adds colour, texture and warmth to the building's aircraft hangar-like form.

The spectacular roof was built with load-bearing Douglas-fir glued-laminated (glulam) and steel composite arches, anchored to concrete buttresses; filler panels were prefabbed from wood recycled from pine beetle–damaged B.C. forests. The roof projects outside, supported

on angled struts above the plaza facing the river. Rain recycling runnels in the buttresses were decorated by Musqueam artist Susan Point with salmon, herons and water patterns that symbolize the river's ecology.

N7 Minoru Chapel
6540 Gilbert Road
1891

Originally Richmond Methodist Mission, this carpenter Gothic chapel was built by volunteers. Its original location at Cambie and River Roads suited worshipers who came by boat. In 1925, it became Richmond United Church. Threatened by a rail spur in 1961, it was bought by the municipality and relocated in Minoru Park, the city's evolving cultural centre. In keeping with handmade buildings (designed and built by those who

would use them) most of the contemporary stained glass was designed by the minister (Reverend Jock Murdoch 1985). The windows are locally themed, many donated by families of pioneers. Minoru Park (opened in 1909 as a race track named for Edward VII's Epsom Derby-winning horse that year) was where the first aircraft flight in Canada west of Winnipeg took place in 1910. An airstrip near Alexandra and Garden City Roads served Vancouver until activity moved to Sea Island in 1931 (N1).

N8 Richmond City Hall
6911 No. 3 Road
Hotson Bakker Architects, Kuwabara Payne McKenna Blumberg Architects, Phillips Farevaag Smallenberg landscape design 2000

This neo-modernist building symbolizes the city's transition from suburbia to urbanism. Its personality is West Coast contemporary with a typical wood, steel and glass vocabulary and a sustainable script emphasized by prominent *brises-soleils*. There are four distinctive components: a circular council chamber and south terrace water garden; a "meeting house," café and galleria; an office tower with main-floor public access to city services; and a civic square and west terraces. Unifying these is a single big idea: a horizontal I-beam raised on concrete slabs. This runs from the War Memorial (a Celtic

N

cross) on the main entrance plaza, along the galleria (where it supports a timber-framed ceiling and north-facing glazing) and exits above the west terraces. Attention to detail and clarity is exceptional throughout, as is the West Coast landscaping. Mature trees by the War Memorial were retained; the south terrace water garden is a layered outdoor public space in the tradition of Robson Square (H50).

N9 Gulf of Georgia Cannery
12138 4th Avenue, Steveston
1894; many subsequent additions

Steveston, on the South Arm of the Fraser River, is named for Manoah Steves, a New Brunswick pioneer, patriarch of the first European family to settle in the area, in 1877. The townsite, surveyed by the Royal Engineers, was promoted by Manoah Steves's son, William Herbert Steves, as a port to compete with Vancouver, a vision that never got further than a map he printed in 1889.

Salmon was Steveston's fame and erratic fortune. The harbour is home to Canada's largest commercial fishing fleet (many fishers were local Japanese before WWII). The community was known as the "salmon capital of the world" with fifteen plants on Cannery Channel in 1900, processing fish for export. Thousands of First Nations, European, Chinese and Japanese men and women worked seasonally in the canneries, before mechanization in the twentieth century (and the Hell's Gate landslide up the Fraser River in 1912, which interrupted salmon runs) reduced employment and put many canneries out of business. Only one plant—Ocean Fisheries (13140 Rice Mill Road)—remained to benefit from the 2010 sockeye run, the biggest since 1913.

The townsite retains some heritage character; **Steveston Museum** (3811 Moncton Street) was the town's first bank (it opened in 1905, the year the interurban railway linked Steveston with Vancouver). Two preserved canneries recall the salmon heritage: Gulf of Georgia Cannery and Britannia Heritage Shipyard (see next entry), both National Historic Sites. The former, a heavy timber structure built on six hundred river-bed pilings, was nicknamed the "Monster Cannery." It closed in 1979. The Gulf of Georgia Cannery Society worked with Parks Canada for over ten years to rehabilitate it as a museum, which opened with a canning line exhibit in 1994.

N10 Britannia Heritage Shipyard
5180 Westwater Drive
1889; 1992 and later

The first salmon shipment from Britannia Cannery (to Europe on the tea clipper *Titania*), proved that Steveston's harbour could accommodate ocean-going sailing ships. The Anglo-British Columbia Packing Company bought the plant in 1891. Fluctuating salmon runs forced its conversion to a boatyard in 1918. The subsequent owner, Canadian Fishing Company (which once owned the Gulf of Georgia Cannery), abandoned the yard in 1979. The City of Richmond acquired the site in 1990, to be part of a waterfront recreational and heritage trail. Since 1992, the Britannia Heritage Shipyard Society has revitalized the yard—which contains a

unique collection of fishery buildings—as a working museum able to accommodate restorations of historic boats.

N11 London Heritage Farm
6511 Dyke Road
c. 1888; 1898

Brothers Charles and William London came to Richmond from Ontario in 1877 and bought 200 acres, which they cleared, drained and diked for this farm. Their enterprise included London's Landing from where their produce was shipped to market at New Westminster. The dock attracted a side-wheel steamer service operating between New Westminster and Victoria. They also ran a general store and Lulu Island Post Office.

The surviving building is Charles London's farmhouse, built in two stages—the back was completed first and the front added in the 1890s—in the hipped-roof American foursquare style, here with porches textured with jigsaw-cut column brackets and balustrades. The house, along with four acres of the London farmland, was bought by the City in 1978 and restored, furnished and managed by the London Heritage Farm Society, to illustrate life in Richmond from the 1880s to the 1930s. The site is a municipal park and a reminder of the homesteads that dotted Lulu Island in the nineteenth century.

N12 Finn Slough
South foot of No. 4 Road

Finn Slough is a tidal backwater sheltered by Gilmour Island, a tidal strip linked to Lulu Island by a quaint drawbridge. The community was founded in 1890 by Finnish settlers who took to fishing. The slough offered a safe harbour; its isolation fostered a let's-stick-together conviviality among stilt shacks, float homes, net lofts and cabins, with fish boats moored outside. The Finn Slough Heritage & Wetland Society, formed in 1993, has helped preserve the community and the wetland habitat. The make-and-mend quality of the buildings takes sustainability to a picturesque extreme.

N13 Richmond Christian School
10260 No. 5 Road
Killick Metz Bowen Rose, Allen + Maurer Architects 2008

Organized with clarity to provide a stimulating learning environment, this restrained building gives students formative exposure to good design. The entrance canopy is the only showy element. Glazing in the classrooms and the multi-

purpose gymnasium/assembly hall—which has a full-height north-facing glass wall—makes the most of Lulu Island's luminous big skies. Flat roofs and projecting wood beams are reminiscent of Vancouver's postwar modernism, reworked in functional contemporary forms.

N14 Lingyen Mountain Buddhist Temple
10060 No. 5 Road
Pacific Rim Architecture 1999

Richmond's No. 5 Road is punctuated with more than twenty churches and temples—an average of one built for each year since the City allowed schools, churches and other community facilities to be built within the Agricultural

Land Reserve. This temple, based on the Lingyen Shan ("Shan" means "mountain" in Mandarin Chinese) monastery in Taiwan, represents one of many faiths along the road that has been nicknamed "the highway to Heaven." A proposed 140-foot-high addition became a controversial palimpsest of change. It was withdrawn pending a review of the city's guidelines, which did not anticipate such heights, however mountainly or heavenly.

N15 East Richmond Nurseries
18431 Westminster Highway

Development on Lulu Island was controlled after the provincial Agricultural Land Reserve was set up in 1974–76, protecting all lands in agricultural use. The intent was to stop the loss of B.C.'s prime farmland to urbanization. Around one-third of Richmond's land area is part of the ALR, but the number of farms continues to decline, a result of socio-economic pressures and the expense of keeping the fluvial land drained. East Richmond

Nurseries, established in 1987, rehabilitated the Beckwith Barn (c. 1919) for office space and storage. The metal siding is not original but has ensured the structure's survival. The barn's gambrel roof is a notable vernacular feature; the adjacent Craftsman house adds period flavour to the site, formerly a dairy farm.

N16 Hamilton Fire Hall No. 5
22451 Westminster Highway
Johnston Davidson Architecture, Sharp & Diamond landscape design 2006

The fire hall's hose tower and fire truck bays are traditional features, but in almost every other respect this Hamilton neighbourhood facility is a reinvention of the typology for a sustainable twenty-first century. Solar technology and geothermal energy are embedded; rainwater is harvested for irrigation and washing fire trucks; wind power is captured for ventilation; there is a green roof. These features were accommodated without compromising primary functions. The structure is load-bearing concrete in the truck bays and wood frame in the staff quarters, with steel posts and beams where required, all visually unified with glulam roof beams. The project was designed to LEED Gold standards.

NEW WESTMINSTER

N17 **New Westminster Armoury**
530 Queen's Avenue
F.C. Gamble 1896

The 127-strong Columbia Detachment of the Royal Engineers, sent from Britain in 1858-59, primarily for survey and public works, was the ancestor of the Royal Westminster Regiment, whose headquarters this is. The regiment evolved from the New Westminster Volunteer Rifles raised in 1863, the year the Royal Engineers' detachment was disbanded after its men constructed the Cariboo Wagon Road (most stayed on, many with families). The armoury, built by contractor David Bain from plans by Dominion Government engineer Gamble, is barnlike in a frontier style that seeks elegance and solidity. The wood building remains a functioning armoury and contains the Regimental Museum, located in a blockhouse in the building where a naval gun was positioned (c. 1896) to fire across the river. The gun is exhibited outside, around the corner from a Victoria Cross memorial that records the regiment's combat in two world wars.

N18 **New Westminster City Hall**
511 Royal Avenue
A C. Smith & Associates 1953

City Hall, set in park-like grounds high above Royal Avenue, gains an authority in excess of its modest modernism, an

early example of the International Style in B.C. The exterior, Council Chambers and the main foyer retain most of their plush original elements. The site was to have been the provincial legislature before Victoria gained capital status. Below the entrance, a war memorial and two nineteenth-century field guns recall the city's military connections. The choice of this location marked a shift of civic affairs uptown. Old City Hall (Agricultural Hall, 1883; converted to City Hall 1891) on Columbia Street was destroyed in the Great Fire of 1898. Carnegie Library (Edwin G.W. Sait 1905; demolished 1958) was built on the site, near the present Law Courts (see next entry). It was replaced by a new **public library** (716 6th Avenue, K.J. Sandbrook 1958; Downs/ Archambault 1978). **Royal City Centre** (610 6th Street, originally developed by Woodward's in 1954) furthered the decline of Columbia as New Westminster's "main street" (N24).

N19 New Westminster Court House
668 Carnarvon Street
George William Grant 1891, 1899;
Gardiner & Mercer 1914; 1990

Sir Matthew Baillie Begbie, B.C.'s first colonial judge and provincial Chief Justice, presided at the opening of this Romanesque Revival courthouse. The brick-and-stone structure survived the Great Fire of 1898 that engulfed downtown. The interior was lost. G.W. Grant rebuilt it to the same plan, adding a roofscape in the fashionable château style; an addition was built by Gardiner & Mercer. The courthouse was superseded in 1980 by **New Westminster Law Courts** (651 Carnarvon Street, Carlberg Jackson Architects), the concrete post-and-beam front elevation influenced by the work of Arthur Erickson. A statue of Begbie stands on the plaza outside. The old courthouse and the adjacent **Land Registry Office** (648 Carnarvon Street, Edwin G.W. Sait, Frank G. Gardiner 1911) were closed but rehabilitated as offices and renamed "Begbie Court" in 1990.

N20 Galbraith House
131 8th Street
c. 1892; 1998

New Westminster's steep topography adds dramatic tension to street corners and the buildings on them. The Galbraith House would be dramatic enough on flat ground. Its Victorian pattern-book elevations are densely draped with shingles, clapboards, cornices, gables and a turret topped with a cast-iron finial. Owner Hugh Galbraith's carpentry and millwork business supplied woodwork for house builders; his home—a rare example of the "Stick Style"—was an advertisement for it. The house became a recreation centre for soldiers awaiting overseas postings during WWII, then a rooming house. New owners rescued it from neglect in 1998 as a B&B; they won an Outstanding Achievement Award from Heritage B.C. in 2000 but later sold it. It is now "Galbraith Manor," an executive office rental facility.

women with histories of homelessness and life skill deprivations. The energy-efficient building (designed for LEED Gold certification) is on steel piles, with a suspended concrete slab at grade supporting a four-storey wood frame. The street elevation's brickwork, horizontal siding and upper twin bays are tough, defensive but not alienating. The contemporary composition and choice of materials is finely balanced and fits planning guidelines for contextual design.

N22 Fraser River Discovery Centre ↑
788 Quayside Drive
Kasian Kennedy Architecture 2001; Boni Maddison Architects 2009

The Fraser River Discovery Centre Society was incorporated in 1989. Its vision—an interpretive centre about the Fraser River's ecology, history, communities and industries—was fully realized twenty years later with this conversion of the Riverboat Casino building, where a preview centre had opened in 2001. Renovations and additions include

N21 Lookout Emergency Aid Society Rhoda Kaellis Residence
1105 Royal Avenue
Boni Maddison Architects 2010

Good, honest, informed design distinguishes this shelter housing, which is oriented around a secure inner courtyard. The project provides twenty-four supportive housing units for men and

multi-use spaces, temporary and permanent displays, educational and audio-visual facilities. The building's main components—drum-shaped like a steamship funnel and shed-like as if part of a boat-yard—fit the waterfront setting without being parodies.

Adjacent on the waterfront boardwalk is **River Market** (810 Quayside Drive, Musson Cattell Mackey Partnership 1985; Hotson Bakker Boniface Haden 2010). This opened with the same formula as the public markets at Granville Island (G6) and Lonsdale Quay (M4) but declined in the 1990s, until a new owner revived it. The market and the **Inn at the Quay** (900 Quayside Drive, Waisman Dewar Grout Carter 1988) were the main components of Westminster Quay, an Expo-era development designed to reconnect city life with the river. The Discovery Centre advances this aim, but the elevated **Front Street Parkade** (1959, 1966), intended to help downtown compete with suburbia and revive Columbia Street, remains a barrier, along with rail tracks that are part of the waterfront's historic character.

N23 Canadian Pacific Railway Station
800 Columbia Street
Edward Maxwell 1899; Gardiner & Mercer 1910; Hopping Kovach Grinnell 1973

This miniature château was designed by Montreal architect Maxwell in the CPR's favoured style, which he had used flamboyantly for the transcontinental terminus in Vancouver (H28). Two wings were added in 1910. Maxwell's original elevations were retained, with twin turrets facing the railway tracks and a gabled entrance on the city side. The building was bought by the Keg Restaurant chain and rehabilitated.

Directly east is the rehabilitated **BCER Station** (774 Columbia Street, Maclure &

Fox 1911; Eric Pattison Architect 2007), a stop on the interurban line to Chilliwack until passenger service was withdrawn in 1950. (Trams ran diagonally through the building until its retail conversion after closure; the BCER's "Market," "Milk," "Mail" and "Owl" trains connected Fraser Valley agricultural producers to markets in metropolitan Vancouver.) The **SkyTrain station** on 8th Street maintains the fragmented zone as a transportation hub, densified above the station with residential towers (VIA Architecture 2010).

N24 Bank of Nova Scotia
728 Columbia Street
Murray Brown, Sharp & Thompson 1939

Columbia Street, with its BCER station (see previous entry), was the Fraser Valley's "downtown" until the post-WWII suburban boom and Highway 1 (Trans-Canada) bypassed it in 1964. It retains

an engaging ensemble of heritage architecture. This Scotiabank branch was designed by collaborating Toronto and Vancouver architects. The front elevation's fluted columns are moderne, with the rest of the building cautious with residual classicism. Decorative bas-reliefs of fishing and logging scenes and a sailing ship symbolize the nineteenth- and twentieth-century commerce and trade that fuelled New Westminster's prosperity. Across the street, reflecting the swagger of the Edwardian era, is the Chicago Style **Westminster Trust Building** (711 Columbia Street, Gardiner & Mercer 1912). Its trendy coffee shop is a sign of Columbia Street's revitalization, by enlightened property owners, niche retail and residential development downtown.

N25 Burr Block †
411 Columbia Street
George William Grant 1892

The Burr Block, now a boutique hotel, belonged to William Henry Burr, a schoolteacher-turned-developer (the family was notable; a descendant was Hollywood actor Raymond Burr). It is one of

only two buildings on Columbia Street to have survived the Great Fire of 1898; the adjacent **Guichon Block** (401 Columbia Street, 1887, also by Nova Scotia-born architect Grant) is the other. The Burr Block's rhythm and texture—asymmetrical elevation, arched windows, rusticated stone, brickwork and floral terracotta details—is robust Richardson Romanesque. A cast-iron balustrade surmounts the cornice. The building's storefronts are much altered, as are those of the Guichon Block. The latter's upper elevations are ebullient, in Victorian Italianate style. Built as the Queen's Hotel (the name and date appear on the pediment above the cornice) it was acquired in 1899 by French-born Laurence Guichon, a Delta landowner.

N26 St. Andrew's Presbyterian Church
321 Carnarvon Street
George William Grant 1889

Architect Grant's pen flowed across a range of styles that included Gothic Revival, displayed here in brick and stone. The corner tower was built with a steeple,

N27 Irving House ↓
302 Royal Avenue
James Syme 1865

removed after a fire in 1930. The interior soars with Douglas-fir hammer beams and a cedar-lined ceiling; there is a rose window; the organ (1891) by Warren & Son of Toronto, was one of the largest to be shipped west of Winnipeg. **The building's predecessor** (A.H. Manson builder 1863), the first Presbyterian church in the mainland colony, stands next door. Its style is carpenter Gothic, a contrast to Grant's polished Gothic Revival. It became the church hall and Sunday school in 1922. The buildings are now occupied by the congregation of Emmanuel Pentecostal Church.

This picturesque house was built for Captain William Irving, a Scottish seaman who came to B.C. in 1859, having worked in San Francisco and Portland, Oregon. His pioneering steamboat services earned him the nickname "King of the Fraser River." His house was one of the finest in the emerging colonial capital and is a remarkable time capsule. The pitched roof, gingerbread bargeboard gables topped by finials, Gothic window and doorway mouldings, and verandah are characteristic features of the "rural Gothic" (also called "carpenter Gothic") cottages popularized by the writings of Andrew Jackson Downing. The Palladian window on the second floor adds a touch of class. Irving died in 1872 and was buried at **Fraser Cemetery** (100 Richmond Street) where his marker is carved with an anchor.

The home's restless Scottish designer, a friend of Irving, had also been drawn to California before moving to B.C.; his

interest shifted to canning Fraser River salmon, an industry he is credited with founding in 1866. The City bought the house in 1950 from Irving's granddaughters. The oldest historic house museum in B.C., it was the first property in New Westminster to receive heritage designation (1981). A recent study (Eric Pattison Architect, Stuart Stark & Associates 2008) focused on restoring the interior, which contains fascinating period features, including plasterwork by Syme. The miniature modernist **Museum & Archives Building** (1964) sits in the garden behind the house.

N28 English Corners
119 Royal Avenue
Maclure & Sharp 1892

Queen's Park Historic District, with tree-lined streets and lovingly preserved heritage homes on the plateau above downtown, was the neighbourhood favoured by the city's social elite. This house was built for Steveston cannery pioneer Marshall English, who started a business in 1877 with a fish plant across the river from New Westminster. The house is also notable for having been an early design by Samuel Maclure (in brief partnership with English-born Richard P. Sharp).

Maclure, son of a Royal Engineer, began his career in New Westminster with modest house designs before moving to grander Tudor Revival residences in Victoria and Vancouver (J3). This transitional design points to the mature Tudor Revival/ Arts and Crafts style for which he is famed. The off-centre layout and lively massing of half-timbered gables and rooflines were features he repeated and refined. Stained glass in the hallway was by Henry Bloomfield & Sons, the first art glass firm in Western Canada (D11), founded in New Westminster in 1890. Queen's Park hosts annually the longest established (since 1979) heritage homes tour in B.C.

N29 Victoria Hill
Royal Avenue at McBride Boulevard
2005–12

Victoria Hill, a "private paradise for a privileged few"—a mix of townhomes and low- and high-rise condos set on "stately" grounds—was the site of Woodlands, the Provincial Lunatic Asylum opened in 1878. The developer of paradise, the Omni Group, understandably distanced it from the past, after buying the property from the provincial government in 2003. The City's rezoning ensured that mature trees and some buildings were saved. Woodlands' old **Centre Block** (1878) was destroyed by fire following the institution's closure in 1996, by then a psychiatric hospital for children. In 2011, the City of New Westminster Council voted to demolish the block's tower, which had survived—it had become a symbol of the abuse patients suffered while incarcerated.

The Arts and Crafts **Nurses' Lodge** (12 East Royal Avenue, Henry Whittaker 1904; Robert Lemon Architect, Douglas R. Johnson Architect, Sharp & Diamond landscape design 2010) is now apartments. The **Carpentry Shop** (245 Francis Way, 1903; Chris Dikeakos Architects, Donald Luxton & Associates 2010) and the Art Deco **Boiler House** (215 Francis Way, Department of Public Works, Henry

spaces above a notable formal stairway. The prison's abandoned burial area is on the west side of Glenbrook Ravine Park; the Pen's bell is preserved at the park's south entrance, off Jamieson Court. This was the first public park in the Colony of British Columbia, established in 1859 by Colonel Moody, who built Government House (demolished 1889) above the ravine the following year.

N30 Justice Institute of British Columbia
715 McBride Boulevard
Henriquez & Partners, IBI Group 1995

The Justice Institute of British Columbia, established in 1978 to consolidate public safety training, expresses a softer approach to public order than when Matthew Bailie Begbie earned the nickname "the hanging judge" for tough justice in the Fraser River gold fields. The Royal City's tradition of conservative civic architecture—which dates from the Begbie-era courthouse (N19)—was overruled with this enlightened postmodern project. Four distinct but connected buildings created a campus-like environment for previously scattered personnel. The built forms—which include a semicircular, almost classical concourse and an expressive, angular atrium—suggest incremental rather than instant construction, a fictional narrative that humanized the institutional building program.

Whittaker 1931; Robert Lemon Architect, Douglas R. Johnson Architect, Sharp & Diamond landscape design 2010; top photo) have been rehabilitated for community recreation. The asylum's grim history informs **Woodlands Memorial Garden** (LEES + Associates landscape design 2007), a reinterpretation of the institution's lost graveyard.

Directly east is the site of the **British Columbia Penitentiary**, also opened in 1878. The high walls, watchtowers, cell blocks and other structures were demolished after the jail closed in 1980 and the site rezoned and redeveloped with houses and low-rise apartments. Two heritage buildings remain: the French Second Empire-style **Gaol Block Building** (65 Richmond Street, 1878; 1990) and the castle-like **Gatehouse** (319 Governor's Court, 1929; 1991; lower photo above), rehabilitated respectively as offices and commercial

N31 St. Mary the Virgin Anglican Church
121 East Columbia Street
Lieutenant J.C. White 1865; 1989

This is one of the hidden architectural treasures of the Lower Mainland, a rustic Gothic Revival church built at the edge of the forest. It was constructed by Royal Engineers after their unit was disbanded in 1863, the year Lieutenant White, a topographical artist and draughtsman, hung out his shingle as an architect (he later moved to San Francisco). The sappers' camp had been at this site, called Sapperton. The name has been in continuous use since—hence Sapperton SkyTrain Station (Hancock Brückner Eng + Wright 2002). The church roof was destroyed and the interior damaged by a fire in 1932. The building was buttressed in 1989 to protect it from vibrations from heavy traffic on Columbia Street. A memorial plaque marks the pew where the colonial governor sat. Stained glass, Gothic wood panelling and an altar screen evoke the village churches of Britain that the engineers remembered.

BURNABY

N32 Simon Fraser University
Burnaby Mountain
Erickson/Massey 1965; many subsequent additions

SFU was named after fur trader and explorer Simon Fraser. It was one of many new universities founded across Canada as the baby boomer generation reached college age. The visionary concept of Arthur Erickson and Geoffrey Massey, with the former as principal designer, was chosen by a competition held in 1963 by Dr. Gordon Shrum, the newly appointed chancellor. Erickson/Massey's linear plan flows along the contours on the ridge of Burnaby Mountain. It reorganized conventional university planning, defining components by use rather than by faculty or college. To meet the building schedule, the four runners-up were invited to participate in the program. Concrete was the primary building material.

The glass-roofed **Mall** (Erickson/Massey), roofed with a mesh of Douglas-fir beams, steel tie rods and glass, is the principal walkway and gathering place. This sublime, classically inspired space (which architect Bruno Freschi remarked would "make an elegant ruin") encouraged both contemplation and student interaction. It was blamed for student unrest in the late 1960s—a tribute to the power of architecture to influence events.

Integrated campus buildings include the **W.A.C. Bennett Library** (Robert F. Harrison), the **Gymnasium** (Duncan McNab & Associates) and the **Shrum Science Centre** (Rhone & Iredale). Also part of the original program was the **Academic Quadrangle** (Zoltan S. Kiss).The original plan anticipated evolution along its terraced spine. The **Student Residences & Dining Hall** (Downs/Archambault & Partners, Davidson Yuen Simpson Architects

THE MALL

ACADEMIC QUADRANGLE

STUDENT RESIDENCES & DINING HALL

ARTS & SOCIAL SCIENCES COMPLEX & BLUSSON HALL

2005) rationalizes a sloping site and extends the campus's east–west plan. Three mid-rise buildings accommodate visiting academics and university guests, and 750 students in single rooms grouped into 23 "student houses." A 300-seat dining hall and administration block steps out from the housing to connect to existing outdoor circulation. The **Arts & Social Sciences Complex** and **Blusson Hall** (Busby Perkins + Will, Fast + Epp engineers 2008) update the original vision of an interconnected learning environment. The neo-modernist design borrows from the Quadrangle's austerity but lightly and with grace, incorporating a courtyard for sociability. The project ticks every sustainable box,

from the use of 50 per cent fly-ash concrete to a green roof.

Erickson's long-neglected call for a townsite for up to ten thousand people is being rolled out east of the campus at **UniverCity**, a sustainable mixed-use, transit-oriented and walkable community. The Official Community Plan was approved in 1996 after SFU agreed to transfer land to the City of Burnaby to more than double the size of the Burnaby Mountain Conservation Area. Site work began in 2001. The neighbourhood's child care facility (Hughes Condon Marler, space2place landscape design 2011) is designed to meet the Living Building Challenge zero-energy sustainability standard.

N33 Overlynn
3755 McGill Street
Maclure & Fox 1909

The Vancouver Heights subdivision, named to disguise its Burnaby location, was marketed to the wealthy—without much success—as an alternative to Shaughnessy. Charles J. Peter, a manager for the Winnipeg-based wholesale tea-importing firm of G.F. & J. Galt, led the development and retained society architects Maclure & Fox to design this Tudor Revival showpiece. It became a convent and girls' school, Seton Academy, run by the Sisters of Charity of Halifax, a Catholic order that had purchased the estate in 1936. Action Line Housing Society bought it in 1974, kept the mansion and built the high-rise **Seton Villa retirement centre** in the garden. Overlynn retains superb decorative detail, which—true to the Arts and Crafts tradition—was integral to Maclure's houses. Designation by Burnaby Council in 1995 included the heritage interior, the first in B.C. to be legally protected.

N34 Woodward Mausoleum, Masonic Cemetery
4305 Halifax Street
1924

The Municipality of Burnaby was named for freemason Robert Burnaby, private secretary of Colonel Richard Moody in New Westminster. The fraternal society's membership was considerable, especially among men of British origin whose Masonic tradition dated from "lodges" constituted in the eighteenth century. This 35-acre cemetery was dedicated in 1924 after the 2½-acre Masonic section at Vancouver's Mountain View Cemetery (F6) filled up. Charles Woodward, the founder of the department store (A25), was a Mason and built this mausoleum for his family. Masons trace traditions to the stonemasons who built the cathedrals of medieval Europe. A feeling of fellowship with the builders of the pyramids may explain the Egyptian Revival style loosely interpreted here.

N35 Brentwood Town Centre SkyTrain Station
Lougheed Highway at Willingdon Avenue
Busby + Associates Architects 2002

This is the most sculptural of the design-conscious stations on the Millennium Line. The look is futuristic, but the inspiration was the traditional ribbed structure of the canoe, upturned. The two platforms sit astride SkyTrain's elevated concrete guideway. Each is shielded by a parallel timber overhang supported on a run of hooped, steel-and-glulam timber ribs. Above the train tracks the overhangs part to admit daylight. The environment is glazed, open-plan, creating spacious circulation. Building codes once prevented the use of mixed-materials seen here, but a combination of performance-enhancing Canadian wood technologies, structural ingenuity and negotiated "equivalency" allowed design flexibility and flair to flourish all along SkyTrain's Millennium Line. The station, which has a pedestrian link to Brentwood Town Centre, is seen by planners as a catalyst for medium- and high-density development, following the Metrotown precedent (N42).

N36 APEGBC Building
4010 Regent Street
Busby + Associates Architects 1997

The Association of Professional Engineers and Geoscientists of B.C. is a governing and regulating body. Every aspect of this steel-framed high-tech glazed box reflects that serious purpose and the analytical nature of those professions. The building stands out from its ho-hum office park surroundings adjacent to the Trans-Canada Highway with transparent functionality achieved with precision, elegance and devotion to detail. The structural engineering (lightweight, stayed ceiling assemblies, slender steelwork) is exposed; the components were beautifully designed (some in the architects' product design studio) and crafted. The

building's microclimate is controlled by energy-efficient design that includes the aluminum solar shields, which are computer monitored to reflect light into (or to shade) the offices. Architect Peter Busby championed "visible technology" and energy efficiency in this building, which set a benchmark in Vancouver in the run-up to the millennium.

N37 The Ismaili Centre
4010 Canada Way
Bruno Freschi 1985

Home of Canada's first Ismaili congregation and the first building of its kind in the country, this Jamatkhana prayer house and community facility was built under the direction of the Aga Khan, the spiritual leader of Shia Ismaili Muslims and patron of the Aga Khan Award for Architecture. For Freschi, the chief architect of Expo 86, it was "by far one of the most fascinating projects." It combines Islamic architectural geometry with refined contemporary design and materials. A fountain and serene courtyard garden lead to an archway and entrance loggia set in a fortress-like sandstone exterior; a social hall is entered, then a prayer hall. The quality of light is subtle, the aspect welcoming. The cast-concrete building's principal floor plans are square; the symbolically inclusive octagon appears in the pavement pattern of the courtyard, turret-like corner staircases, domes and coffered ceilings.

N38 Burnaby City Hall
4949 Canada Way
Fred Hollingsworth 1956; Toby Russell Buckwell & Partners 1999

The location of this building in the centre of the district was a compromise between South and North Burnaby, each of which wanted it. The design, on the other hand, was no compromise at all. Fred Hollingsworth, one of the pioneers of the West Coast style, produced an understated modernist design whose crisp rectangular design symbolized Burnaby's progressive leadership. The building was renovated in 1999 and the grounds landscaped (Phillips Farevaag Smallenberg, Birmingham & Wood 2002), including the Millennium Garden.

N39 Fairacres/Burnaby Art Gallery
6344 Deer Lake Avenue
Robert Percival Twizell 1910

Deer Lake provided a scenic setting for gracious pre-war "country" mansions of Vancouver and New Westminster's social elite. Fairacres, a blend of Tudor Revival and Arts and Crafts, was built by Grace and Henry Ceperley, a Michigan heiress and a Vancouver realtor. His company, Ceperley, Rounsefell & Company,

built a Georgian Revival office building in downtown Vancouver (H37). Subsequent owners of Fairacres included Benedictine monks who lived here from 1939 to 1955 until they built their present spectacular hilltop home at Westminster Abbey, Mission. They were followed by a self-styled prophet and his cult's members. The City of Burnaby bought the mansion for use as the Burnaby Art Gallery, which opened in 1967 as the nucleus of a recreational and cultural precinct that includes five other period houses, all now in public ownership, and the recent Shadbolt Centre (see next entry).

N40 Shadbolt Centre for the Arts
6450 Deer Lake Avenue
Hotson Bakker, Henry Hawthorn 1995

Formerly Burnaby Arts Centre, this arts facility commemorates artist Jack Shadbolt and curator Doris Shadbolt for their lifetime commitment to culture. The building—an expansion of existing facilities—serves many cultural and community functions, with performance and

other spaces accessed from a stone-and-timber atrium. The overall composition is a striking combination of wood, concrete, stone and tree-like struts—unmistakably West Coast. The materials chosen and busily distributed were intended to fit the parkland and the cultural precinct's heritage character that includes **Burnaby Village Museum** (6501 Deer Lake Avenue), which has a collection of heritage buildings, replicas and artifacts—including a BCER interurban tram and a fabulous Edwardian carousel, once a popular ride at the PNE (E17)—presented in a themed setting.

N41 Baldwin House
6543 Deer Lake Drive
Arthur Erickson 1965

Arthur Erickson turned from his dramatic, competition-winning entry for
Simon Fraser University (N32) to this intimate post-and-beam house that seems
to float like a pavilion on the south shore
of Deer Lake. It was commissioned by
Dr. William Baldwin and his wife Ruth,
friends of the architect. All the signs of
Erickson's developing sensitivity to architectural space, landscape and materials can be experienced in the home's
luminous, slightly Japanese spatial interplay, framed within typically squared-up
horizontal massing. Siding is cedar, B.C.'s
most characteristic architectural timber.
There is a Japanese-style reflecting pool
and "rain chains" (also Japanese) in place
of drain pipes. The house is preserved by
the City of Burnaby and The Land Conservancy of B.C., which allows short-stay
vacation or business rentals.

N42 Kingsway Pedestrian Bridge
Kingsway and McMurray Avenue
Busby Perkins + Will, Fast + Epp engineers
2008

Construction of the SkyTrain's Expo Line
(E24) spurred development on this strip
of Kingsway, around Metrotown Sky-
Train station. Two decades on, Metrotown is a dense shopping and entertainment centre with adjacent residential,
office and hotel towers. This density anticipated the regional town centres (M17)
envisaged in the former Greater Vancouver Regional District's (now Metro Vancouver) 1996 Livable Region Strategic
Plan, expanded in its 2001 Sustainable
Region Initiative and recent Regional
Growth Strategy. The intent is to encourage sustainable growth, contain suburban sprawl, maintain the Agricultural
Land Reserve (N15) and promote transit and pedestrian-oriented communities. Metrotown is still auto oriented. This
bridge—a glulam timber–and–steel arch

with a precast concrete walkway tension tie—is an elegantly engineered solution that separates people from Kingsway's six-lanes of traffic, connecting Metrotown with the high-rise residential neighbourhood to the north.

N43 Burnaby Public Library, Tommy Douglas Branch
7311 Kingsway
Diamond + Schmitt Architects,
CEI Architecture 2009

Named for Tommy Douglas, labour activist and the first leader of the federal New Democratic Party, this modest "médiathèque" is one of the new breed of community libraries (M12) that combine traditional book borrowing with new technology, multimedia, online access, courses and events. The building is a glass box. The interior is luminous, double-height like a clerestory-lit temple. Automated windows assist natural ventilation, allowing the extraction of hot air.

Lighting is unobtrusive and energy efficient. Bold colour relieves the modernist hard edges. Tradition is evoked on the main elevation with contemporary reference to classical columns, reminiscent of the Carré d'Art médiathèque in Nimes, France (Foster + Partners 1993), an example of the globalization of design.

GLOSSARY

Note: Terms in *italics* are defined in separate entries

ARCADE: a row of *arches* carried on *columns, posts* or *piers* or set in a wall; also a *galleria*

ARCH-AND-SPANDREL: A wall treatment that emphasizes the play between the vertical wall and horizontal *spandrels* between windows, capped by an *arch* at the top of the windows; a common feature of Richardsonian *Romanesque* architecture

ARCH: a form of construction, usually made of *masonry*, that spans an opening in a curved form, distributing the weight above it to the walls, *columns, posts* or *piers* at either side

ART DECO: a decorative style prevalent in the 1920s and '30s and characterized by zigzag and geometric ornament; popularized by the Exposition Internationale des Arts Décoratifs et Industriels Modernes, held in Paris in 1925 (H34)

ART NOUVEAU: a decorative and architectural style prevalent c. 1900 and characterized by organic compositions and sinuous curves (I10)

ARTICULATION: a distinct and logical expression of architectural elements

ARTS AND CRAFTS: a decorative arts movement, begun in England in the late nineteenth century, that attempted to re-establish the skills of craftsmanship then threatened by mass production and industrialization; its ideals entered Vancouver architecture in the early twentieth century (J20), particularly in the *Craftsman style* and the *Tudor Revival*

BALUSTRADE: a railing with posts (balusters) and a handrail

BARGEBOARD: wooden boards, usually decorated, usually fastened to a *gable*

BAROQUE: a style of seventeenth-century European architecture, animated by assertive *massing*, dynamic curves and lavish decoration; aspects were revived in early-twentieth-century Vancouver architecture (H27)

BAS-RELIEF: French for "low relief"; a sculptural or cast panel on which figures or ornament are raised slightly from the surface

BAUHAUS: a design school in Germany (1919 to 1933), founded by architect Walter Gropius, whose ideal that art and craft should be part of everyday life influenced industrial design, typography and architecture; Gropius, Mies van der Rohe, and other teachers later settled in America, where they spread *modernism* and the *International Style*

BAY window: a window, usually three sided, that projects from a wall

BAY: a window, door or vertical division of an *elevation*

BEAM: a principal horizontal structural member, usually supporting a floor or roof

BEAUX-ARTS: a style (and form of urban planning) named after the École des Beaux-Arts, the architecture school in Paris at which many North American architects studied; characterized by a monumental, often luxuriant *classicism* and formal, hierarchical planning (H27)

BELLE ÉPOQUE: the Edwardian era of gracious living for those who could afford it, largely extinguished by WWI

BOW WINDOW: similar to a *bay window* but curved

BRACKET: a member, often triangular, that projects from a wall and supports another feature, such as a balcony, *eave* or *cornice*

BRISE-SOLEIL: a sunshade, usually louvred

BRUTALISM: a style characterized by massive composition that empha-sizes the solidity of the walls, usually achieved with roughly finished poured-in-place *concrete* (N32)

BUTTRESS: a vertical feature used to support the lateral forces exerted by a wall, *arch*, or vault

BYZANTINE: a style of architecture developed in Byzantium, the Eastern Roman Empire and centred in today's Turkey, and characterized by heavy *masonry* buildings, often capped by *arches* and domes (C24)

CAMPANILE: a bell tower

CANTILEVER: a beam that projects beyond vertical support and is unsup-ported at one end

CAPITAL: the top part of a *column* or *pilaster*, usually decorated, and directly below the *entablature* in *classical* architecture

CARYATID: a sculpted female figure supporting an *entablature*

CAST IRON: in nineteenth-century architecture, an industrial material poured into moulds and used for *columns* and decoration; distinct from *wrought iron*, which is hand formed; *cast iron* has high strength in com-pression, whereas *wrought iron* has moderate strength in tension

CHÂTEAU STYLE: an architectural style prevalent in the late nineteenth and early twentieth centuries, characterized by steep roofs, towers and other features adapted from European castles; promoted as a Canadian national style after its adoption by the national railways for their hotels (H51)

CHEVRON: a V-shaped pattern often seen in *Romanesque* and *Art Deco* architecture

CHICAGO STYLE: a style used for "skyscrapers," developed in Chicago in the 1880s and used widely in Canada in the years before WWI; the composition is usually divided into three parts, inspired by the base, *shaft* and *capital* of a *classical column* (H14)

CLADDING: the external, non-structural material that protects the structure from the weather. *See also curtain wall*

CLAPBOARD: a *cladding* material consisting of horizontal, overlapping boards

CLASSICAL, CLASSICISM: the architecture of ancient Greece and Rome and its many revivals through to the twentieth century; also the classical "orders"—i.e., the *Tuscan, Doric, Ionic* and *Corinthian* orders— distinguished by the decorative details of their *columns, capitals, entablatures* and other features (G16). *See also neoclassical*

CLERESTORY: a row of windows located near the top of a wall or other building feature providing high light to the interior

COLONNADE: a procession of *columns* carrying *arches* or an *entablature*; an *arcade*

COLUMN: a vertical, cylindrical structural member, usually supporting part of a floor, roof or *façade*; in *classical* buildings, it supports the *entablature*

CONCRETE: a construction material composed of cement (primarily burnt lime), aggregate (usually sand or gravel) and water that hardens to attain considerable compressive strength; when steel rods are used, the resultant *reinforced concrete* also attains high tensile strength; *poured-in-place concrete* sets (hardens) in wooden formwork which is later removed; *precast concrete* is fabricated off-site

CONTEXTUAL: in urban design, describes a new building whose scale and materials (or style) fit in with the established streetscape or neighbourhood

CORBEL: a kind of *bracket* composed of a single projecting block or of several projecting courses of *masonry*

CORINTHIAN ORDER: the most ornate *classical* order, distinguished by leaf motifs on the *capitals*

CORNICE: in *classical* buildings, the uppermost component of an *entablature*; the projecting horizontal element at the top of an *elevation*

CRAFTSMAN style: the North American legacy of the *Arts and Crafts* movement, most closely associated with the "Craftsman bungalow" or

"California bungalow," a form of post-WWI mass housing with a clearly expressed structure and which creates the impression of hand-crafted decoration (K11)

CRENELLATIONS: notches in a *parapet*, also called battlements, originally in forts from which defenders could shoot safely

CRESTING: a decorative band, often *wrought iron* or *terracotta*, on the ridge of a roof

CRUCIFORM PLAN: shaped like a cross

CUPOLA: a dome-like feature at the top of a roof or a larger dome

CURTAIN WALL: a non-structural exterior wall commonly composed of glass panels fastened to a building's structural frame; typical of the *International Style*

DORIC ORDER: the oldest *classical* order, characterized by heavy *columns*, usually *fluted*, and plain *capitals*; the *frieze* often features groups of three vertical bars, called "triglyphs"

DORMER: a window projecting from a sloping roof, with a small roof of its own

EAVE: the projecting edge of a roof, frequently supported by *brackets*

EDWARDIAN BUILDER: a style of mass housing of that era, plainer than Victorian precedents; normally two or two and a half stories, with a front porch, wood *siding* and a *gabled roof* (K10); if the roof is *hipped*, it is usually called "*foursquare*" (N11)

ELEVATION: the wall of a building, also called the *façade* if facing forward; the two-dimensional representation of a wall in architectural drawing

ENTABLATURE: the horizontal member above a *column* in *classical* design, composed of an architrave (the lowest part), *frieze* and *cornice*

EXPRESSIONISM: a twentieth-century artistic movement originating in northern Europe in the years around 1900 and fuelled by the aftermath of WWI; used to describe buildings that feature unconventional spaces, shapes and angles (F32)

FANLIGHT: a semicircular window with radiating glass panels above a door, particularly in *Georgian* architecture

FINIAL: an ornamental vertical projection at the top of a *cupola*, *gable*, roof or turret

FLATIRON: a building that is triangular in plan

FLUTING: concave grooves, repeated vertically on a *column* or *pilaster*

FOURSQUARE: *See Edwardian Builder*

FRETWORK: particularly in Victorian houses, a strip of lace-like ornament in wood or iron, often seen on *gables* and porch *brackets*

FRIEZE: the middle part of an *entablature*, or any decorated band

GABLE, GABLED ROOF: a gabled roof slopes on two sides; a gable is the triangular portion of wall at the end of a gabled roof

GALLERIA: an *arcade* or interior passage, sometimes a grand one more than one level

GARDEN CITY: an early-twentieth-century movement that sought to rationalize and beautify urban development with planned, self-contained communities having leafy streets and boulevards, with parks and zones for farming, industry and commerce

GEORGIAN REVIVAL: a revival of the eighteenth-century *classical* British style, which in turn was derived from the architecture of ancient Greece and Rome and from the Renaissance; characterized by elegant and symmetrical *elevations*, typically with *columns*, *pediments* and other *classical* features (J19)

GINGERBREAD: wood ornament carved or cut by jigsaw, e.g., decorated *bargeboards* and *fretwork*

GOTHIC REVIVAL: a revival of the Gothic style of medieval Europe, initially and principally used for churches (I1)

HAMMER BEAM: in a roof, a horizontal timber that projects (is *cantilevered*) from a wall on which the roof structure is supported; its structural function is similar to a *bracket* or a *corbel*

HIGH-TECH: an offshoot of *modernism* that pushes technological boundaries, expressed in visible structural components and systems (H30)

HIPPED ROOF: a roof that slopes on four sides

HISTORICISM: refers to the revival of past styles

INFILL: new construction on an undeveloped part of a property occupied by an existing building or on a vacant urban site adjacent to a building

INTERNATIONAL STYLE: an architectural style developed in a number of European countries in the 1920s and characterized by the work of the *Bauhaus*; migrated to North America in the 1930s to '50s; it is distinguished by flat roofs, glazed *elevations* devoid of historical ornament, rational planning of interior space and use of industrial materials (H33)

IONIC ORDER: a *classical* order, with *capitals* displaying spiral "volutes" or scrolls; the *frieze* may feature *bas-relief* sculpture

ITALIANATE STYLE: a nineteenth-century architectural style featuring windows, often with *arches* of varying shapes (usually circular and segmental-headed) and prominent *cornices*; used especially for commercial buildings (A1)

LANCET WINDOW: a tall, narrow window with a pointed *arch*, typically in Gothic or *Gothic Revival* architecture.

LANTERN: a small turret or *cupola* with windows on all sides, on top of a dome

LINTEL: a small *beam* set directly above a door or window and distributing the weight above it to the walls or *columns* at either side of the opening

LOGGIA: the open side of a *galleria* or *arcade*, or of a partly enclosed balcony; or the open side of a room extending to a garden

MANSARD: a roof that has a double slope, with lower slope steeper and higher than the upper one, usually pierced with *dormers*; a primary feature of the *Second Empire* style; similar to a gambrel roof. The name is derived from the name of French architect François Mansart.

MASONRY: stone, brick, *concrete*, tile or any other inorganic and non-metallic building material

MASSING: in architectural composition, the arrangement of a building's bulk

MISSION STYLE: a relatively plain companion to the *Spanish Colonial Revival*, with stucco imitating adobe; inspired by Spanish mission architecture in California (J21)

MODERNE: an architectural style popular in the 1930s and '40s, with little or no historical ornament and usually finished in white *concrete* or stucco, often with "streamlined moderne" curves suggesting speed and progress; often featuring *Art Deco* ornament (K22)

MODERNISM: the cult of the new in architecture and other arts, especially from the 1920s onward. *See also Bauhaus; International Style*

MULLION: a vertical unit dividing glazed areas in a window

NEOCLASSICAL: an architectural style that continues the *classical* revivals of earlier eras; began in Europe in the late eighteenth century and seen in North America in the early twentieth century; the composition is usually formal and the façade is usually dominated by *columns*; used especially by government institutions and banks (H25)

PALAZZO: a palatial building; especially a *Renaissance* palace in Italy

PALLADIAN: relating to the sixteenth-century Italian architect Andrea Palladio and to the English revival of his style in the eighteenth century; also describes a round-arched window with flanking rectangular windows (M11)

PARAPET: a low wall on the edge of a roof, balcony or bridge

PEDIMENT: a triangular feature, often filled with sculptural groups, at the top of a *portico* in *classical* architecture or above a window; a curved or broken pediment has the upper or lower part removed

PIER: a square or rectangular *post*, usually *masonry*; often used as a support for an *arch* or bridge

PILASTER: a shallow, rectangular *column* set in a wall, often rendered as one of the *classical orders*

PILLAR: an archaic word synonymous with *post*

PILOTIS: structural, stilt-like *columns* or *piers* that support a building and create space open at ground level

PORTE COCHÈRE: a covered entrance for vehicles

PORTICO: a roofed entrance porch, in *classical* architecture, with a *pediment* supported by *columns*, open or enclosed at each side

POST-AND-BEAM: a structural system that emphasizes the use of vertical *posts* and horizontal *beams*, and a defining feature of the *West Coast style*

POST: a generic word for any upright support, used either in a general sense (e.g., *post-and-beam*) or as a specific structural support, such as a *pier* or *column*

POSTMODERNISM: a reaction to the *International Style*, begun in the 1970s, that featured *contextual* design and individuality, with imagery often taken from *classicism* and pop culture (H7)

POURED-IN-PLACE CONCRETE: *See concrete*

PRECAST CONCRETE: *See concrete*

QUEEN ANNE: a North American style, mainly residential, derived but distinct from the British style of that name; it is picturesque and asymmetrical, composed of *gabled roofs*, turrets, *bay* and *dormer windows*, and wrap-around porches (D25)

REINFORCED CONCRETE: *See concrete*

RENAISSANCE: the revival, in the fifteenth and sixteenth centuries, of art and architecture from *classical* sources, begun in Italy and subsequently a pan-European style; its legacy includes *Palladian, baroque, Georgian* and *neoclassicism*

ROMANESQUE REVIVAL: a nineteenth-century style rooted in the Romanesque architecture of medieval Europe, enlivened forcefully by the American architect H.H. Richardson (hence Richardsonian Romanesque); features *rusticated* stonework, round *arches* and intricate decoration on *capitals* and around windows and doorways (A18)

ROSE WINDOW: a circular window, usually coloured, and normally a feature on the front *elevation* of a church

ROUGHCAST: stucco with a textured finish

RUSTICATED: rough-faced stonework chipped on the exposed side, giving a deep texture

SCOTS BARONIAL: a sixteenth-century style noted for crow-stepped *gables* and Loire-style turrets, revived in the nineteenth century; in Canada, often used as a component of the *château style*

SECOND EMPIRE: a *classical* architectural style featuring *columns*, *pilasters*, arched windows and *mansard* roofs; developed in the Second Empire in mid-nineteenth-century France and came to Canada (G24)

SHAFT: the vertical element in a *column* between the base and the *capital*

SHED ROOF: a roof that slopes in one direction

SIDING: Another term for *cladding*

SPANDREL: the portion of wall between the top of one window and the sill above it, usually recessed behind the surface of the wall; also the roughly triangular surface between two adjacent *arches* in an *arcade*. *See also arch-and-spandrel*

SPANISH COLONIAL REVIVAL: an architectural style begun in California in the early 1900s, derived from Spanish missions but more ornamental than the contemporaneous *Mission Style*; stucco walls, semicircular *gables*, round *arches*, iron balcony railings and *terracotta* roof tiles are characteristic (I13, K18)

STEEL-FRAME CONSTRUCTION: steel *posts* and *beams* that form a building's skeleton; early steel frames were clad with brick, stone or *terracotta*, subsequently with glass-and-metal *curtain walls* or *concrete*

STRIP WINDOWS: a horizontal row of windows with common sills and heads, with glass panes separated by thin *mullions*

TERRACOTTA: fired clay ("baked earth" in Italian) shaped in a mould, fired and often glazed; used as *cladding* material valued for its durability and suitability for decoration

TRUSS: a structural framework composed of individual wood or metal members arranged in triangles for stability; able to span wider spaces than beams; also used in bridges

TUDOR REVIVAL: an architectural style characterized by steep roofs, tall chimneys and decorative half-timbering that recalls the heavy-timber frame and *roughcast infill* of buildings from the Tudor period of England (J3)

TUSCAN ORDER: a *classical* order similar to *Doric*, with a smooth *shaft* and no base

VAULTED: a *masonry* ceiling, usually in the form of an *arch* or *arches*; usually found in churches and other public buildings

WEST COAST STYLE: an architectural style, primarily residential, that blends features of the *International Style*, the Prairie School associated with Frank Lloyd Wright and Japanese house forms; characterized by *post-and-beam* construction (mainly wood), flat roofs and open-plan interiors, with generous glazing that diffuses the conventional division of living space from nature (M37)

WROUGHT IRON: *See cast iron*

FURTHER READING

Atkin, John, and Andy Coupland. *The Changing City: Architecture and History Walking Tours in Central Vancouver.* Vancouver: Steller Press, 2010.

Boddy, Trevor. "New Urbanism: The Vancouver Model." *Places* 16:2 (University of California, Berkley) 2004; designobserver.com, 2009.

Davis, Chuck, editor. *The Greater Vancouver Book.* Surrey, BC: Linkman Press, 1997.

Demers, Charles. *Vancouver Special.* Vancouver: Arsenal Pulp Press, 2009.

Greater Vancouver Green Guide. Vancouver: Design Centre for Sustainability at UBC, 2006.

Hayes, Derek. *Historical Atlas of Vancouver and the Lower Fraser Valley.* Vancouver: Douglas & McIntyre, 2005.

Kalman, Harold. *A Concise History of Canadian Architecture.* Don Mills: Oxford University Press, 2000.

Kluckner, Michael. *Vancouver Remembered.* Vancouver: Whitecap Books, 2006.

Luxton, Donald, editor. *Building the West: The Early Architects of British Columbia,* 2nd edition. Vancouver: Talonbooks, 2007.

Macdonald, Bruce. *Vancouver: A Visual History.* Vancouver: Talonbooks, 1992.

Macdonald, Chris. *A Guidebook to Contemporary Architecture in Vancouver.* Vancouver: Douglas & McIntyre, 2010.

Punter, John. *The Vancouver Achievement: Urban Planning and Design.* Vancouver: UBC Press, 2003.

Ward, Robin. *Robin Ward's Vancouver.* Madeira Park: Harbour Publishing, 1990.

——. *Robin Ward's Heritage West Coast.* Madeira Park: Harbour Publishing, 1993.

Windsor Liscombe, Rhodri. *The New Spirit: Modern Architecture in Vancouver 1938–1963.* Vancouver: Canadian Centre for Architecture and Douglas & McIntyre, 1997.

INDEX OF DESIGNERS

This index lists architects, engineers, landscape architects, planners, heritage consultants, and artists. Individuals are listed by surname; firms are listed by their names at the time of project completion

INDEX OF BUILDINGS AND GENERAL INDEX

Italicized page numbers indicate maps.

Strathcona Residents' Association, 44
Strathmore Lodge, 165
Street Light (Miller & Tregebov), 119
streetcar lines, 44, 56, 64, 203, 208, 218, 242–43, 251, 254, 270
Student Residences & Dining Hall (SFU), 292–93
Students' Union Building (Langara College), 95
Sun Tower (A23), 20, 149
Sun Yat-Sen (Dr.), 32, 33, 39
Sunset Community Centre (F18), 96–97
SuperValu stores, 92, 222
sustainability: about, 2–3; Busby as leader, 257; in Downtown/West End, 128, 144, 166; in False Creek area, 105, 109, 111, 112, 113, 116; in Grandview/East Vancouver, 77, 78, 80; in North and West Vancouver, 253, 255, 257, 260; in Richmond, 278, 279, 282, 283; at SFU, 271, 293; in South Vancouver, 98; in Strathcona, 41, 49; Sustainable Region Initiative, 255, 298; at UBC, 227, 230, 232, 238, 239; in West Side, 224. *See also* densification; LEED certification
Swiss chalet style, 178, 254
Sylvia Hotel (I23), 175
Sylvia Tower, 175
Symbols for Education (Thomas & Thomas), 235

Tait, Bob, 45
Tait, William Lamont, 151, 198
Take Root Properties, 45
Takehara, R., 68
Takehara Tenements (D22), 68
Tamura, Shinkichi, and Tamura House (C21), 52–53
Tapestry at the O'Keefe, 217
Tatlow, R.G., and Tatlow Court (K9), 209–10
Taylor, A.J.T., 145, 247
Taylor, Austin, 223
Taylor, Louis D., and Taylor Manor, 20, 84
Technology Enterprise Facility III (UBC, L20), 239
Telus Garden, 128
Telus House (H5), 128
Temple Sholom, 223

Terminus Hotel, 9, 13
Terra Vita, 83–84
Les Terraces (M32), 262–63
Terry Fox Memorial, 116
Themis, Goddess of Justice (J. Harman), 155
Theological Neighbourhood (UBC, L11), 234
"thin house" (4167 West 11th Avenue), 215
Thomas, John ("Navvy Jack") (M28), 261
Thornton Park, 115
Three Greenhorns, 160
Tom, Gregory Henry, 46
Tony's Deli, 75
Toronto Dominion Bank Building (H24), 135, 138
Toronto Dominion Tower, 123, 126, 144
Torre Guinigi (Lucca, Italy), 176
Toy, Chang, 31
Toys "R" Us Sign (D23), 68–69
Trans Canada Trail Pavilion, 248
Translational Research Building, 225
Travelling Crane, 108
Trev Deeley Motorcycles (E22), 84
Trout Lake, 103
True Colours heritage palette, 165–66
Tudor Manor (I8), 167–68
Tudor Revival style: about, 307; in Burnaby, 294, 296; as Maclure's specialty, 290; Modern Tudor style, 226; in Shaughnessy Heights, 189, 191, 192, 193–94, 196, 197, 199; at UBC, 233; in West End, 167–68, 169–70, 177–78; in West Side, 209, 212, 219
Tulk, A.E., 196
Turnbull elevator, 170
TV Towers, 130

UBC Bookstore, 241
UBC Hospital, 240
UBC Medical Student & Alumni Centre, 65
UBC Renew program, 227, 230, 235
Unitarian Church of Vancouver (K41), 223–24
Unity of Vancouver, 224
UniverCity (SFU), 227, 271, 293
Universal Buddhist Temple (F15), 95
University Endowment Lands, 227
University of British Columbia (UBC), 5, 65, 179, 226–28, 229, 230–41, 278. *See also specific buildings* (section L)

SPONSORS

A heartfelt thanks to our donors:

ABBARCH Architecture Inc.

Carolyn Affleck &
Paul McElligott

Susan Alexander

Barbara Armstrong

Peter & Wendy Armstrong

Herbert & Mary Auerbach

Jane Banfield

Dorothy Barkley

Jean Barman

Cinnamon & Galib Bhayani

Margaret Brown

Allan Diamond

Barry & Mary Downs

Judy Ellis

Andrea Elvidge

Elizabeth Esson

Marta Farevaag, Phillips
Farevaag Smallenberg

Marguerite Ford

Kate Gerson, DIALOG

Judith & Poul Hansen

Gordon Harris, SFU
Community Trust

June Harrison

Peter & Joan Hebb

Sholto & Shirley Hebenton

Donna Hellewell

Andrew Hiscox

Jeannette Hlavach &
Bill Buholzer

Marianne Janzen

Karen Jarvis &
Cameron Campbell

Richard & Heather Keate

Margot Keate West
& Ben West

Heather Kennedy

Carolyn Kenton

Sandra Korpan

Denny Lang

Edward Little

Kevin Louis & Emmanuel
Buenviaje, Kevin Louis Design

Bruce Macdonald

Alexander Mackenzie

Mollie Massie & Hein Poulus

Chris Mattock, Habitat Design
Consulting Ltd.

Susan Milne

Rob Mitchell

Paul Nursey

Judy Oberlander & Mark
Wexler

Joyce Ozier

Colette Parsons, Municipality
of West Vancouver

Naomi Pauls, Paper Trail
Publishing

Sheila Petrie

Michelle Pullan

Bill Rapanos, City of Burnaby

Shawna Reibling

Sally Reukauf Warren

Alan Roaf

Elizabeth Roaf

Peter Roaf

Michael & Louisa Roberts

Mitch Sakumoto, Merrick
Architecture/Borowski Lintott
Sakumoto Fligg Ltd.

Jenny Sandy

Nola-Kate Seymoar

Jean Shepherd

Basil Stuart Stubbs &
Brenda Peterson

John Stubbs

Diane Switzer

Melania Taylor & Brian Wawro

Ronnie & Barry Tessler

Mark Tindle & Leslie Cliff

Heather Tremain &
Robert Brown, Resource
Rethink Building Inc.

Diane Walker

Elizabeth Walker

David Whittaker

Constance Wigmore

Yosef Wosk

Jonathan Yardley

Andrew Young

Additional donors are listed at
www.vancouverheritagefoundation.org.